PHONOLOGICAL AWARENESS

CHALLENGES IN LANGUAGE AND LITERACY

Kenn Apel, Barbara J. Ehren, Elaine R. Silliman,
and C. Addison Stone, *Series Editors*

FRAME WORK IN LANGUAGE AND LITERACY:
HOW THEORY INFORMS PRACTICE
Judith Felson Duchan

PHONOLOGICAL AWARENESS:
FROM RESEARCH TO PRACTICE
Gail T. Gillon

Forthcoming

HANDBOOK OF LANGUAGE AND LITERACY:
DEVELOPMENT AND DISORDERS
*C. Addison Stone, Elaine R. Silliman, Barbara J. Ehren,
and Kenn Apel, Editors*

PHONOLOGICAL AWARENESS

From Research to Practice

Gail T. Gillon

Series Editor's Note by Kenn Apel

THE GUILFORD PRESS
New York   London

© 2004 The Guilford Press
A Division of Guilford Publications, Inc.
72 Spring Street, New York, NY 10012
www.guilford.com

Paperback edition 2007

Printed in the United States of America

This book is printed on acid-free paper.

Last digit is print number: 9   8   7   6   5   4   3

Library of Congress Cataloging-in-Publication Data

Gillon, Gail T.
  Phonological awareness : from research to practice / Gail T. Gillon.
      p.   cm.—(Challenges in language and literacy)
  Includes bibliographical references and index.
    ISBN-10: 1-57230-964-4   ISBN-13: 978-1-57230-964-7 (cloth)
    ISBN-10: 1-59385-472-2   ISBN-13: 978-1-59385-472-0 (paper)
    1. Reading—Phonetic method.   2. Language awareness in children.
  3. Children with disabilities—Education.   I. Title.   II. Series.
  LB1573.3.G48 2004
  372.46′5—dc22
                                                      2003016790

About the Author

Gail T. Gillon, PhD, is a senior academic staff member in the Department of Communication Disorders at the University of Canterbury, *Te Whare Wānanga o Waitaha,* in Christchurch, New Zealand. A native New Zealander, she completed her undergraduate qualifications in education, primary teaching, and speech–language therapy in Christchurch in 1983. Following a period of several years working in New Zealand and Australia as a speech–language pathologist, she completed her Doctorate in Speech and Hearing at the University of Queensland, Australia, in 1995. Professor Gillon returned to the University of Canterbury in 1996 to undertake a prestigious 2-year postdoctoral fellowship awarded by the New Zealand Foundation for Research Science and Technology. She currently lectures and teaches in the Department of Communication Disorders, College of Science. Her research focuses on understanding the relationship between developmental spoken and written language disorders, and she has led a series of successful intervention trials investigating the benefits of phonological awareness interventions for children at high risk for literacy difficulties. Professor Gillon's research has been widely published in leading U.S., British, European, Australian, and New Zealand speech–language pathology and reading journals. She has won on three occasions (1995, 2000, 2005) the esteemed American Speech–Language–Hearing Association Editor's award for a research article of highest merit.

Series Editor's Note

This volume in The Guilford Press's series *Challenges in Language and Literacy* provides a clear and lucid account of one of the most important scientific findings of the 20th century for education: that a child's explicit awareness and use of the phonological components of language plays a significant role in reading and spelling development. Dr. Gillon provides an in-depth account of the research on phonological awareness and its implications for the assessment and intervention of reading and spelling deficits. As such, this book will be welcomed by professionals in a variety of fields, including speech–language pathology, general education, and special education.

The principal aim of *Phonological Awareness: From Research to Practice* is to bring together a large body of information, synthesize and evaluate that information, and translate it for students, practitioners, and other scientists. The focus on the prevention and treatment of early reading deficits is particularly timely as more emphasis is being placed on prevention and early intervention for at-risk children both nationally and internationally. What positions this book ahead of others is its simultaneous consideration of both reading *and* spelling, thus melding both literacy skills together into a multiple skill or an integrated approach to treating deficits in these areas. In addition, readers will welcome the attention given to phonological awareness development in children whose first language is not English and in children who present with other deficits such as sensory or motoric difficulties.

This book exemplifies the aim of our series: to integrate interdisciplinary perspectives on language and literacy with empirically based components in order to promote effective learning outcomes in diverse students.

The series is based on the premise that spoken and written language skills are closely intertwined in individual development. To understand the complexity of this relationship, the collaborative contributions of scholars and practitioners from multiple disciplines are required. The series focuses on typical and atypical language and literacy development from the preschool years to young adulthood in order to provide informative, timely resources for a broad audience including practitioners, academics, and students in the fields of language science and disorders, educational psychology, general education, special education, and learning disabilities.

I am certain that *Phonological Awareness: From Research to Practice* will be well received by scientists, practitioners, and students—an unusual phenomenon. This is due entirely to Dr. Gillon's understanding of the relevant research and her ability to translate it into practice. The book represents an excellent addition to anyone's professional library or required course readings. It may also serve as a driving force for practitioners to provide scientifically based, theoretically sound assessment and intervention practices in the areas of phonological awareness, reading, and spelling.

KENN APEL, PHD

Preface

One of the great joys of parenting and teaching children through the early school years is listening to them read a favorite story or receiving their little handwritten notes and cards. With the onset of the formal education process, parents eagerly await such experiences, expecting their child to move from speaking the language to reading and writing it with relative ease. Society also expects that our young children will develop into highly literate adults and provide a reservoir for our knowledge. A myriad of complex and interwoven factors contribute to the realization of these expectations: environment, cognitive abilities, genetic inheritance, motivation, and instructional qualities and access. The contributory "weight" of these variables has intrigued researchers for over a century. But the last quarter of the 20th century has been described as a most remarkable period of scientific growth in understanding reading development and reading disorder (Stanovich, 2000). Stemming from this period the term "phonological awareness" has emerged.

This book is devoted to understanding phonological awareness and its importance to reading and writing. The convergence of a vast array of research that has utilized a variety of methodologies and engaged populations in differing alphabetic languages has led to conclusions related to phonological awareness that have immense practical significance. Phonological awareness has been credited with successfully predicting children's reading ability, causing reading disorder if impaired, and through instruction, rapidly improving reading and spelling for children at risk for reading difficulties as well as children with severe reading disorder. These findings demand that professionals working to develop children's reading and spelling performance (i.e., teachers, reading specialists, speech–language pathologists,

and educational psychologists) acquire an in-depth understanding of phonological awareness development and an ability to accurately identify and
resolve phonological awareness deficits.

Phonological Awareness: From Research to Practice aims to meet
these demands. It is intended for professionals, or students in training, who
work with children with reading and spelling difficulties or those at risk for
such difficulties. The book provides the necessary background knowledge
to understand the role of phonological awareness in reading and spelling,
focuses on linking research to practice, and provides useful frameworks for
phonological awareness assessment and intervention to help ensure that all
children read and write with success.

Chapter 1 defines phonological awareness and discusses the use of this
term since it first began to appear in research literature in the 1970s. The
levels of phonological awareness that are relevant to reading and spelling
are described, and examples of differing phonological awareness tasks presented. The term "phonological awareness" is distinguished from related
terms such as "metalinguistics," "phonological processing," and "phonics."

Chapter 2 presents a theoretical basis for understanding the importance of phonological awareness. Theories of word recognition and spelling
development are presented, and the contribution of phonological awareness to written language acquisition is discussed. Implications from theoretical models for teaching and clinical practices are suggested.

Chapter 3 discusses the development of phonological awareness in
English and in other alphabetic languages. Research related to the predictive power of phonological awareness to later reading and spelling
achievement is reviewed. Current hypotheses as to what contributes to
phonological awareness development are explored, and practical suggestions to promote the emergence of phonological awareness in very young
children are provided.

Chapter 4 discusses the phonological deficit hypothesis for dyslexia.
"Dyslexia" is defined as a language-based disorder, and research investigating the phonological awareness and processing deficits of children with
dyslexia is reviewed. A case study is presented to highlight the language
characteristics of children with dyslexia and to provide insight into the benefits of phonological awareness intervention to accelerate word recognition
development.

Chapter 5 focuses on understanding the relationship between spoken
and written language difficulties and explores the nature of phonological
awareness deficits in children with speech and language impairments. The
role of speech–language pathologists in helping to prevent reading and
spelling difficulties for these children is emphasized.

Chapter 6 addresses the assessment of phonological awareness in children of differing ability levels. A variety of phonological awareness assessment procedures are described and psychometric properties of standardized tests are evaluated. A speech-to-print assessment profile is presented as one method of summarizing assessment data gained from various sources. A collaborative approach to in-depth assessment is advocated.

Chapter 7 focuses on the research evidence for phonological awareness intervention and the clinical implications that may be drawn from this research. Guiding principles are presented for practitioners to consider in the design and implementation of phonological awareness programs. Other important considerations for phonological awareness implementation such as background knowledge required by the instructor, the inclusion of children with differing learning needs and children learning English as a second language, and the acoustic quality of the instructional environment are also discussed.

Chapter 8 describes three instructional frameworks for phonological awareness intervention: the enhancement of early literacy development in all children; the prevention of reading and spelling disorder for children at risk for persistent written language difficulties; and an intervention method for older children and adolescents with reading and spelling disabilities. Practical suggestions for phonological awareness activities within each of these frameworks are provided.

Chapter 9 (coauthored with Sally Clendon, Linda Cupples, Mark Flynn, Teresa Iacono, Traci Schmidtke, David Yoder, and Audrey Young) discusses issues related to the development of phonological awareness in children with special learning needs. The chapter includes assessment and treatment of phonological awareness deficits in children who use augmentative and alternative communication systems, children with Down syndrome, children who are blind and use Braille as their reading medium, and children with hearing impairment.

The chapter summary points and links from research to practice at the ends of chapters are designed to focus the reader's attention on key content areas and to encourage the reader to consider teaching implications from the research discussed.

Acknowledgments

My grateful thanks are expressed to Hugh Catts and Kenn Apel for their detailed reviews of the manuscript in the publication process. Their suggestions for changes were most useful.

I am very grateful to my coauthors of Chapter 9:

Sally Clendon and David Yoder, *Division of Speech and Hearing Sciences, University of North Carolina at Chapel Hill*, for their contributions regarding children with severe speech and language impairments.

Linda Cupples, *Speech, Hearing and Language Research Centre, Macquarie University, Sydney*, and Teresa Iacono, *Centre for Developmental Disability Health Victoria, Monash University, and Communication Resource Centre, Melbourne*, for their contribution to understanding the phonological awareness skills in children with Down syndrome.

Mark Flynn and Traci Schmidtke, *Department of Communication Disorders, University of Canterbury, Christchurch*, for their contribution to the section discussing the phonological awareness skills in children with hearing impairment.

Audrey Young, *New Zealand Ministry of Education, Speech Language Therapy Services*, for her innovative work in helping children who struggle to read using Braille as their reading medium.

My grateful appreciation is also expressed to my colleagues and friends from the University of Canterbury, the New Zealand Speech–Language Therapists' Association, and colleagues from around the world, who have been most supportive of my research endeavors. Thanks are expressed to Nicholas Bankson for his insightful comments on draft chapters and to Barbara Bernhardt for her feedback on specific chapter sections.

Particular thanks are expressed to Barbara Dodd and Ilsa Schwarz for their ongoing mentoring and encouragement in my research work. I would also like to acknowledge the contribution of students in the Department of Communication Disorders at the University of Canterbury who provided feedback on draft book chapters.

My family has been a source of enduring support in writing this book. My two young children, Grace and Lewis, are a constant reminder of how enriched children's lives are through successful reading and writing experiences. They reinforce for me, as I listen to them read each night, that striving to ensure successful literacy acquisition for all children is indeed a most worthwhile pursuit.

Contents

1

Phonological Awareness Defined

Comprehension of information and ideas expressed through a written medium is undoubtedly the primary purpose of reading and writing. There is little value in being able to decode written sentences or write well-formed letters in a sentence if the meaning of those sentences is not accessed. Competency in comprehending and creating written text is a developmental process that spans a lifetime. Even highly literate adults can be challenged by the task of comprehending difficult text in an unknown subject or writing in a less practiced or unfamiliar style.

Acquiring competency in written language is a complex and unnatural process. Simply being surrounded by good models of written text will not ensure its acquisition. Rather, specific skills and knowledge must be developed. Comprehending and composing written text require the integration of a wide variety of knowledge and skills, but the ability to recognize individual words in print (word recognition ability) and the ability to spell words utilizing conventions that can be deciphered by the reader are central to these processes. It is within this context of word recognition and spelling development that the importance of phonological awareness to reading and writing is recognized. A vast body of research employing differing methodologies and conducted in a variety of alphabetic languages has convincingly demonstrated that a powerful relationship exists between phonological awareness and literacy development. Indeed, a child's phonological awareness knowledge has been described as the best single predictor of reading performance (Liberman, Shankweiler, & Liberman, 1989; Lundberg, Olofsson, & Wall, 1980).

Phonological awareness is frequently discussed in texts amidst related concepts such as phonology, phonemic awareness, phonological processing, and metalinguistics. This chapter defines phonological awareness, clarifies the relationship between differing terminologies, and discusses levels of phonological awareness that are relevant to reading and spelling.

The term "phonological awareness" began appearing in the research literature in the late 1970s and early 1980s (Bradley & Bryant, 1983; Leong & Sheh, 1982; Marcel, 1980; Rozin & Gleitman, 1977; Tunmer & Fletcher, 1981; Zifcak, 1981) and refers to an individual's awareness of the sound structure, or phonological structure, of a spoken word. The term replaced earlier descriptors such as "phonetic analysis of spoken words" (Bruce, 1964) and "linguistic awareness" at the phonological level (Mattingly, 1972), which referred to children's knowledge of words as comprised of smaller, discernible units. Phonological awareness typically has been linked to the reading process; indeed, the term stems from early research which indicated that understanding a word's sound structure would enable children to decode (or sound out) a word in print (Calfee, Lindamood, & Lindamood, 1973; Elkonin, 1973; Fox & Routh, 1975; Liberman, 1971; Liberman, Shankweiler, Fischer, & Carter, 1974; Rosner & Simon, 1971). Marcel (1980) was amongst the first researchers to directly link the term "phonological awareness" to spelling, demonstrating that individuals with spelling disorders performed poorly on phonological awareness tasks. Rapid and remarkable growth during the 1990s in research studies investigating the importance of phonological awareness to reading and spelling has led to the wide adoption of the term in the scientific literature and in education, speech–language pathology, and psychology clinical practices.

It is important to gain a perspective of phonological awareness within the broader context of phonology and linguistic theory. Long before children become explicitly aware of the phonological structure of words, they have developed implicit phonological knowledge that allows them to gain mastery of speaking and listening to their native language. Implicit phonological knowledge, for example, enables children to make a judgment about whether a word is part of their native language, allows for the self-correction of speech errors, and enables children to discriminate between acceptable and unacceptable variations of a spoken word (Yavas, 1998).

Phonology is the area of linguistics that focuses on understanding the speech-sound system and the sound patterns of spoken language. The study of language also involves syntax, semantics, morphology, and pragmatics. "Syntax" refers to understanding the grammatical aspects of language and how phrases and sentences are constructed. "Semantics" focuses on vocabulary knowledge or understanding the meaning of words, phrases, and sentences and how these may be associated with each other. "Morphology" relates to understanding that words are comprised of, meaningful units, for example, the word *play*, one morpheme, can combine with another morpheme such as *er, ed, ing,* or *s* to form differing meaningful combinations. "Pragmatics" is the area of linguistics that focuses on how individuals use language to communicate with others. (See Moats, 2000, for detailed explanations of these linguistic areas.) All of these areas of language are important to consider when assessing and intervening with children who have written language disorders.

Phonology, however, is the linguistic domain that has received particular research attention in relation to early literacy development, because explicit awareness of the phonological structure of a word helps children draw connections between the spoken form of a word and its written representation. Understanding the phonological system of the child's language forms a basis from which to interpret phonological awareness development (see Chapter 3). A variety of theories has been posited as to how children acquire the phonological system of their environmental language; Bernthal and Bankson (1998) provide a review of phonological acquisition theories and models for describing disordered phonological systems.

Recent phonological theories focus on the nonlinear or hierarchical nature of phonological form ("nonlinear phonological theories"), rather than viewing the relationship between phonological units in words in a linear fashion. Understanding a word's phonological structure in a hierarchical manner is useful in appreciating the concept that phonological awareness can be represented at distinct levels. For example, in applying nonlinear theory of phonology to children's phonological system, Bernhardt and Stoel-Gammon (1994) explained that a word is "composed of a number of progressively smaller units each with its own representational tier/level" (p. 126). In adapting their illustration of how a word can be represented in a hierarchical structure, Figure 1.1 depicts how separate representational levels form the word *basket*. The word *basket* can be represented according to its stress pattern as having one foot (i.e., has one stressed element). The word can then be divided at the syllable level into a strong or stressed syllable (*bas*) and a weak or unstressed syllable (*ket*). Each syllable, in turn, can be divided further into an onset (i.e., the consonant or consonant cluster that precedes the vowel) and a rime unit (i.e., the vowel and following consonants in the syllable). The onset-rime level can be further segmented into individual speech sounds or phonemes, and the features or characteristics of each phoneme (e.g., that /b/[1] is a voiced sound

---

[1]Letters in slashed lines, such as /b/, represent the sound (phoneme) associated with the letter using IPA phonetic symbols. See the Appendix for further details.

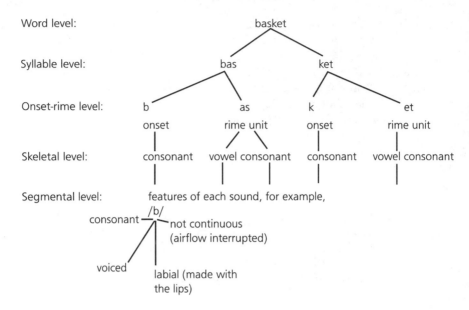

FIGURE 1.1. Representation of the phonological structure of the word *basket*. Adapted from Bernhardt and Stoel-Gammon (1994 p. 127). Adapted by permission of The American Speech–Language–Hearing Association.

made by the lips closing together and interrupting the airflow) are also represented in a hierarchically organized manner. These distinct levels are illustrated in Figure 1.1. Phonological awareness and tasks used to measure phonological awareness ability are consistent with this hierarchical structure of words, as discussed in the next section.

LEVELS OF PHONOLOGICAL AWARENESS

Phonological awareness is a multilevel skill of breaking down words into smaller units (Hoien, Lundberg, Stanovich, & Bjaalid, 1995; Muter, Hulme, Snowling, & Taylor, 1997; Stahl & Murray, 1994; Treiman & Zukowsky, 1991). Just as a word can be described in terms of its syllabic structure, onset-rime structure, and segmental or phoneme structure, so too can phonological awareness be described in terms of syllable awareness, onset-rime awareness, and phoneme awareness. A variety of measures can be utilized to evaluate individuals' knowledge of these three differing levels of phonological awareness. A discussion of each level follows.

Syllable Awareness

Phonological awareness at the syllable level requires an awareness that words can be divided into syllables. Understanding that a word such as *number* can be divided into *num-ber* is an example of syllable awareness. Treiman (1993, p. 18) discussed three principles of syllable division that have been tested in experimental work investigating children's spelling development:

1. Each syllable in a word contains a vowel (or vowel sound, such as that produced by the letter *y* in *baby*).
2. Syllable division follows the stress pattern of a word, with as many consonants as possible beginning a stressed syllable. Thus, *patrol* is divided as *pa-trol* and not *pat-rol*.
3. Syllables are divided to ensure that consonants which cannot be clustered together in English do not begin or end a syllable. For example, *only* is divided at *on-ly*, not *onl-y* or *o-nly*, because *nl* is not a "legal cluster" in English.

Syllable awareness demonstrates a realization of these principles while allowing for some differences in the marking of syllable boundaries. For example, the syllables in the word *hospital* may be verbally segmented (or tapped out by a child) as *hos-pit-al* or *hos-pi-tal*. Both attempts would be considered correct, because both reflect awareness of the vowel principle. It is likely that syllable awareness is initially promoted by the acoustic signal from a spoken word, which provides peaks of energy at the vowel center for each syllable (Liberman et al., 1974). The real-time spectogram in Figure 1.2 illustrates this pattern for the word *baby* (as spoken by a speaker of standard New Zealand English). Such clear acoustic information at the vowel center of each syllable helps in identifying that the word has two syllables, *ba-by*.

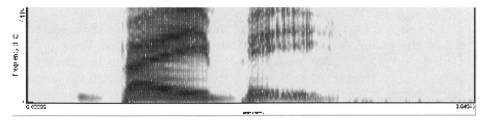

FIGURE 1.2. Real-time spectogram of the word *baby* spoken.

Tasks used to evaluate children's awareness of the syllable structure of words include the following:

- Syllable segmentation—for example, "How many syllables (or parts) in the word *coffee*?" (Dodd, Holm, Oerlemans, & McCormick, 1996).
- Syllable completion—for example, "Here is a picture of a rabbit. I'll say the first part of the word. Can you finish the word *ra_____*?" (Muter, Hulme, & Snowling, 1997).
- Syllable identity—for example, "Which part of *compete* and *compare* sound the same?" (Dodd et al., 1996).
- Syllable deletion—for example, " Say *finish*. Now say it again without the *fin*" (Rosner, 1999).

Onset-Rime Awareness

Demonstrating awareness that syllables and words can be divided at the onset-rime level shows phonological awareness at the intrasyllabic level and is often referred to as "onset-rime awareness" (Goswami & Bryant, 1990; Moats, 2000). For example, in the word *sit* the *s* is the onset of the syllable, and *it* is the rime of the syllable. In the word *start*, *st* is the onset and *art* is the rime unit of the syllable. Most commonly, this level of awareness is measured through rhyming tasks, because in order to understand that words rhyme, there first must be an awareness that the words share a common ending (rime unit) that can be separated from the beginning of the word (onset). Different measures of onset-rime awareness include:

- Spoken rhyme recognition—for example, "Do these words rhyme: shell bell?" (Dodd et al., 1996).
- Spoken rhyme detection or rhyme oddity task—for example, "Which word does not rhyme: *fish*, *dish*, *hook*?" (Bradley & Bryant, 1983).
- Spoken rhyme generation—for example, "Tell me words that rhyme with *bell*" (Muter et al., 1997).
- Onset-rime blending (Wagner, Torgesen, Laughon, Simmons, & Rashotte, 1993).

Other types of tasks, such as spoonerisms, sound categorization, and deletion tasks, also involve awareness that the onset of the word can be separated from the rime unit of the word. However, these tasks are considered under the next level of phoneme awareness when the onset of the word is a single sound and the tasks require specific awareness of this individual sound.

Phoneme (or Phonemic) Awareness

A third way that a word can be broken down into smaller parts is by using the individual sound or phoneme level. A "phoneme" is defined as the smallest unit of sound that influences the meaning of a word. For example, the word *tree* has three phonemes: /t/ /r/ /i/. If one of these phonemes is changed, a new word or a non-word will be created. If the first phoneme is changed from /t/ to /f/, the word *free* would be heard. If the last phoneme in *tree* is changed from /i/ to /ei/, the word *tray* would be heard. Hence each phoneme in a word can change the meaning of the word.

Phonemes are an abstract concept. When words are spoken, the listener does not hear the separated phonemes in words. Rather, phonemes are blended into syllables within the sound stream. Individuals must learn to perceive phonemes in speech (Liberman, Cooper, Shankweiler, & Studdert-Kennedy, 1967). There are a total of 41 phonemes in standard spoken English (25 consonants and 16 vowels), as shown in the Appendix. Phonological awareness at the phoneme level (frequently referred to in the literature as "phoneme awareness" or "phonemic awareness") necessitates understanding that words are comprised of these individual sounds.

Phoneme awareness can be measured with the following types of tasks:

- Alliteration awareness, also referred to as phoneme detection and sound or phoneme categorization—for example, "Which word has a different first sound: *bed, bus, chair, ball?*" (Torgesen & Bryant, 1994).
- Phoneme matching—for example, "Which word begins with the same sound as *bat*: *horn, bed, cup?*" (Torgesen & Bryant, 1994).
- Phoneme isolation—for example, "Tell me the sound you hear at the beginning of the word *food*" (Stahl & Murray, 1994).
- Phoneme completion—for example, "Here is a picture of a watch. Finish the word for me: *wa_____*" Muter et al., 1997).
- Phoneme blending with words or non-words—for example, "What word do these sounds make: *m . . . oo . . . n?*" (Wagner et al., 1999).
- Phoneme deletion, also referred to as phoneme elision,—for example, "Say *coat*. Now say it again but don't say /k/" (Rosner, 1999).
- Phoneme segmentation with words or non-words—for example, "How many sounds can you hear in the word *it?*" (Dodd et al., 1996).
- Phoneme reversal—for example, "Say *na* (as in *nap*). Now say *na* backwards"—*an* (Wagner et al., 1999).
- Phoneme manipulation—for example, "Say *dash*. Now say it again, but instead of /æ/ say /ɪ/"—*dish* (Rosner, 1999).
- Spoonerisms—for example, *felt made* becomes *melt fade*, Dodd et al., 1996).

The Relationship
between Phonological Awareness Levels

The tasks employed to measure ability within each level of phonological awareness are closely related to each other. Stanovich, Cunningham, and Cramer (1984, 1988) demonstrated that tasks tapping skills at the phoneme level, such as phoneme detection, phoneme blending, phoneme deletion, and phoneme segmentation, are strongly interrelated. Their results suggest that despite differences in the cognitive requirements necessary to successfully complete the tasks, the tasks measure a similar underlying construct of phoneme awareness. However, the tasks do differ in their degree of difficulty and level of linguistic complexity (Stahl & Murray, 1994; Yopp, 1988). For example, phoneme detection (i.e., alliteration) requires less explicit phonological awareness than a task such as phoneme deletion (Hulme et al., 2002). Yopp observed that these tasks could be divided validly according to the demands they (i.e., the tasks) placed on working memory. Thus, tasks that require only one operation, such as segmenting, blending, or isolating a sound, are classified as simple phoneme awareness tasks. Tasks that require two operations, with the results from the first operation being held in memory while the second operation is performed (e.g., phoneme manipulation), are classified as compound phoneme awareness tasks.

In a comprehensive analysis of phonological awareness tasks, Schatschneider, Francis, Foorman, Fletcher, and Mehta (1999) administered a battery of seven phonological awareness tasks to 945 U.S. children in kindergarten to grade 2. All of the children were fluent English speakers. The battery included blending onset and rime units, blending phonemes into words and non-words, phoneme deletion, phoneme segmentation, phoneme categorization, and phoneme matching tasks. Analysis indicated that all of the tasks were strongly related to each other but that differing tasks were best suited to measuring phonological awareness ability at differing stages in the child's development (see Chapter 6 for further discussion of this issue). Phoneme segmentation, phoneme blending of non-words, and phoneme deletion proved to be more difficult tasks than blending onset rimes, phoneme matching, and phoneme categorization. These findings were consistent with Stahl and Murray's (1994) earlier findings that phoneme isolation is a much easier task for 5- to 7-year-old children than phoneme blending, phoneme deletion, and phoneme segmentation (the latter task proving the most difficult for this age group).

Six of the seven tasks in Schatschneider et al.'s (1999) study measured phonological awareness skills at the phoneme level. The one measure of onset-rime knowledge (i.e., onset-rime blending) was highly related to the phoneme level tasks. Unfortunately, other measures of onset rime, such as rhyme identity, and measures of syllable awareness were not administered.

Yopp's (1988) analysis suggested that the ability to identify rhyming word pairs was only moderately correlated with performance on phoneme level tasks. Duncan and Johnston (1999) and Muter (1994) also demonstrated that rhyme and phoneme level tasks may represent different constructs of phonological awareness. Thus although syllable awareness, onset-rime awareness, and phoneme level awareness are related to each other (in that they are all require awareness of how a word can be broken down into smaller parts), the strongest relationship among differing types of tasks has been demonstrated for tasks at the phoneme level.

Phonological Awareness above the Word Level

In the past, phonological awareness was sometimes defined more broadly as an awareness of the sound structure of spoken language (as opposed to the sound structure of a spoken word). Researchers may therefore have utilized tasks that measured children's awareness above the word level, such as understanding that sentences are comprised of individual words. There is now little evidence to support a connection between this level of awareness and word recognition or spelling ability; indeed, focusing on developing awareness above the word level is not recommended in phonological awareness intervention (Brady, Fowler, Stone, & Winbury, 1994). Throughout this book, therefore, phonological awareness is discussed in terms of awareness of the phonological structure of a word at the syllable level, onset-rime level, and phoneme level.

PHONOLOGICAL PROCESSING ABILITIES

The term "phonological processing" is frequently found in the literature in relation to reading development and reading disorder. Although the term is sometimes used interchangeably with phonological awareness, the concepts are best seen as distinct from one another. Wagner and Torgesen (1987) clearly defined phonological processing abilities as referring to the use of phonological information in processing spoken and written language. Phonological processing ability encompasses phonological awareness as one construct but also distinguishes two other constructs: (1) coding phonological information in working memory, and (2) retrieving phonological information from long-term memory. Digit span tasks (i.e., recalling series of digits presented by the examiner) and sentence repetition tasks are used to measure the efficiency of phonological coding in memory. Rapid naming tasks (e.g., naming alphabetic letters or common animals as fast as possible) are employed to measure the efficiency of retrieving phonological information. Thus, for purposes of clarification, phonological awareness may be seen as a subset of more general phonological processing abilities, as depicted in Figure 1.3.

METALINGUISTIC AWARENESS

Phonological awareness is one aspect of the broader category of metalinguistics. "Metalinguistic awareness" is a general term that refers to the ability to think about and reflect upon language. Instead of using language in a functional sense, knowledge of metalinguistic awareness demonstrates awareness of, and reflection upon, the structural features of language. Mattingly (1972) was among the first researchers to discuss a relationship between children's awareness of language and their progress in reading development. Mattingly argued that reading is a language-based skill dependent upon awareness of primary linguistic activities of speaking and listening.

Although phonological awareness is the aspect of metalinguistic knowledge that has undoubtedly received the most attention in relation to written language acquisition, other aspects of metalinguistic awareness also influence reading and writing performance. These include syntactic awareness, semantic awareness, pragmatic awareness, and morphological awareness. These latter areas of metalinguistics may be particularly important in word recognition processes once the reader or writer has mastered basic decoding and encoding skills. For example, syntactic and semantic awareness allows a reader or writer to make a judgment about whether a word used makes logical or grammatical sense within the text. Morphological awareness helps children to identify the main part of a word, such as recognizing the word *drink* in *drinking,* and can be an important strategy as spelling knowledge develops (Carlisle, 1995; Masterson & Apel, 2000). Figure 1.3 depicts the intersection of metalinguistic awareness and phonological awareness in relation to word recognition processes.

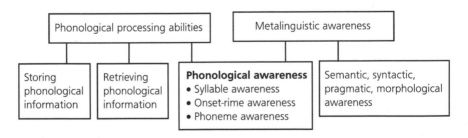

FIGURE 1.3. Phonological awareness in relation to phonological processing and metalinguistic awareness.

PHONOLOGICAL AWARENESS AND PHONICS

From a teaching perspective, the terms phonological awareness and phoneme awareness are sometimes confused with the term "phonics." All these terms have some relationship to sounds within words. *Phonics* refers to teaching sound-letter correspondence for reading and spelling. "*A* is for *apple*, *b* is for *bat*, *c* is for *cat*" or "*s* says /s/" are examples of phonic activities. Such activities clearly differ from phonological awareness tasks that require an awareness of the sound structure of words. For example, understanding that the word *apple* has two syllables, the word *bat* has three phonemes, or that *bat* and *cat* are rhyming words differs from being taught the sound–symbol relationships for *a*, *b*, and *c*. Historically, phonics was taught in a skill-and-drill manner through workbook activities. Little attention was directed to increasing children's explicit awareness of a word's sound structure. That is, phonics was taught in isolation from phoneme awareness. Phoneme awareness also can be taught in isolation, with children asked to segment words into individual phonemes or blend phonemes to make words without any reference to letters. However, research has clearly demonstrated that the best outcomes for reading occur when phoneme awareness and phonics are integrated (e.g., Hatcher, Hulme, & Ellis, 1994, discussed in Chapter 6). Thus, many phonological awareness programs now integrate phonic learning activities into the program.

SUMMARY

This chapter has defined phonological awareness and discussed the terminology associated with it. Clarifying terminology is important from both a research and teaching perspective and influences implications drawn from research. The following summary points highlight the terminologies discussed:

- Phonological awareness refers to the understanding that spoken words can be broken down to smaller parts.
- Phonological awareness is a multilevel skill, typically seen as comprised of syllable awareness, onset-rime awareness, and phoneme awareness.
- Phonological awareness may be viewed as a subset of skills within the broader categories of phonological processing and metalinguistic knowledge.
- *Phonics* and *phonological awareness* refer to different types of knowledge. Phonics refers to the learning of letter-sound associations and is frequently embedded in phonological awareness activities.

FROM RESEARCH TO PRACTICE

A clear understanding of what is intended by the term "phonological awareness" has a variety of practical implications. These include:

1. The interpretation of research related to phonological awareness necessitates an understanding of the level of phonological awareness being addressed in the study. Do the research findings relate to children's phonological awareness knowledge at the syllable, onset-rime, or phoneme level? The linguistic complexity and level of difficulty of each task also needs to be considered in data interpretation. What specific phoneme level tasks have been used to evaluate children's phoneme awareness skills?

2. Clarifying the use of terms such as *phonics*, *phonological awareness*, *phonological processing*, and *metalinguistics* is important when working collaboratively with other professionals in the management of children with spoken and written language disorders. Confusion also may be avoided when professionals involved with a child present a consistent definition of phonological awareness (and related terms) to the child's parents/caregivers and any aides who may be working with the child.

3. Teachers, speech–language pathologists, and reading specialists need to clearly identify the level of phonological awareness they are targeting in an intervention program. Do the teaching activities target skills at only one level, such as onset-rime skills, or are phoneme level skills also targeted during the teaching program?

4. Clinical descriptions in reports of an individual's phonological awareness ability should reflect the differing levels of phonological awareness knowledge. For example, does a report comment that a child has "poor phonological awareness knowledge" mean that the child has poor awareness of the syllable, onset-rime, or phoneme structure of words? Some children show awareness of syllables within words but struggle with awareness of smaller units at the onset-rime and phoneme levels. Specific reference to the level of phonological awareness the child finds difficult provides a more accurate profile of the child's strengths and weaknesses and assists intervention planning.

Understanding the vocabulary associated with phonological awareness is a first step toward gaining an in-depth understanding of phonological awareness and its importance to reading and spelling processes. The following chapters use the terminology presented in this chapter to describe theoretical models of word recognition and spelling, the development of phonological awareness, and phonological awareness assessment and intervention practices.

2

Theoretical Background

The strong interest in phonological awareness currently exhibited in educational, health, and clinical fields has been fueled by a plethora of research studies demonstrating the relationship between phonological awareness task performances and reading ability (reviewed in Chapter 3). In particular, findings from intervention studies, which demonstrate the effectiveness of phonological awareness training in enhancing reading accuracy and reading comprehension performance, have led to a wide pragmatic interest in phonological awareness (see Chapter 7). The importance of phonological awareness to spelling development is also being recognized. Spelling is no longer considered an exercise in visual memorization, as formerly thought. Rather, spelling is now viewed as a language-based skill, in which knowledge of the sound structure of spoken language is an important component (Kamhi & Hinton, 2000; Oerlemans & Dodd, 1993; Treiman & Bourassa, 2000).

Before reviewing the research literature related to phonological awareness and launching into the practicalities of phonological awareness assessment and intervention, it is necessary to discuss a theoretical context for phonological awareness. How does awareness that a spoken word is comprised of smaller sound units contribute to an individual's ability to accurately read and comprehend connected text or to spell words correctly? It is critical for professionals who are expected to have expertise in language development and its disorders to understand the theoretical basis for phonological awareness. Most adults can easily engage a child in simple phonological awareness game activities, such as playing rhyme bingo or sorting pictures together that start with the same sound. However, professionals who assess children's phonological awareness development, interpret assessment findings within the context of other aspects of spoken and written language development, and design and plan phonological awareness interventions to meet individual needs require additional understanding of theories regarding word recognition and spelling development. Strong theoretical knowledge assists in data interpretation and helps ensure that relevant and appropriate outcomes from phonological awareness interventions are achieved.

THEORIES OF WORD RECOGNITION

It is easy to take for granted the quick and efficient way that meaning can be abstracted from a printed word on a page. Consideration of the cognitive processes involved in word recognition brings with it a realization of the subskills involved. Word recognition is the level of the reading process that has been the predominant focus of research during the last few decades. Its relevance to investigations of reading development and reading disorder is fundamental, given that descriptions of poor readers typically emphasize their inability to recognize and pronounce printed words in an accurate manner.

Theories of skilled reading emphasize the importance of efficient word recognition to the development of reading comprehension ability (Gough & Tunmer, 1986; Perfetti, 1985; Stanovich, Nathan, & Zolman, 1988). Although a range of linguistic skills is necessary for written text comprehension, differences in word decoding skills account for much of the variance in reading comprehension performance (Stanovich, 1985). It is predicted, therefore, that inefficient word decoding skills are central to the comprehension problems of many poor readers (Rispens, 1990; Stanovich, 1991b). For example, a basic model of reading comprehension, referred to as the "simple view" (Conners & Olsen, 1990; Gough & Tunmer, 1986; Hoover & Gough, 1990; Juel, Griffith, & Gough, 1986; Tunmer & Hoover, 1992), proposed that two independent factors—word recognition and listening comprehension—account for differences in reading comprehension. Developmental changes in the relative contribution of each of these factors are evident. Word recognition skills are considered critical in early reading acquisition. Listening comprehension may be more important in later stages of reading acquisition, when children have mastered basic decoding skills, and reading texts increase in complexity (Hoover & Gough, 1990).

Researchers have developed a number of competing models to explain word recognition ability. Two models that have dominated the literature are the "dual-route" (Coltheart, 1978; LaBerge & Samuels, 1974; Marshall & Newcombe, 1973; Morton & Patterson, 1980) and "connectionist" (Patterson, Seidenberg, & McClelland, 1989; Rumelhart & McClelland,

1986; Seidenberg, 1989; Seidenberg & McClelland, 1989) models. An understanding of these and related models (e.g., modified dual route models and an analogy model) provides a theoretical context for how phonological awareness may influence the ability to process words at the single word level. Although developed primarily to explain how the ability to recognize printed words is acquired, these models also have been used in reference to spelling skills acquisition. That is, they are used to conceptualize how a person can translate a spoken word into its printed form. Discussions of these models for both reading and spelling follow.

Dual-Route Model

A dual-route theory for explaining how skilled readers access meaning from printed words has been widely used in studies of reading and reading disorder. In recent years this theory has received heavy criticism. Nevertheless, it has been very influential in the development of subsequent models of word recognition and provides an understanding of some current teaching practices.

Dual-route theory, as its name suggests, proposes that there are two routes to accessing the meaning of an isolated printed word: a phonological route and a visual route (Coltheart, 1978; Forster, 1976; Morton & Patterson, 1980). Comprehending a word on a page via a phonological route involves a series of subskills. The first skill engaged is referred to as "graphemic parsing." This process involves analysis of the string of letters in the printed word into those letters or sets of letters that correspond to a single phoneme (e.g., *sh*; two letters are parsed to one phoneme). Next, letter-sound translation rules (grapheme–phoneme conversion) are applied to access the phonology of the word, which involves the subprocesses of maintaining the phonemic codes in working memory and assembling the phonemes into a complete phonological representation. Once the phonological representation of the word is accessed (based upon the individual's experience and knowledge of the word in spoken form), the meaning of the word is realized. Figure 2.1 depicts the process of moving from analysis of the orthographic form of the word, to applying grapheme–phoneme rules, to accessing the word's phonological representation, and finally to attaching meaning to the word. In common terms, the phonological route involves "sounding out the word" or "decoding the word" to access the word's meaning.

Coltheart (1978) proposed that English words that do not conform to regular grapheme parsing or grapheme–phoneme conversion rules (i.e., irregularly spelled words such as *sword*) cannot be encoded phonologically. Rather, an alternate visual route must be used to access the meaning of these words. The visual route is independent of phonological processing and allows the reader to form a direct association between the written form of the word and the meaning of the word from the reader's vocabulary store. The orthographic shape, letter cues, and legality of letter patterns may be used to access the orthographic representation of the word in memory store (i.e., memory for what the word looks like in print). The orthographic representation of the whole word is then used to access the meaning of the word. The association between the visual form of a word and its meaning is arbitrary and must be rote learned, because letter-sound relations are not involved (Ehri, 1992). Figure 2.1 illustrates the direct link from the printed word on the page to an orthographic representation in memory (established from frequent exposures to what the word looks like in print) and to the subsequent meaning of the word.

Skilled readers are considered to have sufficient flexibility to select routes (i.e., phonological vs. visual) depending on the nature of the reading material and the purposes of reading. The phonological route is thought to come into play when reading unfamiliar or low-frequency words. Once words become familiar through practice in reading, they can be accessed directly by sight (i.e., the visual route). Within a dual-route model, phonological awareness would be necessary only when using a phonological route to access the word's meaning. Understanding how a word can be broken

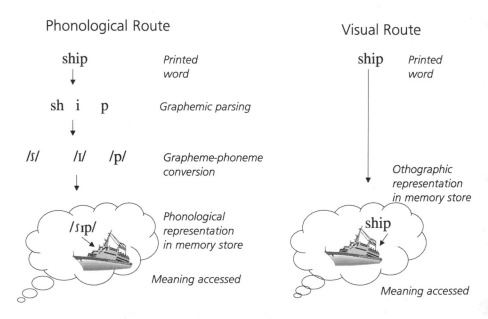

FIGURE 2.1. Illustration of the dual-route theory of word recognition.

down into smaller parts would assist in understanding how letters map onto sounds (the grapheme–phoneme conversion process) and would allow the reader to decode the word. For example, consider the skills involved in reading the following unfamiliar word from a medical dictionary: *ileosigmoidostomy*. Awareness that words can be broken into syllables (syllable awareness), awareness that syllables are comprised of individual phonemes (phoneme awareness), knowledge of which phonemes map to specific graphemes, and phoneme blending skills all contribute to the decoding of the word (which is pronounced *i-le-o-sig-moid-os-to-me*). However, only if the reader has knowledge of medical terminology will a semantic representation then be accessed to attach meaning to the word's pronunciation.

In a dual-route model it would be possible for a person with no awareness of a word's sound structure to access its meaning via the visual route. Learning that a particular pattern of letters represents a particular word through visual rote learning would enable access to the word's meaning. The teaching practice of reading flash cards is an example of visual rote learning; A word is displayed to a child on a card, and the teacher articulates the word. Through multiple repetitions of seeing and hearing the word simultaneously, the child can learn that the visual pattern of the letters on the card is attached to a particular word without any understanding of the word's phonological structure.

A dual-route model of skilled spelling, described by Barry (1994), essentially mirrors the two routes discussed for word recognition. The child may produce the spelling of the word via an assembled (phonological) route or via a lexical (visual) route. The assembled route to spelling involves segmenting the target word and applying a process of converting from sound to letters, based on knowledge of how individual sounds in words are represented in spelling. The spelling of the word is assembled via phonological information and knowledge of phoneme–grapheme relationships. Teaching strategies that encourage children to listen for the sound a word starts with, to break down a word into parts, and to sound out the word when spelling are consistent with the phonological route theory of spelling. This route would facilitate successful spelling of words with regular sound-to-spelling correspondences, such as *hot*, but the alternative lexical route would be necessary for irregularly spelled words, such as *yacht*.

The lexical route to spelling involves the retrieval of the whole word from a stored orthographic representation in memory. Upon hearing or thinking of a spoken word the writer wishes to spell, an orthographic representation of the word is activated. The writer then must engage in the mechanics of writing, typing, or spelling aloud the sequence of letters to match the orthographic representation of the word. In essence, the visual form of the whole word is simply retrieved from memory, without any reference to the sounds in the word. Teaching strategies such as looking at a word, covering the word, visualizing the word, then spelling the word are consistent with the visual route theory for spelling.

Modified Dual Route Models

The standard dual-route model has been criticized by a number of researchers (Barron, 1986; Ehri, 1992; Humphreys & Evett, 1985; Seidenberg, 1985), and several modified versions of the model have been proposed (e.g., Ehri, 1991; Norris & Brown, 1985; Patterson & Morton, 1985). Ehri (1992) criticized this standard dual route theory for its lack of phonological processing attributed to the visual route to word recognition. Ehri pointed out that most irregular words are only partially irregular. For example, in the word *sword*, only the *w* does not follow regular sound-spelling correspondences. Knowledge of the grapheme–phoneme relationships for *s, or, d* may help prompt the recognition of the word. Ehri suggested that the reader can utilize the systemic relations between spelling and pronunciation the word offers to aid memory and thus reduce memory demand, rather than rote learning the entire form. According to Ehri, the rote learning required to access words via a visual route is inefficient, because remembering the orthographic shape of each new word acquired in an arbitrary manner places heavy demands on memory. It is more plausible to hypothesize that once a child has acquired knowledge of connections between graphemes and phonemes, he or she will use these cues, at least partially, to access the stored orthographic representation of the word.

In Ehri's model of word recognition the visual route of the standard dual-route model is modified to include a phonological element. This new route is described as a visual–phonological route. Based on knowledge of letter-sound correspondences and orthographic information, specific connections between the visual form of the printed word and its pronunciation stored in memory (phonological representation) are formed. The connections between the spelling of the word and its pronunciation are immediate, and the individual letter-sound translation rules, or phonological recoding, used in the phonological route are unnecessary. In essence, the reader "sees" the pronunciation of the word, which then creates direct links between the spelling and its meaning (Ehri, 1992, p. 116). This formulation suggests it is not the arbitrary visual cues of the word that are associated with the word's meaning in memory but the letter-sound cues that connect the visual form of the word to its pronunciation in memory. These connections are possible due to the prior phonological recoding knowledge used to read the word by the phonological route when the word was unfamiliar to the reader.

In summarizing the modified dual route theory, it is proposed that children first learn to read a word through the phonological route and decode the word using grapheme–phoneme conversion strategies. After experience in decoding the word, children learn to recognize the word instantly, and it is no longer necessary to decode each grapheme. However, this sight recognition is aided by phonological cues in the word (e.g., an initial phoneme cue), and it is not solely the orthographic shape of the word that provides access to the word's meaning.

This theory highlights the importance of phonological processing skills in the reading process and has important educational implications. According to Ehri (1992), decoding any word requires, to some extent, phonological processing knowledge. For this reason, children with inadequate phonological awareness skills not only will have difficulty recognizing printed words via a phonological route, but will also not reach age-appropriate levels of sight reading. This deficit may become particularly evident as reading texts increase in complexity, and the demands of remembering words visually, without using phonological information to aid memory, become overwhelming. Even by the second year of schooling, children who do not make use of phonological cues in reading, but rely solely on whole word recognition, are likely to be the poorest readers (Stuart, 1995). Spelling strategies that encourage a child to "look at the word, *say the word, listen to the sounds in the word*, cover the word, and then spell the word" are consistent with Ehri's modified model, in which accessing the visual form of the word, based on some phonological cues, is encouraged.

Analogy Model

The visual–phonological route for sight-word reading proposed by Ehri (1992) allows for spelling–pronunciation connections to be formed from knowledge of onset-rime spelling units. Knowledge of other words that have similar spelling patterns and pronunciations may help such connections form (e.g., recognizing the word *fat* because of its spelling and phonological similarities to known words *bat, mat,* and *cat*). Recognizing words in this manner has been described as "reading by analogy" (Goswami, 1991; Goswami & Bryant, 1992; Marsh, Desberg, & Cooper, 1977; Treiman, 1992).

Theories of reading analogy (Glushko, 1979; Goswami, 1994b; Marcel, 1980) suggest that readers access the stored pronunciation of words with similar spelling patterns rather than mapping each individual letter or letter pair to its corresponding phoneme. It is proposed that both regular and irregular words can be processed by analogy. Initial research in this area (Marsh et al., 1977; Marsh, Friedman, Welch, & Desberg, 1980) sug-

gested that analogy may be important in the later stages of reading development, when memory for a range of spelling–pronunciation patterns has
been consolidated through practice at the grapheme–phoneme conversion
level. Evidence to support this view is provided by Marsh and his colleagues' findings that 7-year-old children made fewer analogies of non-
words to real words than 10-year-old readers.

Others have argued that if younger children are given knowledge
about how a word can be divided into linguistic units at the onset-rime
level, then they can apply this knowledge to decode new words (Goswami
& Bryant, 1991). Rather than decoding a new word they encounter
phoneme-by-phoneme, children can use their knowledge of the rime unit.
Goswami and Bryant (1992) hypothesized that children's phonological
awareness at the onset-rime level contributes significantly to their formation of an orthographic category of common spelling patterns. Teaching
children to identify rhyming words, produce rhyming words, and segment
or blend words at the onset-rime unit supports an analogy theory of word
recognition. These activities should assist children in learning to read and
spell new words through analogy to known words.

Connectionist Models

Both the dual-route and the analogy models of word recognition have influenced the development of more recently formulated models, referred to
as "connectionist" or "parallel distributed processing" models of word
recognition. Although not without flaws (see (Coltheart, Curtis, Atkins,
& Haller, 1993, for a critical review), connectionist models may provide
a useful framework to explain typical reading and spelling development
as well as poor patterns of performance (Ehri, 2000; Treiman, 1993). It
is therefore important for professionals working in the area of reading
development and disorders to grasp an understanding of connectionist
models and to evaluate the teaching implications from such models.
Harm and Seidenberg (1999) and Baker, Croot, McCleod, and Paul
(2001) provided detailed explanations of connectionist models and described how these models have been implemented using computer programs.

Connectionist models of word processing that are based on the influential Seidenberg and McClelland model (Seidenberg & McClelland, 1989)
emphasize the importance of phonological information to word recognition. They propose that both regularly and irregularly spelled words can be
processed in the same manner, through a highly interconnected system of
orthographic, phonological, and semantic knowledge acquired by the
reader. Within a connectionist framework, phonological knowledge is nec-

essary to the processing of (1) unfamiliar words (tested by non-word reading), (2) learned words that can be decoded grapheme-by-grapheme (e.g., *sheep*) and (3) known words that involve irregular elements (e.g., *sword*). Connectionist models do not have a specific representation for grapheme–phoneme rule acquisition. Instead, accurate connections between graphemes and phonemes are seen as an emerging property of the learning process (Bjaalid, Hoien, & Lundberg, 1997).

A connectionist model proposes that the relationships between spoken and written words are gradually learned through distributed patterns of activity represented by orthographic, phonological, and semantic processors. For example, in reading the word *shop*, the printed word on the page (orthographic pattern) needs to generate an appropriate phonological representation. This transformation is achieved through excitatory and inhibitory interactions among orthographic, phonological, and semantic units. That is, connections between the letters in the words, the speech-sounds those letters represent, and the individual's vocabulary knowledge are necessary. In early stages of reading acquisition, when limited phonological knowledge is available, the orthographic form of *shop* may, for example, excite *any* phonological representation that starts with /s/. As connections are strengthened between specific graphemes and phonemes through the learning process, and increased phonological information is activated, only connections from the orthographic pattern close to phonological representations (e.g., *ship*, *shoe*, *show*) will be activated. Finally, with continued learning and access to a complete phonological representation of the word *shop*, the correct connections between the orthographic, phonological, and semantic patterns of activity will be strengthened, thereby facilitating the inhibition of all other connections.

In the model that has been simulated via a computer program, the strengthening of these connections is achieved by increasing the "weights" between particular input units (orthographic units to code the letter strings) and output units (to code phonological information). The weights represent learning. With more practice and experience in making a connection between a particular letter or letter string and its phonological form, the stronger the connection becomes. The connections between the input and output units in the computer simulation of the model are made via a set of "hidden units," which allow for complex connections to be made between the orthographic and phonological units. Understanding that one phoneme can be represented by more than one grapheme (e.g., /f/ is represented by *f* and *ph*) is an example of a complex connection.

Harm and Seidenberg (1999) extended an earlier connectionist framework to investigate the role of phonological information in early reading acquisition and to examine how phonological impairment may interfere with learning to read. Using computational modeling of their connectionist theory, they demonstrated that by impairing the phonological unit in the computer model, in which the phonological structure of words is learned (i.e., phonological awareness), the computer was less able to read nonwords and to generalize learning to untrained words. Severe impairment to the phonological unit resulted in marked difficulty in reading both nonwords and irregular words from which the model could not recover.

Connectionist models also might be used to explain poor spelling performance. In their computational model of a connectionist framework, Brown and Lossemore (1994) demonstrated that by reducing the number of connections between activity representing the phonological form of a word and activity representing the orthographic form of a word, the spelling performance of the computer model was very similar to the performance of children with dyslexia.

Some of the texts written on connectionist models can appear very abstract at first reading. It is difficult to immediately grasp an understanding of a model that is expressed in computational terms of "weights" and "hidden units." In comparison a dual-route model that has direct practical meaning—decoding a word letter by letter or visually remembering a whole word—may have more appeal to practitioners. Yet seen in the simplest terms, connectionist models have much relevance for understanding the role of phonological awareness in reading and spelling. Connectionist models are consistent with Ehri's modified dual-route model and the analogy models. These models hold that skilled readers use knowledge about a word's phonological structure (either at that phoneme level or onset-rime level) to recognize both regularly and irregularly spelled words in print. These models are also consistent with practical knowledge gained by professionals who witness the struggle that older poor readers have in acquiring an alphabetic language such as English. Most children who do not make rapid connections between the orthographic and phonological forms of a word do not become fluent readers. Learning words visually by rote may prove a successful technique in the early stages of reading, but as texts increase in complexity, learning the arbitrary visual shape of a word and attaching it to its meaning (without any cues from phonological information to assist memory) becomes unmanageable.

If skilled readers access meaning from a printed word through strong connections between orthographic, phonological, and semantic information networks (as suggested by connectionist models), it is logical to suggest that teaching practices should work to strengthen these connections in children who struggle to recognize words in print. Strengthening phonological awareness knowledge allows a child to use phonological information in making connections with orthographic and semantic information when reading and spelling.

DEVELOPMENT OF WORD RECOGNITION
AND SPELLING

The preceding models have provided theoretical frameworks related to how skilled readers recognize printed words. It is also important to understand the developmental process leading to competency in word recognition and spelling. Developmental models of reading and spelling acquisition typically propose sequential and progressive stages of development. Researchers hypothesize that children pass through defined stages in order to acquire efficient and fluent word recognition and spelling skills (Ehri, 1991; Frith, 1985; Gough & Hillinger, 1980; Marsh et al., 1980).

Stage models suggest that there are qualitatively different cognitive processes involved in each stage (Ellis, 1994). Recently, researchers have challenged this notion (e.g., Treiman & Bourassa, 2000). The failure of stage models to account for the complex interactions between different sources of knowledge in word recognition and spelling also has been criticized. It may be more useful, therefore, to view "stages" as a period in the child's development wherein a particular strategy may dominate, but the use of this strategy does not exclude the possibility of the child concurrently using other strategies or processes (Treiman & Bourassa, 2000).

Stage Models in Word Recognition

Three main stages are typically identified in stage models of word recognition: logographic, alphabetic, and orthographic. The *logographic* phase (Frith, 1985; Ehri, 1991) is characterized by the ability to recognize whole words, predominantly on the basis of salient graphic features. Contextual cues may assist the reader in attempting the word, but letter order and phonological factors receive little attention. Children as young as 2 and 3 years of age may effectively read environmental print such as advertising logos (Clay, 1991). For example, when a 2-year-old child recognizes the advertising sign for "McDonald's," he or she is demonstrating word recognition at the logographic stage. The child does not require any level of phonological awareness or letter-sound knowledge to demonstrate word recognition at this stage. Share (1995) argued that because positive correlations between "logographic reading" and skilled reading have *not* been demonstrated, it is best to consider it a prereading activity.

The next phase of word recognition relates to the acquisition of alphabetic knowledge and grapheme–phoneme correspondence. This stage has been described (Frith, 1985) as the alphabetic phase of word recognition development and conceptualized further (Ehri, 1991) into the rudimentary alphabetic phase and then the alphabetic stage. In the rudimentary alphabetic phase (also termed "phonetic cue reading"), the reader begins to learn connections between the written and spoken forms. Partial spelling–sound connections (initially with only one or two letters) are made, causing the substitution of words that have similar visual–phonetic cues—for example, *jail* for *jewel* (Ehri, 1992). Unlike the logographic stage wherein the connections are arbitrary, the reader is beginning to form systematic connections between some letters and sounds. Initially children make many errors as the letter cues used appear in a number of other words. As reading experienced is gained, however, attention is focused more closely on the spelling-to-sound relations and these are then established in memory (Ehri, 1992).

Corresponding to Firth's (1985) alphabetic stage is Ehri's (1991) mature alphabetic stage. Here children acquire the ability to analyze spellings fully, permitting the accurate translation of graphemes to phonemes. Thus words with similar pronunciations that may have been confused in the rudimentary alphabetic stage are now discriminated. Phonological awareness skills are crucial at both the rudimentary and mature alphabetic stages of word recognition development, because they allow the reader to analyze the word at the sub-word level.

In the final orthographic phase (Frith, 1985; Ehri, 1991), children develop the ability to instantly recognize the morphemic parts of words, taking letter order into account. Through experience at the alphabetic stage, readers begin to recognize common letter patterns such as *ing, ment, ed*. At the orthographic stage of development, they can read these segments as whole units based on phonological knowledge, rather than using grapheme–phoneme conversion strategies for each letter in the unit. This phonological knowledge allows speed and efficiency in reading to be achieved. However, in contrast to the logographic stage, the connections are analytic and systematic.

Stage Models in Spelling Development

Based on early research that analyzed and categorized children's spelling attempts (e.g., Henderson & Beers, 1980; see Ellis, 1994, for a review), distinct stages of spelling development have been identified. As with stage models of word recognition, the concept of defined developmental stages in spelling also has been criticized (Treiman & Bourassa, 2000; see further discussion later in this section). A general understanding of spelling stages, however, provides a useful framework by which to describe developmental aspects of children's spelling attempts.

Ellis (1994) proposed that children pass through precommunicative, semiphonetic, phonetic, and transitional stages of spelling before reaching well-established correct spellings of words. These stages generally follow the same stages as those described for word recognition. Models of spelling and word recognition proposed by Ehri (1986) and Frith (1985) reflect the interactive links between reading and spelling and suggest that the processes mutually influence each other. This section summarizes each of the stages in spelling development, relates the stages in spelling to those of word recognition, and comments on the involvement of phonological awareness at each stage. The summaries are based on descriptions of spelling stages discussed by Ellis (1994) and Ehri (2000).

Precommunicative Spelling

At this stage of spelling development, children's writing attempts may be scribble-like in nature with only partial resemblance to letter forms. The child may know how to form some letters (such as the letters in his or her name), and these letters may be included in writing attempts. The letters used for creative spelling, however, bear no resemblance to the phonology of the intended word. Rather, the spelling attempts are random strings of letters. A young child may accurately spell a word, such as his or her name by visually copying a whole word as a result of teaching, but the child has no understanding of the relationship between the letters he or she is forming on the page and the phonemes they represent. This stage of spelling relates to the prealphabetic stage of word recognition, in which a child's reading attempt is based on associated visual features and environmental contexts of the word and involves no use of phonological information. Likewise, there is no evidence of phonological awareness knowledge in the child's writing attempts at the precommunicative spelling stage.

Semiphonetic Spelling

Children who are beginning to show evidence that they understand how letters are used to represent sounds in words demonstrate the use of semiphonetic spelling strategies. Partial mapping between letters and sounds is evident, and the use of a letter-name strategy is common (e.g., the word *are* spelled as *R*, or *you* represented by *U*; Ellis, 1994). The salient consonants in words are the likely sounds to be represented, and incomplete representations of the word's sound structure is evident. This stage in spelling corresponds to the rudimentary alphabetic stage or phonetic cue stage of word recognition where partial-decoding attempts of words in print is apparent. Evidence of emergent phonological awareness knowledge is seen in semiphonetic spelling attempts. Initial phonemes in words or stressed syllables may be accurately represented, indicating the child's awareness that words are comprised of individual phonemes. Complete phoneme segmentation ability is not evident, however.

Phonetic Spelling

Phonetic spelling attempts involve closer approximations to spelling the word the way it sounds. The main phonological features in the word are represented in the spelling, but knowledge of complex phoneme–grapheme connections and spelling conventions, such as representing final /k/ in back with a ck, and knowledge of vowel diagraphs are not well established (Ellis, 1994). Marking of vowels in unstressed syllables may be absent. Ehri (2000) also noted that orally segmenting the word and spelling the segmented form (e.g., adding additional vowels) is characteristic of the phonetic spelling stage. Children are using their knowledge of the alphabet and regular phoneme–grapheme relationships. This level of spelling ability relates to the alphabetic stage of reading development, in which children are able to use alphabetic knowledge in decoding words. Phonological awareness skills are clearly evident in children's phonetic spelling attempts. They can use knowledge about a word's sound structure to relate the phonemes they hear in the word to associated graphemes or to close approximations. Phonological awareness knowledge gained at the prephonetic and phonetic stages of spelling positively influences the use of the alphabetic strategy in reading (Ellis, 1994; Frith, 1985).

Transitional Stage

The transitional stage (or consolidated alphabetic stage, as described by Ehri, 2000) is marked by the speller's closer adherence to orthographic conventions. Reading experience and exposure to correct orthographic sequences help to facilitate spelling skills at the transitional stage (Ehri, 1994; Frith, 1985). Syllable awareness in spelling multisyllabic words is evident, and each syllable is marked with a vowel. Differences in vowel sounds are marked with the use of diagraphs—for example, spelling *cake* as *caik* or *caek*. The overuse of final *e* spelling pattern also may be evident at this stage. Morphological knowledge is applied to spelling though the use of phonological cues such as representing *ed* as *id* or *ment* as *mint*. The transition from phonetic spelling to morphological and orthographic spelling apparent at this stage (Ellis, 1994) suggests that the child is integrating phonological awareness knowledge with visual orthographic knowledge.

   With the development of complete orthographic and phonological representation of words, the mastery of correct spellings emerges.

Spelling Examples

Figure 2.2 displays the spelling of two children who started formal schooling at 5 years. The spellings were collected after approximately 18 months

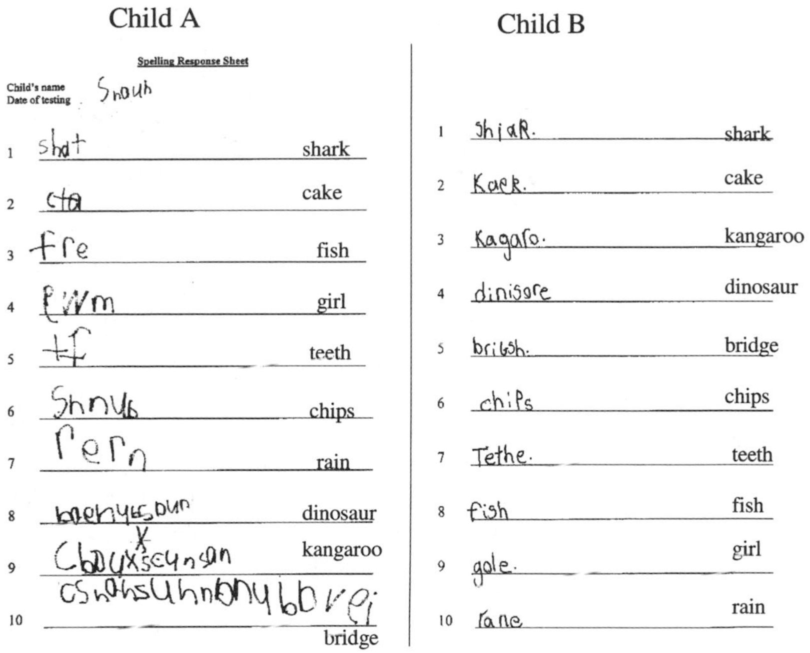

Child A

Spelling Response Sheet

Child's name
Date of testing . Shauh

1. shat   shark
2. cta   cake
3. fre   fish
4. Pwm   girl
5. tf   teeth
6. Shnub   chips
7. Pern   rain
8. baehyesbun   dinosaur
9. Cbaux5cynan   kangaroo
10. cSnehsUhnbnybbvei   bridge

Child B

1. ShjaR.   shark
2. Kaek.   cake
3. Kagaro.   kangaroo
4. dinisore   dinosaur
5. brilsh.   bridge
6. chiPs   chips
7. Tethe.   teeth
8. fish   fish
9. gole.   girl
10. rane   rain

FIGURE 2.2. The spelling attempts of two 6-year-old children

of classroom reading and spelling instruction. The children were of comparable nonverbal ability, and both received scores within the normal range on a measure of receptive language ability. The children participated in similar classroom reading and spelling programs, and their teachers implementing the same language curriculum. The children's spelling attempts clearly indicate different stages of development. Child A's attempts may be described as predominantly semiphonetic. Partial phoneme-to-grapheme mapping is evident on items 1–7 (item 4 shows a reversal form of the letter *g*). Evidence of spelling at the precommunicative stage is also apparent. Items 8, 9, and 10 appear as random strings of letters, with the possible exception that the C in item 9 relates to /k/ for kangaroo. Letters from the child's name (Shaun) also commonly appear in these spelling attempts. The spelling attempts for *teeth* (which the child pronounced as *teef*) and *rain* suggest development toward the phonetic stage with the marking of the salient consonant sounds of the word in the correct order and attempt at the vowel sound in *rain*.

Child A's spelling attempts suggest limited phonological awareness knowledge. The child is developing an awareness of the initial phoneme in words and how this phoneme maps to a grapheme, but more advanced phonemic awareness skills are not evident. This was confirmed by Child A's poor performance on standardized tests of phonological awareness.

Child B's spelling is predominantly at the transitional stage (although there is evidence of both phonetic and correct spellings). The spellings contain vowels in each syllable, vowel diagraphs are attempted, and there is an overuse of silent *e*. Attention to correct orthographic forms and conventions of English are evident. Strategies from the phonetic stage of development are also apparent. The spelling attempt for *bridge* (*brigsh*) suggests the child is drawing out the sounds in the words to access the word's phonology. The use of a phoneme segmentation strategy is also suggested by the child's attempt at *shark* (*shi-a-k*) *kangaroo* (*ka-ga-ro*), and *dinosaur* (*di-ni-sore*). Child B demonstrated strong phonological awareness skills on a standardized assessment measures.

The stages of spelling development are useful to provide a broad description of these children's current abilities. However, the observation that the children were using multiple strategies across stages supports Treiman and Bourassa's (2000) contention that spelling development cannot be viewed strictly according to defined stages. One strategy may be predominant at a given point in time, but some children can use multiple strategies and integrate different types of knowledge from the onset of spelling development. The stage model also does not account easily for why children can read and spell some types of words more accurately than other words in the process of learning to read and spell. In the spelling example, it was obvious that the words *dinosaur*, *kangaroo*, and *bridge* presented much more difficulty for Child A than the other stimulus items. Child B had more difficulty spelling particular phonemes (i.e. vowels and *dge* in the word *bridge*) than other phonemes.

The following discussion of the "self-teaching model" addresses these word- and phoneme-specific differences in children's development of word recognition and spelling.

Self-Teaching Hypothesis

The self-teaching hypothesis (Share, 1995; Share & Stanovich, 1995) presents an item-based rather than a stage-based model for decoding words in print. Share hypothesized that children become efficient in recognizing printed words through a self-teaching process rather than passing through well-defined stages in a predetermined manner. That is, from each successful decoding attempt, children learn specific information about the word's orthography from which they acquire an orthographic representation of the word. A relatively small number of successful decoding experiences is necessary to establish an orthographic representation that can be accessed in future encounters of the word. Words that a child decodes frequently in early reading experiences (high-frequency reading words) gain well-established orthographic representations that the child can access efficiently, with little decoding required. In contrast, less familiar words, for which an orthographic representation has yet to be established, require decoding until sufficient exposures of the word enable the orthographic representation to be accessed (or "self-teaching" to take place).

The child may begin the self-teaching process by learning simple one-to-one phoneme–grapheme correspondences, but with increased decoding experiences and exposure to words in print the child learns more complex relationships between phonemes and graphemes as they occur among other orthographic and morphemic constraints. In reviewing the literature, Share (1995) discussed how the phonological and orthographic complexity of the word influences the decoding attempt. In early development consonants are more likely than vowels to be decoded successfully, because grapheme–phoneme connections for consonants are generally less variable. (Practitioners who have worked with older poor readers will immediately relate to the enormous struggle some children have in efficiently decoding vowels.) Successful decoding of initial consonants may be established prior to final consonant decoding, but decoding of initial consonant blends pose difficulties in early self-teaching attempts.

The self-teaching model proposes that the ability to decode words using knowledge of grapheme–phoneme relationships is the primary component involved in the development of fluent word reading. The ability to process visual information (i.e., store and retrieve orthographic information) is regarded as a secondary component that is heavily dependent on successful phonological processing. This view is consistent with Ehri's (1992) modified dual-route model of word recognition, in which skilled sight reading is based on making systematic connections between phonological and orthographic information and not arbitrary rote learning of visual word shapes or other such orthographic cues. Within the self-teaching model, the development of the ability to recognize words by sight (as opposed to decoding each word letter by letter) may be viewed as the product of accumulated phonological and orthographic word knowledge developed in response to successful decoding attempts.

Phonological awareness skills are central to the self-teaching hypothesis. Phonological awareness, together with letter-sound knowledge, allows for the initial successful decoding attempts of printed words on which visual and orthographic processing are dependent. Children with poor phonological awareness skills will struggle in their early attempts to decode words. They will be exposed to far fewer decoding attempts than early successful readers, and they will become less likely to be exposed to more complex phoneme–grapheme relationships. Thus their opportunities to engage in a "self-teaching process" are severely restricted. In contrast, children who approach decoding with an awareness of the sound structure of words and how letters map onto sounds will gain success from early decoding attempts. This successful decoding will increase their knowledge of how phonemes in words can be segmented and blended together, which in turn will allow for increased success in decoding and the establishment of accurate orthographic representations of words.

Consistent with Shares self-teaching hypothesis for word recognition is Treiman's (1993) description of children's spelling development. Treiman discussed how spelling development occurs in relation to frequency of exposure to the phoneme–grapheme relationships in words. In a comprehensive study involving detailed analyses of the spelling abilities of 43 6- to 7-year-old children, Treiman drew a number of important conclusions about children's early spelling development. Among these conclusions are points that reflect Share's hypotheses about word recognition development. For example, Treiman demonstrated that first-grade children were more likely to spell words correctly to which they had received frequent exposure in print. The frequency of the word's exposure, rather than its perceived spelling difficulty, also determined how often a child attempted to spell a word. Context of the phoneme within the word also influenced children's spelling development. Treiman reported that complex connections such as one phoneme but two letters in the grapheme (e.g., *sh*) or one phoneme but multiple spellings (e.g., /f/: *f* or *ph*) were harder to strengthen (i.e., developed later) than simple connections such as /t/ that is only represented by the letter *t*. Connections between initial and final phonemes were stronger then those with medial phonemes. Treiman also emphasized the importance of analyzing children's misspellings. Careful analysis of spelling attempts provides important information about a child's spelling development, particularly his or her acquisition of phoneme–grapheme knowledge.

From a practical perspective, understanding both stage and self-teaching models of word recognition and spelling development is useful. If a "weaker" position of the stage models discussed in the previous section is adopted (i.e., stages describe the dominant strategies used in word recognition and spelling but do not exclude interaction with other strategies and processes), then they can provide a useful framework for a broad description of children's reading and spelling development. Stages also provide a common vocabulary that can be used among practitioners to describe dominant strategies used by a child. Understanding the self-teaching hypothesis draws attention to word-specific and phoneme–grapheme-specific information. This model provides deeper insight into the development of word recognition and spelling processes and highlights the importance of analyzing children's reading and spelling errors. The model places importance on examining the types of words that are successfully or unsuccessfully read and spelled and suggests the need for more detailed assessment of the child's reading and spelling strategies than would be gained by simply categorizing a child at any particular stage of reading or spelling development.

Understanding children's phonological awareness development is critical to both stage and self-teaching models of word recognition and spelling. Poor phonological awareness skills severely restrict children's progress through the stages of development. Firth (1985) hypothesized that the development of children with reading disorder is largely arrested at the alphabetic stage of word recognition due to inadequate phonological processing ability. The self-teaching model holds that poor phonological awareness precludes children from engaging in the self-teaching processes that skilled readers and spellers employ.

CONNECTED TEXT READING MODEL

The previous models of word recognition discussed in this chapter depict how words might be read or spelled in isolation. However, contextual features also can facilitate word recognition when reading connected text. In addition to single word recognition, a variety of linguistic skills contribute to the comprehension of text, such as understanding semantic relationships in sentences, semantic association skills, using context to determine the appropriate meaning of words with multiple meanings, and utilizing knowledge of sentence and narrative structure to enhance comprehension (Roth & Spekman, 1989). Integrating information from word-level and higher-order processing is generally now considered within an interactive model.

The interactive model described by Rumelhart (1977) integrates two strongly opposing views that dominated earlier research. These views were referred to as the *bottom-up* and *top-down* processing views. The bottom-up model (e.g., Gough, 1972) depicted reading in a linear fashion that involved a series of hierarchical steps. This sequential process emphasized decoding skills in translating the printed string of letters to spoken form and accessing meaning. In contrast, the top-down model emphasized the centrality of meaning and the importance of higher cognitive processes, such as syntactic and semantic skills, in governing lower-level information processes (Smith, 1971). This view described reading as a psycholinguistic guessing game (Goodman, 1970). Researchers hypothesized that semantic knowledge and knowledge of syntactic structures helps readers narrow down the possibilities of what is to come next in the text and make plausible guesses at the words; that is, contextual knowledge provides "cues" for the reader in the word recognition process (Athey, 1977; Goodman, 1985).

The extremity of these two positions has been strongly criticized. For example, Rumelhart (1977) and Danks (1978) discussed a number of experimental findings related to the effects of semantic and syntactic contexts on word recognition that cannot be explained by the bottom-up serial stage model, because the bottom-up model provides no mechanism whereby higher-level processes can influence lower-level processes (Stanovich, 1980). The prediction, from the top-down view, that skilled readers should be more dependent on contextual information to speed word recognition has been disproved (Stanovich, 1984). Contextual cues to facilitate word recognition are just as likely to be used by poor readers.

Most researchers now support some form of interactive model to conceptualize reading of connected text. An interactive model holds that skilled readers use information from different processing levels simultaneously when engaged in the act of reading; lower-level processes are not necessarily completed before higher-level processes are initiated. Rather, several sources of information simultaneously are synthesized. Such synthesis of information increases reading accuracy. For example, given an early reading book about farm animals, a child may read: "The horse likes to eat _____," with the last word, *grass*, being unknown to the child. If only employing top-down strategies, the child may call upon his or her knowledge about what horses like to eat: hay, carrots, oats, straw, or grass. This strategy would result in a high chance of error, as a number of words would make semantic and grammatical sense. Indeed, Share (1995) argued that children are twice as likely to guess words wrong than choose the correct word if only using semantic, syntactic, or pragmatic information. However, if the reader also integrates phonological and orthographic information—knowing, for example, that the letters *gr* make a /gr/ sound and understanding that the word *grass* starts with a /gr/ sound—then the child is more likely to select the correct word: *grass*.

Failure to use phonological information but draw only upon contextual cues will result in a higher rate of reading errors that do not even partially resemble the target word. Teachers who work with children with reading disorder easily identify this "wild guessing" type of strategy. Such a strategy may become a source of frustration to parents of poor readers, particularly parents of older children, as it may be interpreted as lack of effort or cooperation by the child. Parents may perceive these wild guesses as an indication that the child is not even trying to read the words on the page, but is simply making up words as he or she reads. Knowledge of children's phonological awareness and, more generally, phonological processing skills will provide insight into why children are unable to use phonological information when reading text. Interventions to develop phonological processing skills focus on improving children's ability to use phonological information and developing both accuracy and comprehension of connected text.

SUMMARY

This chapter has presented theoretical contexts for understanding the importance of phonological awareness to reading and spelling. The following points emphasize key issues discussed in this chapter:

- Phonological awareness contributes to reading comprehension via its importance to word recognition ability.
- Phonological awareness contributes to writing via its importance to early spelling.
- Phonological awareness is critical to word recognition because it helps readers decode words and use phonological information to access orthographic representations of words and their meaning.
- Phonological awareness is critical to early spelling development because it helps the speller map phonemes to graphemes and recognize common spelling units within words.
- Phonological awareness is an important component of each model of word recognition and spelling development presented in this chapter. It contributes to:
  1. The decoding of regular words by the phonological route, as proposed by the dual-route theory.
  2. The recognition of both regular and irregular words, as proposed by modified dual-route theory and connectionist models.
  3. Understanding common spelling units, noted in analogy models.
  4. The prealphabetic stage of word recognition, facilitating development into the alphabetic and orthographic stages of word recognition.
  5. The semiphonetic stage of spelling development, permitting progress into the alphabetic and transitional stages of spelling.
  6. The successful decoding attempts that are the foundation of the self-teaching hypothesis for word recognition acquisition.
  7. The ability to integrate phonological information with semantic and syntactic knowledge when reading connected text.

FROM RESEARCH TO PRACTICE

A variety of practical implications can be drawn from the research and theoretical models discussed in this chapter:

1. It is important to consider the type of knowledge children need to draw upon in a class reading or spelling activity. For example, a visual approach to spelling—"Look at the word, cover the word, visualize the word,

then spell the word three times"—does not bring attention to the phonological cues in the word. This absence limits the use of a critical strategy typically employed by skilled readers and spellers and reflects a theoretical model (dual route) that has been heavily criticized in the literature. In contrast, teaching young children a spelling strategy that requires them to (1) articulate the word, (2) listen to the sounds in the word, (3) identify the initial and final sounds in the word, and (4) observe the visual aspects of the word, encourages the integration of phonological and orthographic information. Such a strategy is well supported by current theoretical models of spelling (e.g., connectionist models).

2. Teaching practices that focus on enhancing children's strengths and talents in learning are obviously to be encouraged. Caution, however, in applying these practices to the development of word recognition and spelling skills is necessary. Teaching children to read or spell words solely using a visual approach because they are considered to have stronger visual than phonological processing skills will ultimately restrict their reading and spelling development. Interactive theories, connectionist models, and modified dual-route models dictate that children need both phonological and orthographic knowledge. Thus focusing on enhancing a learning strength (i.e., visual processing) at the expense of resolving a deficit (i.e., phonological processing) is unlikely to result in long-term reading success.

3. Children need many experiences in successfully decoding text. The concept of the self-teaching model and the systematic strengthening of phoneme–grapheme relationships proposed by connectionist and modified dual-route models all suggest that word recognition and spelling development are established from such experiences.

In planning curriculum activities, it is essential that sufficient teaching time is devoted to providing opportunities for *all* children to engage in successful reading and writing experiences. Children with differing learning needs and children with language learning difficulties who are integrated into mainstream classes frequently require more teaching time devoted to fostering successful decoding and encoding experiences than children with typically developing skills. For example, difficulty accessing text or processing information for a child with severe physical impairments is likely to result in far fewer successful decoding experiences in any given time period than a child without such impairments. Therefore, although a balance in curriculum activities is essential, the importance of establishing successful reading and writing experiences in the early school years needs to be considered against other curriculum and extracurricular activities that all compete for class time.

4. Ensuring that early reading books are an appropriate level for the child will foster successful reading experiences. If spelling lists are used,

providing lists of regular spelling patterns at levels appropriate to the child's ability also will foster successful decoding and encoding of words.

5. It is critical to develop the underlying skills in spoken language upon which written language is based. Although phonological awareness is central to the decoding and encoding of text, other aspects of spoken language also must be developed. Teaching practices that strongly foster children's spoken language abilities in a variety of areas, in particular, working to strengthen semantic, syntactic, and phonological awareness skills, are consistent with interactive theories of word recognition when reading connected text.

6. Developing children's phonological awareness skills and knowledge of letter–sound relationships in preschool and the first year at school will contribute to the building of a strong foundation for decoding and encoding print. Such practices are consistent with the "self-teaching" theory which views efficient decoding as central to fluent word reading development.

Understanding the theoretical contexts of how phonological awareness helps foster word recognition and spelling knowledge, and, in turn, how enhanced word recognition ability promotes reading comprehension provides the framework within which to evaluate instruction in phonological awareness. Interventions to promote phonological awareness that result in improved word recognition and spelling abilities and, ultimately, improved reading comprehension performance can be considered successful interventions.

3

Phonological Awareness Development

Many factors may potentially influence reading and writing development. Factors extrinsic to the child, such as cultural, socioeconomic, and instructional methods, as well as intrinsic factors of intellectual ability, sensory and physical functioning, oral language skills, and knowledge of print concepts all undoubtedly influence literacy development. Phonological awareness is only one component that contributes to written language competency. However, its well-established importance to reading and spelling acquisition necessitates a careful understanding of how children develop an explicit awareness of a word's sound structure. Knowledge of factors that influence phonological awareness development is also critical. This chapter explores the development of phonological awareness in children and discusses literature that supports the predictive relationship of phonological awareness to word recognition and spelling success.

THE DEVELOPMENT OF PHONOLOGICAL AWARENESS IN ENGLISH

Children first learn about the sound structure of language as a result of their biological predisposition to acquire a spoken communication system. Sensitivity to the sound structure of a native language begins early in life. By only 4 months of age, a range of speech perceptual skills that contribute to the child's representation of the sound structure of adult words has developed. These skills have been summarized by Jusczyk (1992): By 4 months of age, infants are able to (1) discriminate their mother's voice from other female voices, discriminate between speech contrasts, (2) distinguish utterances in their maternal language from those in foreign languages, (3) recognize the same syllable in different utterances, (4) detect intonation changes, and (5) represent some speech contrasts over short delay periods when attention is directed to the relevant dimensions.

The perception of speech sounds from infancy occurs at an unconscious level. In contrast, phonological awareness requires children to make explicit the knowledge they have gained about the sound structure of spoken words and to consciously reflect upon elements of spoken language in a manner that is separate from word meaning (Mattingly, 1972). A developmental progression in the emergence of this ability to become consciously aware of a word's sound structure is apparent. Liberman et al. (1974) provided the first direct evidence of a developmental sequence in the emergence of phonological awareness abilities. Based on extensive research in speech perception, they hypothesized that segmenting a spoken word into syllables would be mastered earlier than segmenting a word into individual components. The acoustic signal of a spoken word cannot be segmented, in any easy manner, to correspond with the phonemic segments of a word. As discussed in Chapter 1, the acoustic energy that marks syllables in spoken words provides audible cues that may help a child segment a word into its syllabic parts, thereby facilitating awareness of a word's syllabic structure at a younger age (Liberman et al., 1974).

In testing their hypothesis, Liberman et al. (1974) recruited 135 children in nursery, kindergarten, or first-grade classes in middle socioeconomic areas of Connecticut. The children at each grade level were randomly divided into two experimental groups. There were no group differences in age or intellectual abilities. Children with speech, hearing, or behavioral problems were excluded from the experiment. Children in group 1 were engaged in a phoneme segmentation task in which they were required to tap out the number of phonemes in stimulus items containing one, two, or three phonemes (e.g., *I* = one phoneme, *out* = two phonemes, *book* = three phonemes). Children in group 2 tapped out the number of syllables in a word of one-, two-, or three-syllable length (e.g., *dog*, *birthday*, *superman*). The results clearly demonstrated a task and age effect. Children more readily segmented words into syllables at each grade level. At the nursery level (average age 4 years, 11 months) 46% of the children could segment words into syllables. That is, they reached criterion level of six consecutive correct items. None of the children in this age group reached criterion when attempting to segment words into phonemes. By the end of first grade (average age 6 years, 11 months) 90% of the children had mastered the syllable segmentation task and 70% successfully completed the phoneme segmentation task.

Subsequent research has confirmed a developmental progression in phonological awareness; an awareness of larger units in words develops prior to awareness of smaller units (Caravolas & Bruck, 1993; Chaney, 1992; Fox & Routh, 1975; Johnston, Anderson, & Holligan, 1996; Stanovich et al., 1984; Treiman & Zukowsky, 1991). In the most comprehensive study of phonological awareness development in young children from the United States, Lonigan, Burgess, Anthony, and Barker (1998) investigated the syllable, onset-rime, and phoneme levels. A total of 356 children, between 2 and 5 years of age, participated in the study: 238 predominantly Caucasian children from middle- to high-income families, and 118 predominantly African American children from low-income families. Analyses of participants' ability to detect rhyme and alliteration oddity, blend letters to form words, and blend words to form a compound word (e.g., *b* + *a* + *t* = *bat*; *cow* + *boy* = *cowboy*) and delete part of a word (e.g., say *batman* without the *bat*; say *heat* without saying /t/) revealed the following:

- Age influenced performance on all tasks for children from middle-income families. Accelerated growth in phonological awareness was evident between the ages of 3 and 4 years for these children. Increased rate of growth over time was less evident for children from low-income families.
- The linguistic complexity of the task influenced performance. Children across age groups showed stronger performance on blending and deleting items at a whole word level (e.g., *cow* + *boy* = *cowboy*), followed by success at the syllable level (e.g., *sis* + *ter* = *sister*), with the weakest performance evident at the phoneme level (e.g., *b* + *a* + *t* = *bat*).
- There were no significant differences in performance between girls and boys.
- Performance on the phonological awareness tasks was moderately correlated with performance on receptive and expressive language tasks at the 4- and 5-year-old levels, but not at the 2- and 3-year-old levels.
- Children from middle-income families performed better than children from low-income families, even after controlling for differences in oral language abilities.

Stability in phonological awareness task performance emerged only from 4 years of age. Two- and 3-year-old children generally showed low performance on all tasks and wide variability both within and across tasks. It was only in the 5-year-old age group that the majority of children (75%) in the middle-income families scored significantly above chance level on the rhyme oddity task. Almost half of the 5-year-old children from middle-income families demonstrated confidence on the phoneme detection task. In contrast, a clear majority of 5-year-old children from low-income families failed to score above chance level on the rhyme oddity, phone detection, and blending tasks.

Analysis of recent normative data on phonological awareness assessment measures for young British and Australian children indicated that most 4-year-olds exhibited very limited phonological awareness other than syllable segmentation and the emergence of rhyme (Dodd & Gillon, 2001). Data from screening assessments of approximately 1,000 6-year-old New Zealand children demonstrated that although rhyming knowledge was established in this age group, phoneme segmentation and blending ability was only emerging (Gillon & Schwarz, 1999). Such data are consistent with findings involving children from the United States and suggest general, universal trends in phonological awareness development for the English language.

Although at a group level, stability in phonological awareness performance is not evident in children younger than 4 years, some 2- and 3-year-old children can demonstrate phonological awareness knowledge. Maclean, Bryant, and Bradley (1987) produced the first evidence that a moderate percentage of 3-year-old children can perform competently on a rhyme detection task. In assessing 66 British 3-year-old children (average age 3 years, 4 months) the researchers adapted a rhyme oddity task developed by Bradley and Bryant (1983). Pictures were introduced to reduce the memory demands of the task. Children were asked to name three pictures (e.g., *cat, hat, bell*) and point out which picture did not rhyme. Ten stimulus items were presented following the two training items. Close to 25% of the children scored significantly above chance level (i.e., at least seven of the 10 items were correct). In Lonigan et al.'s (1998) study the same rhyme detection task was presented to 55 2-year-old children from the United States (average age 2 years, 6 months) and again 25% of the group scored significantly above chance. Thus, some very young children can demonstrate phonological awareness knowledge.

Some researchers have questioned the progressive theory of phonological awareness development (i.e., syllable awareness emerges before rhyme awareness, which emerges before phoneme awareness; Duncan & Johnston, 1999; Muter, 1994). Individual case reports of older poor readers who performed better on phoneme manipulation tasks than on rhyme judgment tasks (Duncan & Johnston, 1999) are contrary to the general trend in phonological awareness development exhibited by most children. Understanding whether there is a smooth progression from one level of phonological awareness to the next, and whether awareness of larger units is necessary to facilitate awareness of smaller units for all children, requires continued research. Heterogeneity among good and poor readers must be considered in phonological awareness development, and understanding the influence of reading and spelling experiences on mediating shifts between levels of phonological awareness is critical.

PHONOLOGICAL AWARENESS DEVELOPMENT IN SPEAKERS OF OTHER ALPHABETIC LANGUAGES

In comparison to other languages, English has an inconsistent relationship between phonemes and graphemes. Although only about 14% of common English words may be considered phonetically "irregular" (Moats, 2000, p. 96) examples of variations between phoneme–grapheme associations are easily found. Orthographically similar words that do not rhyme (e.g., *through, rough*; *beard, heard*) and orthographically different words that do rhyme (*tea, key, me, see*) are examples of these variations. Mayringer and Wimmer (2000) discussed how alphabetic languages that have more consistency between phonemes and graphemes, such as German, Dutch, Spanish, Italian, Portuguese, Greek, and Turkish, are easier than English to read using a phonological strategy. These languages may not demand the same level of phonological awareness competence in the early stages of reading and spelling that English demands.

Investigations have established the same developmental sequence of phonological awareness emergence in other alphabetic languages. Prereading Spanish-speaking children demonstrated early knowledge of syllables, rhyme, and alliteration, but phoneme segmentation ability typically developed after exposure to reading (Carrillo, 1994; Denton, Hasbrouck, Weaver, & Riccio, 2000; Gonzalez & Garcia, 1995). Grade 1 Spanish-speaking students were competent in segmenting Spanish words into syllables and blending syllables to form words. They demonstrated more difficulty, however, in segmenting and blending words at the onset-rime and phoneme levels (Durgunoglu, Nagy, & Hancin-Bhatt, 1993). Syllable segmentation ability also has been shown to develop prior to phoneme segmentation in Italian children (Cossu, Shankweiler, Liberman, Katz, & Tola, 1988).

Children learning English as their second language are able to demonstrate phonological awareness skills in English after a relatively short period of study (Chiappe & Siegel, 1999), suggesting that the development of phonological awareness skills in one alphabetic language transfers to understanding phonological awareness in a second alphabetic language. Chiappe and Siegel reported that grade 1 children who spoke English as a second language demonstrated comparable phonological awareness skills to children for whom English was a first language. In this study, 50 English-speaking Canadian children (from Toronto middle-class suburbs) were compared to 38 Punjabi-speaking children from a similar neighborhood level on a range of phonemic awareness tasks. The average age of the children at the assessment trial was 6 years. The Punjabi-speaking children spoke Punjabi at home with both parents but had been exposed to English at preschool since 4 years of age. The phonological awareness tasks were presented in English. Results indicated no significant group differences based on language groups for any of the phonological tasks. This competency in phonological awareness was evident despite the incomplete mastery of the English language for the Punjabi-speaking children. They performed significantly worse on a measure of syntactic ability in English compared to native English speakers. There also were significant group differences on the phonological tasks based on reading ability. That is, good readers who were native Punjabi speakers demonstrated the same level of phonological awareness ability as good readers who were native speakers of English. Both of these groups demonstrated significantly stronger phonological awareness skills than native English and native Punjabi speakers who were poor readers.

These results support other findings in the literature. Children who were bilingual in French and English displayed comparable phonological awareness skills in their native language and in their second language (Comeau, Cormier, Grandmaison, & Lacroix, 1999). The development of phonological awareness, then, is not strictly language specific. Rather, the cognitive processes involved in developing an awareness of the sound structure of words in one language can be applied to other alphabetic languages (Comeau et al., 1999).

Language experiences, though, can influence (1) performance on specific phonological awareness tasks, (2) the rate at which phonological awareness increases, and (3) the use of phonological awareness knowledge in the reading and spelling process. Cossu et al. (1988) observed that Italian children developed stronger syllable awareness skills at an early age compared to English-speaking children. English speakers showed superior phonological awareness abilities compared to Cantonese speakers (Cheung, Chen, Lai, Wong, & Hills, 2001) and Japanese speakers (Mann, 1987) at the prereading or early reading level. Differences in the dominant language—English, Mandarin, or Bahasa Indonesia—influenced the performance of multilingual Chinese children on tasks that required use of phonological knowledge (spelling and reading non-words) (Liow & Poon, 1998). Holm and Dodd (1996) also reported that students from Hong Kong whose first language was a non-alphabetic script (and who had English as their second language) had difficulty using phonological information to decode non-words in English. The researchers suggested that adequate exposure to an alphabetic script, as opposed to a logographic script, appears necessary for the use of phonological knowledge. Further, a transparent alphabetic script (i.e., one that shows regularity in grapheme–phoneme connections) may provide an advantage in learning to use phonological knowledge in reading and spelling (Liow & Poon, 1998; Mayringer & Wimmer, 2000).

PREDICTIVE POWER OF EARLY PHONOLOGICAL AWARENESS DEVELOPMENT

The ability to predict which children in kindergarten will experience difficulty with reading and spelling has tremendous social, economic, and educational value. No parent or teacher likes to see a child struggle to acquire knowledge that is considered fundamental in a literate society. The identification of young children who may be at risk for reading and spelling problems holds the promise of intervention to prevent the academic difficulties these children may otherwise encounter, and has therefore received much deserved attention in the research literature. In particular, the predictive power of phonological awareness in relation to later reading and spelling performance has been examined.

Stemming from earlier research that established a relationship between awareness of the sound structure of words and reading achievement (e.g., Liberman, 1971), Lundberg et al. (1980) implemented the first comprehensive investigation into the possibility of predicting reading and spelling based on measures of phonological awareness at preschool. In this study, 133 Swedish children were followed from kindergarten (approximately 6–7 years of age) through to grade 2 (8–9 years of age). In kindergarten the children were administered a battery of tests that included phonological awareness tasks at the syllabic level (syllable segmentation and blending tasks), onset-rime level (rhyme production task), and phoneme level (phoneme segmentation and blending tasks, phoneme detection and manipulation tasks). Measures of general cognitive ability and preschool reading tests also were included in the assessment battery. Word recognition and spelling tests were administered in grade 1 and in grade 2. The results indicated that performance on phoneme manipulation tasks in kindergarten was a strong predictor of reading and spelling in grade 2; indeed, it was the most powerful predictor of reading ability among the tests administered (Lundberg et al., 1980, p. 165).

Bradley and Bryant (1983) extended the findings of Lundberg et al. (1980) by demonstrating a causal connection between phonological awareness and reading and spelling performance. In utilizing both longitudinal and training study designs, they investigated whether phonological awareness ability at preschool level influenced later reading and spelling success. British 4-year-old (n = 118) and 5-year-old (n = 285) children participated in the study. All of the children were nonreaders at the first assessment. The phonological awareness task employed in the study tapped knowledge at the phoneme level. Children were required to listen to a group of words and decide which word started with a different sound. The 4-year-old children were presented with items containing three words (e.g., *hill, pig, pin*) whereas the 5-year-olds were presented with four words (e.g., *bud, bun, bus, rug*).

A significant relationship was found between scores on the preschool phonological awareness measure and scores on standardised reading and spelling tests 3 years later. This relationship held even when differences in intellectual ability and memory performance were controlled. The influence of phonological awareness was specific to reading and spelling outcomes; there was no relationship between phonological awareness ability and performance on a standardised mathematical test.

To establish that this predictive relationship between phonological awareness and reading and spelling success was causal in nature, Bradley and Bryant (1983) designed a training study for 65 children who had demonstrated weak phonological awareness ability in the longitudinal study. The children were divided into four groups matched for age, verbal intelligence, and their performance on the initial phonological awareness assessment tasks. Group 1 received training on categorizing words based on common phonemes (e.g., finding pictures of words that start or end with the same sound); group 2 received this same training and were taught letter sound knowledge in addition; group 3 received training in semantic categorization (e.g., "Find all the farm animals"); and group 4 received no training outside their regular class program.

The children received 40 training sessions over a 2-year period of the study. The results from the final reading and spelling tests revealed that those children whose education had included the 40 sessions of phonological awareness combined with specific letter-sound learning (group 2) were significantly better spellers than children in the other groups and better readers than children in the two control groups. There was no difference in reading performance between the two groups who received the phonological awareness training (groups 1 and 2), and both group of children had developed into stronger readers than children who received no phonological awareness training. The researchers concluded that phonological awareness ability prior to preschool has a powerful influence on both reading and spelling achievement.

A variety of subsequent studies has confirmed the predictive power of phonological awareness ability in relation to literacy success. In a comprehensive investigation of factors that may influence reading ability, Share, Jorm, Maclean, and Mathews (1984) administered a large battery of tests, including measures of oral language, social behavior, and motor skills, to 543 Australian children at the beginning of their kindergarten year (average age, 5 years, 3 months). Information also was collected on the children's home and preschool environments. Standardised reading and spelling tests were administered at the end of kindergarten and again at the end of grade 1. Performance on a phoneme segmentation task and knowledge of letter names were found to be the two strongest predictors of reading performance at the end of kindergarten and of the combined reading and spelling performance score at the end of grade 1.

Torneus (1984) specifically examined the causal relationship between phonological awareness knowledge and spelling. As part of a larger investigation, the relationship between Swedish children's performance on phoneme segmentation and blending ability and later spelling of 30 phonetically regular words was measured. The results supported the hypothesis that early spelling development (i.e., phonetic spelling) is dependent upon phonological awareness ability at the phoneme level.

Torgesen, Wagner, and Rashotte (1994) addressed some of the research limitations identified in earlier longitudinal correlational studies. These researchers also examined how differing constructs of phonological processing may contribute to reading ability. In this study, 288 children from the United States (predominantly Caucasian, with approximately 25% African American) were assessed, 12 months apart from kindergarten to grade 2, on both phonological processing and reading measures on three assessment trials. The average age at the first assessment was 5 years 8 months. Five constructs of phonological processing were measured:

1. Phoneme awareness involving analysis skills (e.g., identifying sounds in words).
2. Phoneme awareness involving synthesis skills (e.g., blending sounds together to form a word).
3. Phonological memory.
4. Rapid serial naming (e.g., accessing phonological information when items are presented in a series).
5. Rapid isolated naming (e.g., accessing phonological information when items are presented in isolation).

The significant correlations between the five phonological constructs studied in kindergarten and grade 1, and kindergarten and grade 2, indicated a stable and enduring pattern of individual differences in phonological processing performance in the early grades. Wagner et al. (1993) concluded that "phonological processing abilities have the kind of relative stability that is required for them to play causal roles in the development of reading ability and disability" (p. 100).

In support of this conceptualization of phonological processing skills, their research demonstrated that all five constructs of phonological processing were significantly correlated with subsequent reading development in grades 1 and 2. Of the five constructs, kindergarten phoneme analysis performance was the strongest predictor of word recognition in grade 1, and phoneme synthesis ability in grade 1, was the strongest predictor of word recognition in grade 2.

MacDonald and Cornwall (1995) also found that phonological awareness is a stable predictor of later literacy success. The word recognition and phoneme awareness skills of 24 Canadian children were measured 11 years after their participation in a study during their kindergarten year, which investigated their early phonological awareness, reading, and spelling development. The average age of the children at follow-up assessment was 17 years. Examination of results revealed that performance during kindergarten on a 40-item phoneme deletion task was significantly correlated with performance on word decoding and spelling ability at 17 years of age (differences in socioeconomic levels and receptive vocabulary scores were controlled). There also was a trend for kindergarten phoneme awareness skills to predict non-word reading ability at 17 years, but socioeconomic status and receptive vocabulary measures in kindergarten did not predict later academic achievement.

Predictive Power of Onset-Rime Awareness

Many studies that have demonstrated a predictive role of phonological awareness in relation to reading acquisition have investigated phonological awareness skills at the phoneme level, such as phoneme segmentation, identity, or deletion tasks. Consistent results from a variety of studies have supported the importance of phoneme awareness to reading and spelling development. Studies that have examined the predictive power of phonological awareness skills at the onset-rime and syllabic levels, however, provide less consistent results. Some researchers have argued that rhyme knowledge is important for reading and spelling development (Bryant, Bradley, Maclean, & Crossland, 1989; Goswami & Bryant, 1990; Wood & Terrell, 1998). These researchers have demonstrated that rhyme awareness in preschool can predict reading and spelling performance in the early school years. It is hypothesized that knowledge of rhyme units helps children to read and spell new words through analogy to known words (Goswami, 1994a; see the discussion of analogy theory in Chapter 2, pp. 19–20). Further, researchers have suggested that developing sensitivity at the onset-rime level during the preschool period promotes awareness at the phoneme level in young school-age children. That is, onset-rime awareness may be a developmental precursor to phoneme awareness (Bryant et al., 1990).

In contrast to this school of thought, other researchers have concluded that rhyming knowledge has little predictive power for literacy development and is not sensitive to discriminating between good and poor readers (Carrillo, 1994; Duncan & Johnston, 1999; Hulme et al., 2002; Muter,

Hulme, Snowling, & Taylor, 1997; Muter & Snowling, 1998). It is important, therefore, to carefully examine findings related to rhyme knowledge. The following three issues related to the influence of rhyme knowledge on reading and spelling acquisition are discussed next:

1. Clarification of measures of rhyme knowledge.
2. The role of nursery rhymes in facilitating early phonological awareness.
3. The predictive power of onset-rime knowledge in comparison to phoneme knowledge at differing stages of development.

Clarification of Rhyme Knowledge

Deciding what constitutes rhyme knowledge helps clarify some of the confusion regarding the importance of rhyme to written language development. The common understanding of rhyme, derived from our knowledge of nursery rhymes, is that rhyming words sound the same at the end of the word (the rhyme unit). Thus, *bag, rag,* and *wag* are rhyming words because the rhyme unit sounds the same. Consistent with understanding the phonological structure of words as having a distinct representation at the onset-rime level, researchers have also described children's ability to isolate the onset from the rhyme unit as a measure of rhyme knowledge (Goswami & Bryant, 1990). For example, in a test item that asks "Which word starts with a different sound: *fan, fit, sun,*?" it may be argued that the child is required to isolate the onset from the rime unit (*f-an, f-it, s-un*) to decide which word starts with a different sound. Muter et al. (1997) noted that this type of task is not a "clean" measure of rhyming skill. As presented in Chapter 1, this task may best be considered within early phoneme level awareness because it requires awareness or discrimination of a single phoneme within a word. Thus, some findings that have reported "rhyme knowledge" is important for reading have demonstrated that awareness of initial phonemes in words influences early word recognition ability. A careful examination of the types of "rhyme tasks" employed by researchers (e.g., identifying whether the task involves rhyme detection, rhyme production, onset awareness of single phonemes, onset awareness of phoneme clusters, blending, segmenting, or manipulating words at the onset-rime level) is important when interpreting the research findings.

Nursery Rhymes Facilitate
Early Phonological Awareness Development

Bryant et al. (1989) demonstrated that knowledge of nursery rhymes may be important to reading and spelling because such knowledge helps the child develop early phonological awareness skills. In a longitudinal study the development of 64 British children was monitored from the ages of 3–6 years. At the start of the project the researchers assessed the children's ability to recite five popular nursery rhymes (e.g., "Humpty Dumpty," "Twinkle, Twinkle, Little Star"). The children also were presented with a rhyme detection task. At 5 and 6 years of age the children were given measures of phoneme awareness and reading and spelling. The results indicated that children's knowledge of nursery rhymes at 3 years was strongly correlated with performance on rhyme detection at 4 years and with phoneme detection at 5 and 6 years of age. Rhyme detection performance at age 4 years, 7 months, also strongly predicted reading and spelling performance at 5 and 6 years. Variables that may have influenced this relationship (i.e., intelligence, socioeconomic status, and initial phonological awareness ability) were controlled. The researchers concluded that knowledge of nursery rhymes enhances phonological awareness knowledge, which in turn is linked to success in reading and spelling.

Rhyme Knowledge Compared to Phoneme Level Knowledge

Muter and Snowling (1998) considered whether differing levels of phonological awareness (onset-rime and phoneme levels) as well as short-term memory skills would predict later reading and spelling development. British children (*n* = 34) were seen at 4, 5, 6, and 9 years of age. Their results indicated that early rhyme detection ability (e.g., "Which word rhymes with *cat*: *fish*, *gun*, *hat*?) did not predict reading accuracy ability at 9 years of age, nor was rhyming ability sensitive in predicting good-versus-poor reading ability at age 9. Phoneme deletion ability (e.g., "Say *bus* without the /b/") at 5 and 6 years, however, did significantly predict individual variation in reading ability at 9 years. Phoneme deletion ability and phonological memory (i.e., non-word repetition) proved the strongest predictors of later reading achievement.

Muter, Hulme, Snowling, and Taylor (1997) argued that skills at the phoneme level, not rhyming skills, predict reading progress. Although these researchers did find rhyming ability had some influence on spelling ability during the second year of schooling, the ability to detect rhyme failed to predict reading and spelling performance in older age groups. In contrast, phoneme segmentation ability proved to be a strong predictor of both reading and spelling performance. Consistent with Muter et al.'s conclusions, Duncan and Johnston (1999) also failed to find a relationship between rhyme oddity and rhyme judgment tasks and reading ability in 10-year-old good and poor readers and suggested that rhyming tasks lose their "predictive power" in older age groups.

Hulme et al. (2002) demonstrated that awareness of the initial phoneme in a word, as opposed to awareness of an initial phoneme cluster, was a strong predictor of early reading development. Utilizing a novel design, the researchers used one set of 10 stimulus non-words to measure differing levels of phonological awareness and differing types of operations (detection, deletion, and oddity tasks). Awareness of onsets in words was measured by a cluster sound (e.g., "Which word starts the same as *blaip*: *bleug*, *suk*, *tad*?"), whereas phoneme awareness was measured via the initial phoneme in a cluster (e.g., "Which word starts the same as *blaip*: *beug*, *smuk*, *tad*"). The results indicated that (1) initial phoneme awareness was the strongest predictor of reading ability in 5- and 6-year-old British children, and (2) taken together, awareness of initial and final phonemes in non-words was a much more powerful predictor of children's reading ability than awareness of onset (i.e., initial cluster sound) and rime units in non-words.

Thus, a general pattern regarding the relationship between rhyme and written language development in English may be drawn from the literature. Knowledge of nursery rhymes positively influences rhyme awareness. In turn, rhyme awareness in prereaders (e.g., 4-year-old children) has some influence on early reading and spelling development, possibly via its contribution to stimulating phoneme awareness. In young school-age children (e.g., 5 and 6 years old) phonological awareness skills at the phoneme level are much stronger current and long-term predictors of their reading and spelling performance than measures of onset-rime awareness.

Predictive Power of Syllable Awareness

Few studies have directly investigated the predictive power of phonological awareness at the syllable level to reading and spelling. Wood and Terrell (1998) failed to find a predictive relationship between syllable awareness in preschool children and literacy performance during the first 2 years at school. In contrast, Engen and Hoien (2002) found that syllable awareness explained unique variance in both word recognition and reading comprehension performance in average and poor grade 1 readers who were native Norwegian speakers. However, the impact of syllable awareness on reading development for these children was very low in comparison to the strong influence of phoneme awareness on literacy development. Denton et al. (2000) noted that syllable knowledge may be a more important predictor in languages that are phonetically regular, such as Spanish, than in English. In their review of studies investigating phonological awareness in Spanish-speaking children, they highlighted the mixed findings in relation to syllable knowledge. Gonzalez and Garcia (1995) speculated that syllable segmentation ability may be an important predictor of proficiency in reading Spanish, a language characterized by a high number of multisyllabic words and a well-defined syllable structure. However, the researchers concluded that continued research is necessary to understand the importance of syllable awareness to written language acquisition in Spanish.

Phonological Awareness in Context with Other Important Variables

The research findings convincingly demonstrate that phonological awareness is crucial for reading and spelling success. Skills at the phoneme level, such as phoneme analysis and deletion skills, have the strongest predictive power for long-term reading and spelling achievement. It is important, however, to keep phonological awareness in perspective with other necessary skills for reading and spelling. It would be incorrect to assume that all a child needs to read and spell are strong phonological awareness skills. The words of Tunmer, Herriman, and Nesdale (1988, p. 50) that "phonological awareness is necessary but not sufficient for acquiring phonological recoding skill" are a reminder that other variables also contribute to word recognition and reading comprehension performance. Scarborough's (1998) analysis of research that investigated the correlations between kindergarten performance on a range of variables and later reading performance confirmed the importance of phonological awareness but also highlighted the contribution of other aspects of language proficiency and print knowledge. Scarborough reported that measures of children's performance on letter identification, print concepts, rapid naming, vocabulary naming, verbal memory (sentence/story recall), and syntactic/morphological comprehension tasks also contributed to the prediction of reading achievement.

Roth, Speece, and Cooper (2002) utilized a 3-year longitudinal design to investigate the predictive relationship of a range of oral language skills (including syntactic, semantic, morphological, and phonological awareness) on later word recognition and reading comprehension in children with typically developing skills. As predicted, children's performance on the phonological awareness tasks in kindergarten predicted their word decoding performance in grades 1 and 2. However, the children's semantic knowledge combined with print awareness knowledge in kindergarten was a stronger predictor of reading comprehension performance. Two measures of semantic knowledge proved important for reading comprehension in this study. The first measure, oral definitions of words (i.e. the oral vocabulary subtest of the Test of Language Development—Primary: 2; Newcomer & Hammill, 1988) tapped the children's decontextualized language requiring them to reflect upon language in a conscious manner. Other researchers have also found evidence of the importance of decontextualized language skills for successful reading and spelling achievement (Snow, Gonzalez, & Shriberg, 1989; Snow, Tabors, Nicholson, & Kurland, 1995). The second measure of semantic knowledge that predicted reading comprehension was a measure of word retrieval (i.e., Boston Naming Test, Goodglass & Kaplan, 1983) in which children were required to name pictures of familiar objects. As word retrieval does involve phonological coding ability (see discussion in Chapter 4), Roth and associates concluded that reading comprehension in the early grades could be seen as a convergence of both phonological knowledge and semantic knowledge.

Researchers also have discussed the importance of other linguistic variables in relation to successful spelling development. Bourassa and Treiman (2001) discussed the role of letter-name, orthographic, and morphological knowledge as well as phonological knowledge in spelling development. The authors described a "morphological deficit hypothesis" to explain some children's spelling difficulties. This hypothesis holds that in addition to having delayed development in phonological awareness, children with spelling disorder may have particular difficulty in using a morphological strategy in their spelling attempts. This may be a consequence of failing to understand how spelling reflects the morphological structure of words or an inability to use morphological information to generate correct spellings. Continued research is required to understand the contribution of morphological knowledge in oral language to spelling development. In support of the importance of other linguistic variables to spelling, Apel and Masterton (2001) reported an integrated spelling intervention that simultaneously developed orthographic knowledge and morphological awareness with phoneme awareness produced significant benefits for an older child with spelling disorder. Thus, the influence of phonological awareness on subsequent reading and spelling development should be viewed in context with other linguistic variables that affect literacy development as well as extrinsic factors, such as home literacy environment, that show positive relationships to children's reading performance (Scarborough, 1998).

VARIABLES CONTRIBUTING TO THE DEVELOPMENT OF PHONOLOGICAL AWARENESS

Influence of Reading and Spelling Experiences

A reciprocal relationship exists between phonological awareness and literacy development. The previous section reviewed literature that demonstrated the importance of phonological awareness in relation to reading and spelling performance. In addition, experiences in reading and spelling also play an important role in phonological awareness development (Burgess & Lonigan, 1998; Cataldo & Ellis, 1988; Ehri, 1987, 1989; McGuinness, McGuinness, & Donohue, 1995; Morais, Cary, Alegria, & Bertelson, 1979; Perfetti, Beck, Ball, & Hughes, 1987; Read, Zhang, Nie, & Ding, 1986). Preschool children who are nonreaders find it difficult to

complete a number of tasks at the phoneme level, such as phoneme manipulation, segmentation, and deletion tasks. They can, however, demonstrate
some awareness of individual sound segments in words. For example, qualitative scoring of phoneme segmentation tasks in a group of Scottish preschoolers who were nonreaders revealed that although the children could
not successfully segment an entire word, many could segment the first phoneme in the word (Johnston et al., 1996). Similarly, Wood and Terrell
(1998) demonstrated that preschool nonreaders achieved, on average, 25%
accuracy on a phoneme deletion task.

Exposure to formal reading and spelling instruction appears to more
fully develop phoneme awareness knowledge (Perfetti et al., 1987). Cognitive maturation alone cannot easily account for later developing competency at the phoneme level; illiterate adults, for example, also show poor
phonological awareness knowledge at the phoneme level but can demonstrate competency in phoneme awareness once they have received reading
instruction (Morais et al., 1979).

Cataldo and Ellis (1988) explored the sequence of interactive development not only between phonological awareness and reading development
but also the influence of spelling on reading and phonology. The researchers pointed out that although early instruction in reading may apply a visual whole word strategy, the early stages of learning to spell are more
likely to focus on developing explicit awareness of words' phonological
structure. Such experience may facilitate the child's ability to understand
the relationship between spoken and written forms. Their findings indicated that global awareness of the sound properties of words (i.e., implicit
phonological awareness as measured by a sound categorization task) directly affected early reading development. However, explicit awareness of
phonemes within words (i.e., segmentation skills) may come to reading
through spelling experience. Thus, spelling may play an important role in
early reading development by promoting the use of explicit phonological
processing knowledge. This may be particularly evident for children who
enter school with limited phoneme awareness (Frost, 2001).

Given that phonological awareness encompasses differing levels of
skills, it is reasonable to assume that these levels are influenced by differing
variables. Learning to read an alphabetic language affects the development
of phoneme awareness, but syllable and onset-rime awareness may develop
spontaneously with spoken language and be only weakly influenced by
reading (Cheung et al., 2001; Morais, Bertelson, Cary, & Alegria, 1986).
Overall, research indicates that a general awareness that words can be broken down into smaller parts is a necessary base on which to build successful word recognition and spelling skills. Experiences in decoding and encoding print further develop knowledge about word sound structure,
particularly at the phoneme level, and increased proficiency in word recog-

nition allows children to successfully complete complex phonological tasks, such as phoneme manipulation and deletion tasks. Thus, following an initial impetus from phonological awareness to reading and spelling, the relationship becomes mutually supportive (Perfetti et al., 1987).

Alphabet Knowledge

Another important influence on phonological awareness development is that of alphabet knowledge (Bowey, 1994; Burgess & Lonigan, 1998; Johnston et al., 1996; Stahl & Murray, 1994; Wagner, Torgesen, & Rashotte, 1994). Learning the names of the alphabetic letters and their associated common phonemes may help children understand the sound structure of words. Johnston et al. (1996) argued that letter knowledge may be the trigger for phoneme awareness in preschool children, because explicit phoneme awareness ability develops *after* children have gained at least partial alphabetic knowledge. Letter knowledge also has been shown to be a strong predictor of later reading ability (Adams, 1990; Share et al., 1984). Yet a simple linear progression from letter knowledge to phoneme awareness to reading cannot be supported. Training in letter knowledge alone, for example, does not result in improved word decoding (Adams, 1990), and there is evidence that an initial level of phonological awareness is necessary for children to be able to use letter-name knowledge in word recognition (Tunmer et al., 1988). Furthermore, phoneme awareness makes a unique contribution to predicting reading, even when letter knowledge is taken into consideration (Elbro, Borstrom, & Petersen, 1998, p. 39).

The findings of Burgess and Lonigan (1998) provided important insights into understanding the influence of prereading abilities such as letter knowledge to phonological awareness development. Growth in letter-name, letter-sound, rhyme detection, and phoneme detection, blending and deletion tasks was examined over a 12-month period in 97 4- to 5-year-old American children from middle-class families. A bidirectional relationship between letter-name and phoneme awareness skills was demonstrated. Consistent with previous research, letter-name knowledge made a unique contribution to growth in phoneme awareness. However, a larger effect size was evident for the composite phonological awareness measure in predicting growth in letter knowledge. The performance of the 4- to 5-year-old children on the phonological awareness tasks contributed to their growth over the following year in both letter-name and letter-sound knowledge. Detailed analyses suggested that both rudimentary phonological awareness skills (e.g., rhyme, syllable, and word-level awareness tasks) and more complex phoneme level skills contributed to growth in letter knowledge. The researchers concluded that the bidirectional relationship between phoneme awareness and literacy growth evident in school-age children is also evident at the preschool level in relation to prereading skills such as letter knowledge.

An interactive relationship between phoneme awareness and letter knowledge is further supported by the results of training studies that have demonstrated stronger effects on enhancing reading when phonological awareness training is combined with letter-sound knowledge training than when phonological awareness training occurs in isolation (Ball & Blachman, 1988; Bradley & Bryant, 1985; Hatcher et al., 1994). It is important to consider letter knowledge and phonological awareness as two separate variables that influence literacy development. Although interactions in growth between the two are evident, both make individual contributions to predicting literacy achievement and are not measures of the same underlying construct (Burgess & Lonigan, 1998).

It is also important to consider how letter knowledge is measured since some tasks are easier than others. Dodd and Carr (2003) studied letter-sound knowledge development in a group of 83 British children between the ages of 4 years, 11 months, and 6 years, 4 months. All of the participants had received at least 1-year of literacy instruction. The children found letter-sound recognition (e.g., "Show me /s/") an easier task than letter-sound recall (e.g., "What sound does this letter make?"). Letter production (e.g., "Write down the letter /s/") proved a particularly difficult task for children from lower socioeconomic backgrounds (approximately 50% of the group), whereas the children from higher socioeconomic backgrounds showed no group differences in performance between the letter production and the letter-sound recall task. There was no statically significant difference in performance on any of the tasks based on gender.

Influence of Underlying Phonological Representation

Researchers have advanced the hypothesis that the "distinctness" or quality of a child's phonological representation for a given word may influence the child's explicit awareness of the word's phonological structure (Elbro et al., 1998; Snowling & Hulme, 1989; Swan & Goswami, 1997). To be able to break down a word into its individual phonemes, a child requires a distinct phonological representation for the target word stored in memory as well as the ability to access this representation in a conscious manner. In segmenting the word *ship*, for example, the child is required to access a phonological representation of the stored word that is distinct from words with similar phonological segments, such as *shape, sheep, sip, chip*. Elbro et al. described the distinctness of a phonological representation in terms of its separation from words with similar phonological properties and discussed how a word may have multiple levels of distinctness. For example, the word *February* can be represented at one level as *Fe-bre*; similarly, *library* can be represented as *li-bre*. However, in successfully completing a phonological awareness task for these words, such as syllable segmentation, the child needs to access a distinct or more "fully specified" form of the word *February* (feb-u-ar-y or feb-ru-ar-y).

Access to a distinct phonological representation of the spoken word may be particularly important in applying phoneme–grapheme knowledge. Utilization of a phonological strategy to spell a word like *butter* (which can be represented as *budda* or *butta* in some English dialects) necessitates access to its most distinct form—one that identifies the medial /t/ phoneme and the final /er/ phoneme. It is important to understand the concept of phonological representations and how they may influence phonological awareness development.

Definitions of the phonological representations that underlie spoken language are debated in the literature (Stemberger, 1992). Nevertheless, a phonological representation is generally considered to be an abstract concept that "captures the true essence of the sounds in words and sentences" (Clark & Clark, 1977, p. 188). As an infant's ability to recognize spoken words rapidly develops, phonological representations of spoken words stored in memory become increasingly segmental as whole word representations move to phoneme size units (Elbro, 1996; Fowler, 1991). This process helps reduce the burden on memory. Consider the memory capacity required if every spoken word a child recognized was stored in memory as a holistic unsegmented unit. Rather, a very limited number of phonemes need be stored in memory, which can then be utilized to comprise numerous phonological representations. The experience of trying to recall a word or name from memory where only parts of the word (i.e., some phonological segments) can be correctly recalled on the first attempt provides a practical example of how spoken words are represented in memory as phonemic segments rather than as holistic units.

Phonological segments consisting of distinctive features that are not predictable from other features comprise the phonological representation of a word. For example, the phonological representation of the spoken word *spin* that is stored in memory comprises the segments /s/ /p/ /ɪ/ /n/. Each phoneme in a language differs from all other phonemes by at least one distinctive feature—that is, /p/ and /b/ differ from each other by the distinctive feature of voicing (/p/ is a voiceless sound, and /b/ is a voiced sound). All the features of each segment are not necessarily conveyed by the initial phonological representation. Phonological "rules" that change and further develop the representation to specify its pronunciation prevent confusion. For example, English phonotactic constraints would allow /sp/ but not the initial consonant combinations of /fp/ or /sb/. Knowledge of phonotactic constraints is necessary for a fully developed phonological representation (Jusczyk, 1992).

The process by which the representations of spoken words change over time from holistic units to more fine-grained segmental units is described by Metsala and Walley (1998) as the lexical restructuring model (also see Walley, Metsala, & Garlock, 2003). Walley et al. hypothesized that this restructuring of phonological representations depends largely on vocabulary growth and that restructuring to segmental units is necessary for the development of explicit phoneme awareness. That is, unless the child has a phonological representation of a spoken word that is segmental in nature, he or she could not be expected to identify or manipulate individual phonemes of the word in a conscious manner. Metsala (1999a, 1999b) also demonstrated that variables important for spoken word recognition influence phonological awareness development. Metsala observed that young children performed better on phonological awareness task items that involved highly familiar real words than they did on test items involving words that are lower in familiarity or non-words. Furthermore, the proximity of a non-word to a real word influenced phonological awareness task performance, and words and non-words that have many real words that are phonologically similar (e.g., *vat*: *cat*, *hat*, *mat*, *sat*) are easier target items in phonological awareness tasks than words that have very few phonological "neighbors." Such findings may be interpreted to signify that spoken words for which children are likely to have fully specified phonological representations can be more easily accessed in phonological awareness tasks.

Metsala (1999a, 1999b) found positive correlations between the size of the child's receptive vocabulary and performance on phonological awareness tasks at the onset-rime and phoneme level for 4-, 5-, and 6-year-old children. Metalsa concluded that phonological awareness emerges from basic language (phonological) development, and that developmental models of how children recognize spoken words are relevant to understanding the source of phonological awareness development. The importance of vocabulary size, however, may only be significant in the preschool years during the period of rapid vocabulary growth and early development of phonological awareness. Elbro et al. (1998) found that vocabulary size at 6 years of age did not predict later phoneme awareness performance for Danish-speaking children.

The ability to access a fully specified form of a spoken word does not appear to be influenced by dialectic differences. Hart, Guthrie, and Winfield (1980) demonstrated that there was no significant difference between average readers who were speakers of African American English dialect and those who were speakers of standard American English in their ability to identify mismatches between spoken and written forms of words (e.g., saying *fine* for the written word *find*). Although the speakers of African American English deleted final consonants in their own speech, as part of their dialect, they appeared able to access the most distinct phonological representation of the word. This finding is consistent with other researchers' claims that modest variations in dialect are unrelated to reading and writing success (Elbro et al., 1998, p. 53). However, dialect may have some influence on spelling attempts. In support of the role of phonology in spelling development, differences were found in the types of spelling errors made by British and American children (Treiman, Goswami, Tincoff, & Leevers, 1997) and adults (Treiman & Barry, 2000), based on participants' pronunciations of the target word. For example, British participants were more likely than Americans to delete the final letter *r* in spelling a word such as *leper* (adult target word) or *tiger* (child target word), misspelling these words as *lepa* and *tiga*. This error was consistent with the participants' dialect: British adults and children pronounced the final syllable in *leper* as a vowel sound, whereas the Americans articulated the final /r/ sound.

Elbro et al. (1998) further explored the influence of children's underlying phonological representation on phoneme awareness and reading. These researchers designed a novel test to measure 6-year-old Danish children's most distinct pronunciation of multisyllabic words. Typically developing children and children at risk for dyslexia were shown a puppet that had "speech difficulties" and could therefore not pronounce some words correctly. For example, the puppet may have pronounced *crocodile* as *co-di*. The children were asked to teach the puppet the correct articulation of the word. They were instructed to say the word as clearly and precisely as possible for the puppet, because the puppet also had hearing difficulties. A distinctness score, based on the vowels in the word, was obtained from the words that the children pronounced correctly for the puppet. That is, the distinctness score was the percentage of vowels that were given a maximally distinct pronunciation. Statistical analyses indicated that this measure of distinctness in the child's phonological representations significantly contributed to the prediction of the children's phoneme awareness and reading performance. The results supported the researchers' hypothesis that early differences in the distinctness of phonological representations provide a unique contribution to the development of phoneme awareness in the early school years. If a child has a very distinct phonological representation of a spoken word, then he or she may more easily access the phonological segments of the representation in order to use phonological information in the reading and spelling process.

Continued research into the source of phonological awareness is required. As Elbro et al. noted phonological awareness is likely to emerge from more than one source. Basic language development, quality of phonological representations that underlie spoken language, letter knowledge, spoken language experiences, and reading and spelling instruction may all facilitate a child's ability to reflect upon the sound structure of spoken words.

SUMMARY

This chapter has discussed the development of phonological awareness in English and in other languages and has reviewed literature demonstrating the predictive power of phonological awareness to reading and spelling performance. Variables that influence the development of phonological awareness have been identified. Attention is drawn to the following summary points:

- Phonological awareness generally emerges in a developmental sequence from awareness of larger units, such as syllables and onset-rimes, to awareness of individual phonemes in words.
- There is wide variability in the phonological awareness performance in very young children; in the general population, stability in phonological awareness performance is evident only after 4 years of age.
- Most 4-year-old children can demonstrate knowledge of syllable aware ness and begin to show awareness of onset-rime knowledge.
- The developmental sequence of phonological awareness in English is also evident in other alphabetic languages.
- Phonological awareness skills in a native language can transfer to the learning of a second alphabetic language.
- The native language to which the child is exposed influences performance on specific phonological awareness tasks and, in particular, affects a child's ability to use phonological information in reading and spelling.
- Phonological awareness ability at preschool level has a powerful influence on early reading and spelling acquisition.
- Phoneme awareness performance is a strong predictor of long-term reading and spelling success and can predict literacy performance more accurately than variables such as intelligence, vocabulary knowledge, and socioeconomic status.
- School-age children's phoneme awareness skills are stronger predictors of later reading ability than rhyme awareness skills.
- There is a reciprocal relationship between phoneme awareness and reading and spelling development.
- The distinctness of children's phonological representations of spoken words that are stored in memory influences phonological awareness performance.

FROM RESEARCH TO PRACTICE

The research literature provides evidence of typical trends in children's development of phonological awareness and clearly establishes its predictive power in relation to literacy achievement. Research also has identified factors that influence phonological awareness development as well as the originating source of this capacity. These research findings contain several important implications for practitioners working to enhance children's reading and spelling development:

1. Understanding typical development of phonological awareness is critical for practitioners who work with children at risk for reading disability or children experiencing written language difficulties. Knowledge of typical developmental patterns provides a guide for the interpretation of assessment results. For example, a 7-year-old child who is unable to detect rhyming words should receive further assessment, given that most 5-year-old children succeed on rhyme detection tasks.

2. The wide variation in phonological awareness performance by 2- and 3-year-old children makes it inappropriate to classify children in this age group as having delayed or disordered phonological awareness development. However, phonological awareness development can be monitored during early preschool years in children with diagnosed impairments that place them at risk for reading disorder. Research suggests that accelerated development in phonological awareness occurs from 3 and 4 years of age. If a child fails to show this accelerated pattern, further assessment and specific intervention to enhance the development of phonological awareness prior to the child starting school would be appropriate.

3. Knowledge of phonological awareness development in English can generally be applied to understanding a child's phonological awareness development in other alphabetic languages.

4. Children learning English as a second language can be encouraged to practice or develop phonological awareness skills in their native language as well as in English (if their native language is alphabetic), because transfer of phonological awareness skills across languages can be expected. Children who have unexpected and persistent difficulty in learning to read and spell in English (as their second language) are likely to have poor phonological awareness skills in both their native language and in English.

5. Individuals whose native language is a logographic rather than an alphabetic script require adequate exposure to literacy instruction in English and may require direct phonological awareness training in English before they can use phonological information in the reading and spelling process.

6. Given the predictive power of phonological awareness in relation to later literacy achievement, it can be concluded that children who perform poorly on phonological awareness tasks should receive further attention (see Chapter 6). If necessary, sufficient instruction should be provided to ensure the development of strong phonological awareness skills at the phoneme level (see Chapter 7).

7. A variety of factors contributes to phonological awareness development. Some of these variables can be strengthened in very young children. Oral language enrichment is particularly valuable for children who have diagnosed disabilities that place them at risk for reading disorder. Engaging toddlers in the following types of activities helps build a strong foundation from which phonological awareness can emerge:

- Enhancing oral language development through meaningful language experiences, in particular, those that enhance vocabulary and phonological development.
- Teaching and reciting nursery rhymes with a toddler or infant.
- Encouraging a young child to provide the rhyming word at the end of a sentence in a favorite nursery rhyme.
- Bringing toddlers' attention to the rhythm and pattern of speech through rhyming songs or rhythmic storytelling patterns.
- Teaching young children the relationship between relevant letters and sounds, such as the link between the first letter and sound in their name.
- Developing toddlers' print awareness by drawing their attention to words in the environment (stop signs, exit signs, advertising signs) and to the meaning of large, clear print in storybooks. For example, pointing to the words while reading the title of a storybook; finding the main character's name each time it appears in print (assuming the use of large print in a children's book), and bringing the child's attention to the initial letter/s and sound in the character's name; observing how rhyming words often look the same and sound the same at the ends of words in rhyme stories such as Dr. Seuss's *The Cat in the Hat*.
- Introducing alphabet books, large alphabet puzzles, animated computer software with alphabet letters, or alphabet friezes that are specifically designed for young children. The toddlers' attention needs to be directed to the name of the letters and to common letter-sound relationships.
- Bringing young children's attention to beginning sounds in words such as sorting toys by sound or finding pictures in a favorite book that start with the same sound.

- Engaging young children in picture-naming activities, first providing a very clear model of the correct articulation of given words. The parent or early intervention teacher can encourage the child to attempt closer and more precise approximations of the target production. (When engaging in this latter activity, the constraints of the child's speech abilities need to be considered. For some children, this exercise should be enacted only under the guidance of a speech–language pathologist.)

Such activities with very young children should always be presented in a warm and encouraging manner. Rather than viewing these activities as a teaching endeavor, they should be viewed within the context of a positive language interaction between the caregiver and young child.

Understanding phonological awareness development and factors that influence it provides practitioners with the necessary background knowledge to engage in appropriate assessment procedures and assists in the accurate interpretation of assessment findings. Such procedures lay the foundation for relevant and meaningful teaching and intervention programs that ensure children develop an explicit awareness of a word's sound structure.

4

A Phonological Deficit
Hypothesis for Dyslexia

Developmental dyslexia has been a topic of research for more than 100 years. The immense struggle that an otherwise normally developing child displays when confronted with reading and writing has fascinated researchers since the condition was first described as "word blindness" around the turn of the 20th century (Hinshelwood, 1900; Morgan, 1896). A variety of factors such as visual–perceptual deficits, verbal memory deficiencies, neurological damage, genetic differences, and language deficits, has been explored in attempts to identify the cause of dyslexia (see Catts & Kamhi, 1999a, for a review). However, the relationship between phonological awareness (and more broadly, phonological processing skills) and dyslexia has dominated reading research literature in the last few decades. Understanding the role of phonological processing deficits as a cause for dyslexia has fueled much of the widespread interest in phonological awareness.

This chapter provides an overview of literature that has contributed to a "phonological deficit hypothesis" for reading disorder and discusses phonological awareness in the context of other aspects of spoken language that are related to reading disorder. A case study is presented that highlights the persistent nature of word recognition and phonological processing difficulties, frequently encountered by children with dyslexia.

DYSLEXIA DEFINED

Dyslexia has traditionally been defined by exclusionary criteria. The term is used to describe a child's significant difficulty, for no clearly apparent reason, in acquiring efficient reading skills. The difficulties cannot be attrib-

61

uted to sensory, intellectual, or neurological impairments, obvious speech and language disorders, emotional or behavioral disorders, or lack of educational opportunity (Vellutino, 1979). Terms such as "specific reading disability" and "reading disorder" have been used interchangeably to refer to this condition.

This exclusionary definition of dyslexia is fraught with assumptions that have yet to be proven. It assumes that children who have reading difficulties in the presence of average intellectual ability (i.e., reading discrepancy criteria) have different types of difficulties than children whose reading difficulties are commensurate with their lower intelligence. As Prior (1989) and Siegel (1992) argued, there is little consistent evidence to validate this hypothesis. For example, children diagnosed as having dyslexia exhibited very similar decoding processes to children whose reading difficulties were consistent with their lower intellectual abilities (Seidenberg, Bruck, Fornarolo, & Backman, 1985). A large-scale developmental study (Hurford et al., 1993) demonstrated that the performance of two groups of young children with reading disability, who also demonstrated differing levels of verbal intellectual ability, did not differ on a number of phonological awareness tasks. Furthermore, not only has the validity of intelligence tests been questioned, in general, but their relevance to the reading-disabled population is problematic, because they include tasks whose performance may be fostered by reading experience itself (Stanovich, 1991a). It is established, however, that dyslexia can be present in individuals who have markedly superior intellectual abilities. Thomas Edison, Albert Einstein, George Patton, Harvey Cushing, and Auguste Rodin are examples of "men of eminence" who all struggled with acquiring efficient reading or spelling skills (Thompson, 1971).

Excluding children with behavioral disorders from a classification of dyslexia on the assumption that attention problems may cause reading failure is also doubtful. Based on the findings of a 5-year longitudinal study, Wood and Felton (1994) concluded that attention deficit disorder could not be causally linked to the development of word identification skills. Swanson, Mink, and Bocian (1999) also reported that attention and hyperactivity variables were not good predictors of reading performance. Furthermore, Swanson et al. demonstrated that the phonological processing difficulties experienced by poor readers with attention-deficit/hyperactivity disorder (ADHD) are no greater than those of poor readers without an attention disorder.

The most obvious limitation of the exclusionary criteria is that it provides no description, other than to refer to a reading difficulty, of what elements *do* characterize the disorder (Catts & Kamhi, 1999c). Nevertheless, the exclusionary definition has provided some degree of consistency in limiting how participants have been selected for inclusion in studies on reading disorder, and it is still used in the research as a functional convenience.

During the past 30 years, in an attempt to explain and more adequately define dyslexia, researchers have increasingly focused their attention on the relationships between children's linguistic skills and their reading performance. This shift represented a significant deviation from the visual–perceptual theories that had enjoyed popularity for a number of years (e.g., Birch, 1962; Myklebust & Johnson, 1962) and perhaps is best captured in Catts and Kamhi's definition of dyslexia that emphasizes the language basis for the disorder:

> Dyslexia is a developmental language disorder whose defining characteristic is difficulty in phonological processing. This disorder, which is often genetically transmitted, is generally present at birth and persists throughout the lifespan. Phonological processing difficulties include problems storing, retrieving, and using phonological codes in memory as well as deficits in phonological awareness and speech production. A prominent characteristic of the disorder in school age children is difficulties learning to decode and spell printed words. These difficulties, in turn, often lead to deficits in reading comprehension and writing. (1999b, pp. 63–64)

This definition is consistent with the definition of dyslexia presented by the International Dyslexia Association (IDA; 1994). IDA describes dyslexia as a specific language-based disorder and identifies phonological processing deficits as central to it. Educators, speech–language pathologists, and other specialists working with children who have dyslexia need to understand the language basis for the disorder and the relevant research that has contributed to the formulation of this definition. The role of phonological processing in reading disorder that is highlighted in recent definitions has frequently been referred to as a "phonological deficit hypothesis" for dyslexia. This hypothesis holds that a deficit in the phonological language domain results in children experiencing difficulty in two areas: (1) understanding the sound structure of spoken language, and (2) holding phonological information in short-term memory. Reading and spelling difficulties are the result (Rack, Snowling, & Olsen, 1992). The following section discusses literature that has contributed to the phonological deficit hypothesis for reading disorder.

PHONOLOGICAL AWARENESS DEFICITS IN CHILDREN WITH DYSLEXIA

Two approaches to identifying phonological awareness deficits in poor readers are evident in the literature. One approach has studied the predictive ability of phonological awareness in relation to reading and spelling performance (discussed in Chapter 3). This body of research has clearly demonstrated that children with poor phonological awareness knowledge in kindergarten and the early school years are far more likely to become poor readers than young children with strong phonological awareness skills. The second approach, discussed in this section, has investigated the phonological awareness skills of children already identified as having dyslexia. Numerous investigations of children with reading disorder have included a comparison between chronologically age-matched good and poor readers on measures of phonological awareness. These comparisons have consistently demonstrated that the phonological awareness performance of older children who have specific difficulty reading and/or spelling is significantly inferior to that of their peers (Swan & Goswami, 1997; Beech & Harding, 1984; Bowey, Cain, & Ryan, 1992; Bruck, 1992; Catts, Gillispie, Leonard, Kail, & Miller, 2002; Dodd, Sprainger, & Oerlemans, 1989; Duncan & Johnston, 1999; Fawcett & Nicholson, 1995; Fletcher et al., 1994; Gillon & Dodd, 1994; Joanisse, Manis, Keating, & Seidenberg, 2000; Kroese, Hynd, Knight, Hiemenz, & Hall, 2000; Lenchner, Gerber, & Routh, 1990; Manis, Custodio, & Szeszulski, 1993; Pratt & Brady, 1988; Vellutino & Scanlon, 1987).

Weak performance in phonological awareness has been demonstrated in poor readers at a group level on a variety of tasks. For example:

- 7- to 9-year-old poor readers performed poorly on phoneme deletion tasks (Fletcher et al., 1994; Bruck, 1992) and in counting the number of syllables and phonemes in non-words (Bruck, 1992).
- 10- to 14-year-old poor readers performed poorly on syllable segmentation, rhyme judgment, phoneme identity, and phoneme segmentation tasks (Swan & Goswami, 1997).
- 8- to 10-year-old poor readers performed poorly on phoneme manipulation tasks (Pratt & Brady, 1988).
- 8-, 13-, and 17-year-old children with dyslexia all performed poorly, compared to age-matched controls, on rhyme, phoneme identification, and syllable and phoneme deletion tasks (Fawcett & Nicholson, 1995).

Longitudinal investigations of children with dyslexia (e.g., Gillon & Dodd, 1994; Manis et al., 1993; Snowling & Hulme, 1989) and investigations of adults with developmental reading difficulties (Bruck, 1992, 1993; Pratt & Brady, 1988) indicate that poor readers' deficits in phonological awareness persist over time and are not readily resolved through classroom instruction.

Duncan and Johnston (1999) reported that although poor performance was evident across phonological awareness tasks for children with dyslexia in their study, the greatest disparity found between the 10-year-old good and poor readers was at the phoneme level (as demonstrated by a phoneme deletion task). Lenchner et al. (1990) also concluded from their comparison of good and poor decoders on six measures of phonological awareness that more complex phonological awareness tasks may best predict word-decoding ability. Tasks that require the blending and manipulation of phonemes, in addition to segmentation, are examples of such complex tasks. Similarly, Kroese et al. (2000) found that phoneme deletion and reversal measures were stronger predictors of both spelling and reading achievement in 8–12-year-old poor readers than tasks that required only phoneme blending or only phoneme segmentation skills. It also has been found that although 11–12-year-old poor spellers performed significantly below children with good spelling ability on a spoonerism and phoneme segmentation task, their performance was comparable to good spellers on a rhyme judgment and syllable segmentation task (Dodd, Sprainger, & Oerlemans, 1989).

This difficulty in manipulating sounds exhibited by poor readers and spellers is specific to the context of speech. Poor readers performed as well as good readers on nonspeech tasks that required the manipulation of tones, such as reproducing the last three notes from a sequence of four notes played on a xylophone (Morais, Cluytens, & Alegria, 1984), and manipulating colored blocks to represent changes in the number and order of a sequence of tones (Pratt & Brady, 1988).

Reading-Age-Matched Design

A limitation of comparing good and poor readers or spellers of the same chronological age is that observed differences in phonological awareness ability may be the result of differences in reading experience. For example, a 10-year-old good reader will have had a vast deal more experience in processing written text than a 10-year-old poor reader. This increased experience and exposure to text also may strengthen children's phonological awareness skills. To control for this difference, Bradley and Bryant (1978) introduced the reading-age-matched design. They compared the performance of 10-year-old poor readers with typically developing children who were 3 years younger in chronological age but who were reading at the same level (i.e., reading age average was 7 years, 6 months). Remarkably, the older poor readers were significantly worse than the younger readers in judging which word did not rhyme (from a series of four words presented orally), identifying which word ended with a different sound, and identifying which word started with a different sound. They showed particular difficulty on this latter task (e.g., "Which word starts with a different sound: *sun, see, sock, rag?*").

Subsequent studies have frequently utilized the reading-age-matched design (often in combination with the chronological-age-matched design). Some studies have reported no statistical differences between older poor readers and younger readers matched for reading ability on phonological awareness tasks (Beech & Harding, 1984; Johnston, Andersen, Perrett, & Holligan, 1990; Stanovich, Nathan, & Vala-Rossi, 1986; Vellutino & Scanlon, 1987). In contrast, more recent studies have reported significant group differences, with researchers concluding that poor readers have a specific deficit in phonological awareness (Swan & Goswami, 1994; Bowey et al., 1992; Duncan & Johnston, 1999; Gillon & Dodd, 1994; Manis et al., 1993). Methodological differences help to explain the apparent inconsistencies in findings (Bowey et al., 1992). Furthermore, differences in the phonological awareness tasks administered and changes in educational practices may have influenced results. Recent studies (e.g., Duncan & Johnston, 1999) have typically observed group differences only on tasks that require phoneme level knowledge, with similar rhyme judgment performances among groups. A change in educational practices, in which language activities in the preschool and junior school years have focused on bringing children's attention to rhyme, may influence children's knowledge of rhyme. Alternatively, as discussed in Chapter 3, some rhyming tasks may not be particularly discriminatory for older poor readers.

A meta-analysis of phonological awareness abilities from studies utilizing a reading-age-matched design provided clear evidence for a phonological awareness deficit hypothesis (Fletcher-Flinn & Johnston, 1999). The researchers conducted a meta-analysis on 21 studies published from 1978 to 1997 that reported appropriate statistical data from comparisons of older poor readers and younger good readers on phonological awareness tasks. The researchers concluded that, with the exception of rhyme production, older children with reading disorder do not perform as well as younger, typically developing children on phonological awareness tasks.

Phonological Decoding Deficit

The difficulties poor readers experience in phonological awareness restrict these children's ability to use phonological information in the decoding process. Researchers (Rack et al., 1992) utilized a non-word reading task to directly examine readers' phonological decoding ability and hypothesized that children with dyslexia have specific difficulties in non-word reading. Rack et al. addressed whether difficulties with non-word reading reflect delayed development (i.e., develop at a slower rate but are consistent with level of reading ability) or the presence of a specific deficit (i.e., performance is lower than expected for reading ability). They conducted a comprehensive review and analysis of 16 studies that employed a matched reading level design on non-word reading tasks. The older poor readers did not perform better in any of these studies than the younger readers in their ability to read non-words. In 10 of the 16 studies there was clear evidence that poor readers demonstrated a specific deficit in non-word reading ability, with their performance significantly inferior to that of typically developing readers. The researchers concluded that the research reviewed provided "extremely strong evidence for the phonological deficit hypothesis" for dyslexia (p. 49).

Rack et al.'s conclusion was supported by a meta-analysis of the research findings from the studies reviewed by Rack et al. (van Ijzendoorn & Bus, 1994). This analysis quantified the differences in phonological skills between the good and poor readers as well as tested the accuracy of the reading-age-matched design. Combining the subject groups from the studies resulted in analysis for 1,183 individuals (approximately half of whom were dyslexic). The meta-analysis demonstrated that the performance of children with dyslexia on non-word reading tasks was inferior to that of younger children matched for word recognition ability. The hypothesis that children with dyslexia have a phonological coding deficit (as opposed to a phonological delay) can therefore be considered an established fact (van Ijzendoorn & Bus, 1994, p. 273).

An alternative method to phonologically decoding an unknown word phoneme by phoneme is the use of an orthographic analogy strategy—that is, by decoding an unknown word based on spelling pattern knowledge of a known word (e.g., using the known word, *kite*, to read the unknown word *bite*, as discussed in Chapters 1 and 2). Phonological awareness at the onset-rime level is closely related to the ability to use an analogy strategy (Goswami & Mead, 1992). Therefore, it can be predicted that poor readers with weak onset-rime knowledge will struggle to make analogies between words. In support of this prediction, Hanley, Reynolds, and Thornton (1997) demonstrated that 9–11-year-old children with dyslexia were less likely to use an analogy strategy than reading-age-matched children who were good readers. Thus a phonological awareness deficit may restrict the use of both phonological decoding and the use of orthographic analogies in word recognition development.

SUBGROUPS OF POOR READERS

Children with reading difficulties are not a homogenous group. Inspection of individual data within group studies demonstrates unexpected patterns of development for some individuals. For example, although at a group level the poor readers in Duncan and Johnston (1999) study showed adequate rhyme awareness and poor phoneme awareness (as expected from the typical developmental sequence of phonological awareness), two participants demonstrated the exact reverse pattern, struggling on rhyming tasks while showing competency at phoneme tasks. In addition to phonological awareness deficits, poor readers may display a range of other types of processing and linguistic difficulties. Processing skills that underlie rapid naming ability and, most recently, the speed at which poor readers can process information are areas that have attracted particular attention for their potential to clarify the factors that make unique contributions to reading achievement (Catts et al., 2002; Wolf & Bowers, 1999; Wolf, Bowers, & Biddle, 2000). Thus the question arises as to whether there are clear subgroups of poor readers that present with differing patterns of linguistic processing abilities and development. The clinical implication of such subgroups would be the need for different treatment methods to accommodate the type of reading disorder exhibited.

Various methods for identifying subgroups of poor readers have been described in the literature (Morris et al., 1998, detail these methods). Based on observations of adults with acquired dyslexia (e.g., a reading disorder emerging as a result of brain injury suffered during a stroke) and models of word recognition, subgroups of *phonological dyslexia* and *surface dyslexia* were identified. Phonological dyslexia involves particular difficulty in decoding words and is often exhibited by poor performance on reading nonwords (suggesting a break down in the phonological route, as discussed in the dual-route model of word recognition). Surface dyslexia involves difficulty reading irregular words (i.e., words that cannot be completely decoded using a phonological decoding strategy). The pattern of difficulty for this latter group suggests that these individuals have difficulty accessing the orthographic representation of the word stored in memory (i.e., there is a breakdown in the visual route to word recognition; Coltheart et al., 1993).

A second method of subgrouping children with reading disorder was based on a "phonological-core variable–difference" model developed by Stanovich (1988). The qualifier *specific* reading disability was used to describe poor readers whose difficulties were restricted to the phonological language domain and whose reading disabilities were inconsistent with their average or above-age intelligence quotients (IQ). The descriptor *garden variety* poor readers was used to refer to those readers who had language and cognitive problems in addition to phonological problems and whose lower reading scores were consistent with lower IQs. Subgrouping children based on whether their reading achievement is consistent with their intellectual ability has been challenged in recent years. As Catts, Hogan, and Fey (2003) noted, there is little research evidence to support qualitative differences in children's reading behaviors for groups with or without a reading IQ discrepancy, and such a model provides little direction for intervention. Stanovich (2000) provided an in-depth discussion of his phonological-core variable difference model and IQ discrepancy sub-grouping of poor readers. He concluded that continued research is necessary to ascertain whether children with dyslexia and garden variety poor readers have differing educational prognoses and, importantly, whether they respond differently to various treatment approaches.

In more recent years a third grouping model has been developed based on the types of processing difficulties the poor reader exhibits (Wolf & Bowers, 1999). Numerous studies have demonstrated that poor readers also have deficits in the processes that support the ability to rapidly name common objects, letters, or numbers, referred to as rapid automatized naming tests (RAN) (Denckla & Rudel, 1976a, 1976b; Wolf & Bowers, 1999, review this literature). Such a test would present a child with a series of printed letters and ask him or her to the name the letters as quickly as possible. Children who have both phonological awareness deficits and deficits in the processes that underlie rapid naming ability (referred to as a "double deficit") may exhibit greater impairment in reading performance than children who have deficits in only one of these areas (Wolf & Bowers, 1999).

A fourth grouping model is based on the simple view of reading (Gough & Tunmer, 1986). As discussed in Chapter 2, this model views word recognition and listening comprehension as two critical components of reading comprehension. Grouping poor readers within this model separates children with reading disability who have word recognition problems only, those who have listening comprehension problems only, and those who have both word recognition and listening comprehension problems (see Catts & Kamhi, 1999c; Catts et al., 2003). In examining the validity of this type of subgrouping, referred to as the Reading Component Model, Catts et al. explored the word recognition and listening comprehension abilities in a group of 183 second-grade children. All of the children performed at least one standard deviation below the mean on a composite reading comprehension measure. Although the children's performance scores did not naturally cluster into clearly identified groupings, imposing cutoff values on group test performance resulted in groupings predicted by the model. The results indicated that 35.5% of the poor readers displayed poor word recognition skills in the absence of significant listening comprehensions difficulties. A similar proportion of the sample had both word recognition and listening comprehensions difficulties. Approximately 15% of the poor readers could be grouped according to poor listening comprehension but adequate word recognition skills, and 13% of the sample did not show significant deficits in either word recognition or listening comprehension. Profiling children's performance by utilizing this reading component model may prove useful in intervention planning. Children who show a strong pattern of poor word recognition skills but good listening comprehension (i.e., the dyslexic profile) are likely to benefit from intervention that directly targets phonological and orthographic processing skills.

Morris et al. (1998) also attempted to identify subgroups of poor readers more clearly, based on theoretical models of the reading process and reading disability. They administered a comprehensive battery of tests to 376 children (ages 7–9) identified as having a disability in reading, math, or both reading and math, and 123 children representing nonlearning-disabled children. The battery included measures of phonological awareness, verbal and nonverbal short-term memory, rapid naming, vocabulary, speech production, visuospatial and visual attention tasks. Detailed analysis of the children's performance on the tasks revealed seven subtypes of children with reading disability. Consistent with the strong evidence of a phonological deficit model, all poor readers demonstrated weakness on some aspect of phonological processing. Six of the seven subtypes exhibited impairment on the phonological awareness measures, and the last subgroup demonstrated weakness in retrieving phonological information and in phonological production. The identified subtypes of children with reading disability follow. Note that poor readers classified as subtypes 3, 4, 5, or 6 all demonstrated weakness on phonological awareness measures but varying degrees of strengths and weakness on other measures:

- Subtype 1 ($n = 26$)—global deficits across all assessment measures.
- Subtype 2 ($n = 35$)—global deficits across tasks but a relative strength on visual tasks compared to performance on language tasks.
- Subtype 3 ($n = 31$)—strength on rapid naming.
- Subtype 4 ($n = 43$)—a particular weakness on rapid naming.
- Subtype 5 ($n = 15$)—strength on visual attention.
- Subtype 6 ($n = 18$)—strength on speech production.

Children classified as subtype 7 ($n = 15$) were poor readers who did not show a weakness on phonological awareness measures but a deficit on rapid naming, speech production and nonverbal memory.

These findings suggest that most poor readers show a deficit in phonological awareness. However, it is also important to consider poor readers' performance on other cognitive and linguistic tasks, as wider variability in these areas may be expected. The following section focuses on the relationship between deficits in phonological awareness and deficits in other aspects of the linguistic system: semantic, syntactic, and morphological deficits.

SYNTACTIC, SEMANTIC, AND MORPHOLOGICAL KNOWLEDGE

The importance of phonological awareness skills to the reading process is now firmly established. Other aspects of spoken language, however, also make important contributions to the processing of written text. In particular, semantic, syntactic, and morphological knowledge of spoken language is brought to bear in the reading and spelling process. Knowledge of word order and vocabulary help children predict and comprehend text and morphological awareness helps children recognize relationships between base words and derived words (e.g., understanding the word *angry* from the base word of *anger*). As discussed in Chapter 2, the interactive model of word recognition holds that semantic, syntactic, and phonological knowledge work in an interactive manner to produce recognition of words in connected text. Researchers therefore have investigated to what extent deficits in semantic and syntactic knowledge at a young age contribute to later reading difficulties (Sawyer, 1992; Scarborough, 1990; Vellutino & Scanlon, 1987). The role of morphological knowledge in literacy development has received increasing attention. Although data related to children's morphological awareness have sometimes been integrated with data on their syntactic knowledge, morphological knowledge warrants direct discussion. This section provides a brief summary of research related to semantic, syntactic, and morphological knowledge in children with reading disabilities and draws attention to the relationship between these linguistic skills and phonological awareness.

Syntactic Knowledge

One of the earliest studies to investigate the syntactic abilities in children with dyslexia was conducted by Vogel (1974). In this study the syntactic abilities in oral language of 20 7- to 8-year-old males with dyslexia were compared to those of their age-matched peers who were good readers. The results indicated that the poor readers' performance was significantly below that of good readers on seven of the nine measures of syntactic ability. Vogel concluded that syntactic impairment in spoken language and dyslexia are closely related. Consistent with Vogel's findings, other studies have demonstrated that poor readers' syntactic and morphological skills are inferior to those of good readers (Morice & Slaghuis, 1985; Semel & Wiig, 1975; Siegel & Ryan, 1984; Wiig, Semel, & Crouse, 1973).

Morice and Slaghuis's (1985) study is notable in its use of spontaneous speech samples to assess the oral syntactic proficiency of 54 8-year-old children. Children who could be classified as having dyslexia used structurally less complex speech and made frequent syntactic errors compared to average and good readers. Significant correlations between performance on syntactic *awareness* tasks (compared to syntactic *usage*) and measures of reading comprehension also have been found (Bowey, 1986). Scarborough's longitudinal study showed that deficiencies in syntactic complexity and receptive language skills of children later diagnosed as dyslexic were apparent when the children were as young as 2 and 3 years of age (Scarborough, 1990).

Semantic Knowledge

Researchers have examined various elements of children's semantic system in relation to reading disability. Early researchers suggested a link between oral language difficulties and reading disability and reported poor readers' limited spoken vocabularies, verbal concept formation problems, and word-finding difficulties (Fry, Johnson, & Muehl, 1970; Rabinovich, 1959, 1968). The relationship between retrieval of word knowledge and reading ability received particular attention (Denckla & Rudel, 1976a, 1976b; Denkla, 1972; Perfetti & Hogaboam, 1975; Rudel, 1983; Spring, 1976; Spring & Capps, 1974). Findings that poor readers had difficulty retrieving words were initially interpreted as indicating a deficit within the semantic system. Subsequent research, however, suggested that poor readers fail to name objects rapidly and accurately as a consequence of their inability to establish phonological representations of these names in memory and to process phonological representations (Katz, 1986; Snowling, van Wagtendonk, & Stafford, 1988). Zecker and Zinner (1987) argued that poor readers may have the same amount of semantic information available to them as good readers but are slower in being able to access this information. Rapid access to word meanings is considered particularly important for reading comprehension (Perfetti & Lesgold, 1979). Rapid naming difficulties encountered by poor readers are now generally discussed in association with phonological processing abilities and in relation to investigations of speed of processing (Catts et al., 2002; Wolf & Bowers, 1999).

Nevertheless, other areas of semantic delay are evident in the oral language skills of children with reading disability. Wiig and Semel (1984) described poor readers as having difficulty interpreting semantic relationships in complex sentences, difficulty perceiving and interpreting specific types of verbal analogies, and deficits in word relationships and figurative language. Sawyer's (1985) description of children with reading disability included comments on their limited vocabularies and their difficulty interpreting semantic relationships in more complex sentences. Older children (12–16 years) with dyslexia also exhibited difficulty understanding the rules governing word combinations when relayed to memory (Wiig & Roach, 1975). They showed a rapid decrease in their ability to recall sentences verbatim that violated semantic rules or were syntactically complex. Only some of these difficulties may be accounted for by poor phonological representations.

Syntactic and Semantic Knowledge in Relation to Phonological Knowledge

Utilizing both a longitudinal and reading-age-matched design, Gillon and Dodd (1994) demonstrated that 8–10-year-old poor readers had concurrent difficulties in semantic, syntactic, and phonological processing skills that persisted over time. Importantly, the study demonstrated that although performance was impaired in all three language domains, the poor readers exhibited a pattern of particular deficit in phonological processing, whereas their semantic and syntactic abilities showed general delayed development that was consistent with their level of reading experience. Thus weaker semantic and syntactic skill development evident in older poor readers may largely be a consequence, rather than a cause, of reading disability. This view was further supported by a series of training studies implemented at the completion of the 2-year longitudinal study. Gillon and Dodd (1995, 1997) demonstrated that training that was successful in improving these poor readers' semantic and syntactic spoken language had little effect on enhancing their reading ability. In sharp contrast, training in phonological processing dramatically improved both the reading accuracy of connected text and reading comprehension performance for these readers.

A further interesting finding from the Gillon and Dodd (1994) study was the identification of semantic and syntactic delay in older children with dyslexia. The performance of the poor readers on three assessments, administered at 12-month intervals and measuring semantic and syntactic/morphological skills, from a standardised test of language development (Clinical Evaluation of Language Fundamentals—Revised [CELF-R]; Semel, Wiig, & Secord, 1987), remained well below the average standard score expected for their age. At the first assessment these children's ability to orally formulate compound and complex sentences placed them in the severely delayed range. Yet these difficulties were not readily identified in their conversational speech. Class teachers had not reported any of these children as having spoken language difficulties, nor had parents or previous teachers referred the children to speech–language pathologists for spoken language evaluation. Rather, in-depth assessment by a speech–language pathologist was required to adequately identify the weaknesses present in the spoken language system of these poor readers.

Morphological Knowledge

A child's awareness of morphemes within words is referred to as morphological awareness and is useful in both reading and spelling (Elbro & Arnbak, 1996; Windsor, 2000) (Carlisle, 1995; Masterson & Apel, 2000; Moats, 2000; Treiman & Bourassa, 2000). Morphological awareness allows children to understand the relationship between a base or root word and its derived forms such as realizing that the word *biking* is derived from the root word *bike*. Elbro and Arnbak (1996) reported that adolescents with dyslexia used knowledge of morphemes as a compensatory strategy and that awareness of morphemes in spoken language influenced their ability to utilize such a strategy. However, the relationship between spoken and written morphological knowledge is bidirectional. Poor morphological awareness in spoken language restricts the use of a potentially useful reading and spelling strategy. Poor word recognition and spelling knowledge restrict exposure to, and experience with, morphologically complex words and thus limit the development of morphological awareness (Derwing, Smith, & Wiebe, 1995; Fowler & Liberman, 1995).

Distinct forms of morphological awareness influence the relationship between morphological knowledge and reading and spelling in differing ways. Fowler and Liberman (1995) explored morphological awareness in a group of 48 children who had a range of reading abilities. The children all spoke English and were 7–10 years of age. The children's ability to identify the base word from a phonologically complex derived form (e.g., identifying the base word *five* from the derived word *fifth*) proved to be the morphological awareness task that best predicted word recognition performance. However, the opposite pattern was observed for predicting spelling scores: The ability to produce the derived form *fifth* when given the base word *five* was a stronger predictor of written spelling. Fowler and Liberman further reported that 10 poor readers performed significantly worse on these types of morphological tasks than skilled readers, but that they only showed difficulty compared to good readers with words that were phonologically complex (i.e., the derived form involved a phonological change, such as *decide* to *decision*, in contrast to an unaltered base form, such as *suggest* to *suggestion*). There also were no differences between poor and average readers on any of the morphological production tasks when the researchers employed a reading-age-matched design. The researchers concluded that poor readers' difficulty with identifying morphological relationships in some types of words might be a consequence of their weak phonological processing skills.

Windsor (2000) also found that performance with phonologically complex or opaque derivatives that necessitate a vowel or stress change (e.g., *acid* to *acidic*) are more strongly related to word recognition and reading comprehension than derivatives that are more transparent. Twenty-three children, 10–12 years of age, who had spoken and written language impairments, performed significantly worse than age-matched controls on the phonological complex derivates but not on transparent derivatives. In agreement with Fowler and Liberman (1995), Windsor concluded that the ability to analyze the phonological changes associated with these complex derivations might be an important factor in linking morphology to reading in children with language disabilities.

CASE EXAMPLE

An 8-year-old boy (pseudonym Ben), presented with many of the typical features of dyslexia discussed in the literature. Ben's spoken and written language development was monitored for a 4-year, 4-month period. Aspects of his phonological processing and semantic and syntactic skills were assessed on six occasions during this period, and his reading accuracy and reading comprehension performance were measured on seven occasions. This case example is presented here to add a clinical perspective to the literature reviewed and to help readers draw links between theory and practice. Gillon and Dodd (1998) provide further details of this case study in comparison to a matched control group with typical language skills. This case example highlights many findings reported from group studies in the research literature. The following points are exemplified in the case example:

- Children with dyslexia may have superior nonverbal intellectual abilities.
- Children with dyslexia may come from supportive homes and be immersed in language-rich environments at both home and school.
- Children with dyslexia may not have obvious speech and language difficulties; rather in-depth assessment of spoken language skills, including phonological processing skills, is essential.
- Children with dyslexia have persistent phonological processing and word recognition deficits.
- Children with dyslexia have particular difficulty using phonological information, as evidenced by non-word reading or non-word spelling difficulties.
- Children with dyslexia may have concurrent weaknesses in phonological, semantic, and syntactic aspects of spoken language, but it is the domain of phonological processing that plays a causal role in restricting word recognition ability.
- Children with dyslexia may develop behavioral problems that are associated with their frustration in written language acquisition.

- Children with dyslexia can respond very quickly and positively to phonological awareness intervention.
- Children with dyslexia require more than 12 hours of phonological awareness intervention to consolidate skills and ensure continued accelerated learning.

Background

Ben was a participant in a longitudinal, and intervention study investigating the spoken language skills of children with dyslexia (Gillon & Dodd, 1994, 1995). He was close to 8 years, 10 months of age when selected for inclusion in the study. Ben had attended the same private primary school (in Australia) since school entry; at the commencement of the study, he was described by his teachers as a "pleasant boy of neat appearance." Despite his literacy difficulties, his attitude toward school and reading was generally positive. He particularly enjoyed the social aspects of school and was well liked by his peers. He gained recognition from his sporting achievements, which helped to foster positive self-esteem. However, Ben did express frustration with his learning difficulties and, on occasions, would break down in class and cry. This behavior persisted throughout the intervening years, to follow-up at 13 years of age.

At the commencement of the study, Ben's teachers described him as a nonreader. Despite nearly 3 years of education at a private school (with a good educational reputation), Ben was unable to read simple connected text at an independent level. He could, however, read a few words in isolation. Ben had not previously been seen by a speech–language pathologist for any developmental speech or language difficulties. Prior to the initial assessment, the teachers considered Ben to have average spoken language skills and commented on his excellent conversational and social skills.

The teachers described Ben's parents as supportive. They attended periodic consultancy meetings with the school's reading specialist and also had attended a parent-training program to help Ben study reading at home. Ben's siblings (two younger brothers) were reported to have some general learning difficulties and were in the lower-average range for their class level. However, they did not present the specific reading disability Ben displayed.

Cognitive assessment established that Ben's literacy difficulties were not consistent with generally lower abilities. His standard score of 121 on the Test of Nonverbal Intelligence–2 (Brown, Sherbenou, & Johnsen, 1990) placed him within the superior intellectual range. He also gained an average standard score (SS = 94) on a measure of receptive vocabulary: Peabody Picture Vocabulary Test—Revised (Dunn & Dunn, 1981).

Assessment and Intervention Structure

Ben's spoken and written language development was assessed on three occasions at approximately 12-month intervals, from ages 8 to 10 years. During this time Ben participated in the regular class program and received individual support from the school reading specialist. Reading strategies attempted by the teachers to enhance Ben's reading during this period included traditional phonics-based strategies, whole word recognition strategies, and a language experience approach to reading and writing. Shortly after the third assessment period, Ben entered the Gillon and Dodd (1995) intervention study. He was randomly assigned to receive 12 hours of phonological awareness intervention, followed by 12 hours of semantic–syntactic oral language intervention. Each intervention was implemented over two 1-hour individual sessions per week until 12 hours had been completed.

The phonological awareness intervention focused on developing phoneme segmentation and blending skills, phoneme manipulation skills, and linking speech to print through identifying sound changes in words with letter blocks (see Chapter 7). The semantic–syntactic training developed vocabulary knowledge through semantic mapping, language theme approaches, and a series of exercises to enhance Ben's ability to formulate sentences of increasing length and complexity. Assessment data were collected prior to and following each intervention period.

Two further assessments were administered following intervention, when Ben was 12 and 13 years of age. During this time period, Ben received a further 3-month period of phonological awareness intervention implemented by the school's reading specialist. Data reported in this section highlight Ben's struggle to use phonological information in the reading and spelling process.

Word Recognition Development

Ben's reading performance was measured at each assessment trial using a standardised test: The Neale Analysis of Reading Ability—Revised (Neale, 1988). This test consists of a series of graded prose passages that are read aloud by the child. Ben's reading accuracy performance (i.e., the accuracy at which Ben recognized words in print) is shown in Figure 4.1. Improvement in his word recognition ability from 8 to 13 years of age was not the result of steady progress over time. Rather, most of the progress made coincided with his participation in the 12-hour phonological awareness intervention. The only other period of growth coincided with a revision of this program. Other types of individual remedial programs that were imple-

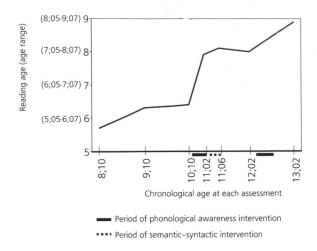

FIGURE 4.1. Ben's reading accuracy performance as measured by the Neale Analysis of Reading Ability—Revised.

mented during the 4-year period and general classroom instruction were largely ineffective in accelerating Ben's reading accuracy performance.

The majority of Ben's reading errors prior to the phonological awareness intervention were substitution errors. Some substitution errors involved visually similar words but were not semantically or grammatically correct. For example: Ben read "We are taking part in a road safety lesson, they said" as "We are *talking* part *of* a road safety *learning, that* said." Other substitutions included semantic associations (e.g., *arrived* read as *returned*) and substitution of phrases (e.g., *They were what* read as *when they had*). Error analysis also showed an increasing pattern of omission of more complex words. Ben showed little evidence of attempting to decode unfamiliar words phonologically. With increasing age, his reading became characterized by a relatively fluent style of presentation, whereby he rapidly substituted words, giving little attention to the printed word's phonological structure or meaning. At age 10 years, 10 months Ben's reading rate was close to the normal range expected for his age, whereas his reading accuracy performance showed severe delay, as indicated in Figure 4.1.

Reading error analysis following the phonological training program indicated an increase in the number of mispronunciations, with closer attempts at phonologically decoding the word (e.g., *sheltered* read as *seltered, amazement* read as *amament*). There was a decrease in the number of phonologically unrelated substitutions word errors. Ben did not omit any words during the postintervention reading assessment. Rather, he appeared to focus more on the orthographic and phonological structure of the words. His overt decoding of some words, read successfully, was apparent.

Ben's comprehension of written text was constrained by his inaccurate word recognition ability. Although his reading comprehension scores were delayed for his age, they were consistently better than his reading accuracy scores, because he was able to utilize information from picture cues, general knowledge, and contextual cues to gain meaning. Thus it was apparent that Ben's reading difficulties were associated with very poor decoding ability rather than more global difficulties in language comprehension.

Spelling Development

Ben's spelling of real words and non-words was evaluated at each assessment. The non-words were derived from the real words by changing one or more graphemes, as shown in Table 4.1. With the exception of the words *strong* and *island*, the non-words maintained the same type of consonant–vowel structure as the real words (e.g., real word = *brisk*; non-word = *plisk*). Table 4.1 illustrates Ben's spelling attempts. Inspection of his spelling errors revealed that the majority of errors for both real and non-words during the first three assessments (prior to phonological awareness intervention) occurred predominately at the semiphonetic stage of spelling development (see Chapter 2). He was beginning to show development of initial phoneme–grapheme connections (particularly for simple connections such as *m* and *b*). What is remarkable, however, is the distinct lack of improvement from 8 to 10 years in his spelling attempts. With the exception of initial consonants, most of his attempts at spelling non-words exhibited little phonological resemblance to the stimulus word (e.g., *slonk - coht*; *cila - serte*). There was little evidence of analogy strategies in Ben's spelling non-word attempts, but the surprising, phonetically correct spelling of one non-word in the first assessment (*bellTom*) indicates his use of known words to assist in the spelling attempt.

Inconsistent attempts at words over time were apparent. For example, the only real word Ben spelled in a phonetically plausible, manner in year 1, *sity* for *city*, was subsequently spelled *sated* and *crety* in years 2 and 3, respectively. Ben utilized verbal mediation strategies to assist him in spelling. Phonological errors were noted in his pronunciations of the non-words, but his spelling attempts were not consistent with his misarticulations. Prior to phonological awareness intervention, he showed severe spelling disorder and a persistent inability to use phonological cues in spelling attempts. However, even a short period of phonological awareness training appeared to have a very positive effect on his spelling development: His spelling attempts showed a much greater number of phonetically plausible and correct spellings for both real and non-words. His improvement

TABLE 4.1. Ben's Spelling Attempts over Time

Target	8 years, 10 months	9 years, 10 months	10 years, 10 months	11 years, 2 months[a]
		Real words		
strong	sogon	stonlod	stong	stronge
ocean	oshn	once	ocian	ocen
enough	enust	enaft	e-	**enuf**
went	when	**went**	whart	**went**
swept	shet	smant	sh	**swept**
hasty	hety	hamed	honset	**haste**
city	**sity**	sated	craty	**city**
brisk	brik	prest	Breter	bresk
sword	sint	slosed	sawer	**sword**
liquid	litwod	lwet	lenter	likrod
height	hitet	hietd	high	**hight**
spirit	scat	srend	speach	spreat
seldom	stad	sramd	sread	sloud
social	sotsh	sonad	sreat	soeswer
island	land	liand	**island**	island
worst	west	went	wrent	**worst**
number	nant	namer	namber	**number**
move	nosh	mrove	move	**move**
		Non-Words		
Flong (strong)[b]	faslh		siont	
ecean (ocean)	airsenst	alnfe	esteder	earst
alough (enough)	flats	alaft	elfarlt	**alaf**
mest (went)	—	meast	sester	**mest**
Frept (swept)	frat	—	fresd	**frept**
fisty (hasty)	fith	feame	fresed	**fiste**
cila (city)	serte	stela	scared	sheel
plisk (brisk)	pink	plast	prest	**plisk**
swird (sword)	shent	stent	srend	sword
biquid (liquid)	bitew	bweik	brekerd	**biquid**
meighft/peight[c] (height)	mitan	miced	pipeted[c]	**piet**[c]
skirit (spirit)	afou	strgerat	srech	seak
beltom (seldom)	**bellTom**	belltollt	bredted	bout
ricial (social)	shlf	rendst	rested	riosh
slonk (island)	coht	**slonk**	slond	slonk
morst (worst)	metf	plast	nerd	**morst**
wumber (number)	whap	wape	wreap	wonb
sove (move)	soodt	sreond	srend	**soov**

Note. Bold text indicates that Ben's spelling attempts were phonetically plausible or were correct, "—" indicates that no repsonse was given.
[a]After phonological awareness intervention.
[b]Word in brackets is the real word that the non-word was derived from. The non-word was articulated in a consistent manner to the real word (e.g., *sove* rhymed with *move*, *morst* rhymed with *worst*).
[c]The non-word *peight* was introduced instead of *meighft* at assessment 3.

in spelling was consistent with his improvement in reading and suggested he was learning how to use both phonological and orthographic information in decoding and encoding print.

Phonological Processing Skills

Ben's phonological awareness skills were measured at each assessment at the onset-rime level (rhyme recognition task) and phoneme level (phoneme manipulation). A measure of speech production (unfamiliar polysyllabic word repetition) was also included. The observation that Ben appeared unable to use grapheme–phoneme conversion strategies to accurately decode or encode text was confirmed by his persistent difficulties on phonological processing skill tasks. Prior to phonological awareness intervention, Ben exhibited a consistent pattern of difficulty and on some tasks showed negative growth. Figure 4.2 shows his performance on a spoonerism task. This is a complex task that requires segmentation, manipulation, and blending skills (e.g., *big dog* changes to *dig bog*). Improvement following phonological awareness training indicated transfer of skills to a novel task, since learning how to spoonerize words was not taught during the intervention period. Compared to average readers in the study, Ben also showed particular difficulty in accurately articulating unfamiliar polysyllabic words such as *swashbuckling, spasmodically, comprehensively,* and *misappropriate*. Although he had never experienced any obvious delay in speech production, he demonstrated limited ability to rapidly form a new phonological repre-

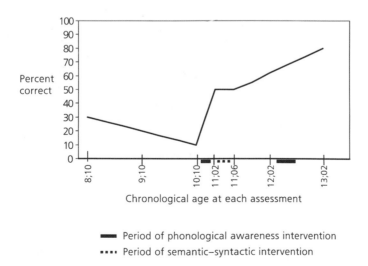

FIGURE 4.2. Ben's performance on a spoonerism task (no. of stimulus items = 10).

sentation for an unfamiliar word and to access this representation to articulate the word correctly.

Semantic and Syntactic Skills

Subtests from the Clinical Evaluation of Language Fundamentals—Revised (CELF-R) (Semel et al., 1987) were selected as tasks to measure Ben's semantic, syntactic, and short-term memory skills. One receptive-language task (*Word Classes*, primarily probing semantic skills) and two expressive-language tasks (*Formulated Sentences*, targeting integrated semantic and syntactic skills, and *Recalling Sentences*, probing syntactic, semantic, and memory skills) were selected. Ben demonstrated persistent difficulty in his ability to formulate grammatically correct compound and complex sentences; his standard score on this subtest was well below the average range on the three assessments prior to intervention training. However, on two other subtests, *Recalling Sentences* and *Word Classes*, he showed steady growth toward the population mean on subsequent assessments. At two further assessments at ages 11 years, 6 months and 13 years, 2 months (following semantic–syntactic intervention), Ben's standard scores placed him within the average range expected for his age level on all three subtests.

Linking Theory to Practice

Ben's profile of literacy and spoken language acquisition during the 2 years prior to his participation in the phonological processing skills training program suggested either that he was using logographic strategies, as described by (Frith, 1985), or that he was at the rudimentary alphabetic stage of reading development, as described by Ehri (1991). He demonstrated use of some letters in the words to form visual–phonetic connections, but accurate connections between spellings and pronunciations in memory were not made. This inability led him to substitute words that had similar visual–phonetic cues. His failure to adopt strategies from the alphabetic stage of word recognition was further evident in his spelling performance. Early development of real word spelling was demonstrated in his ability to detect initial and some final sounds. However, incorrect knowledge of phoneme sequence and inability to identify the phonemes within words and nonwords were clearly apparent. Such difficulties indicate a failure to acquire the alphabetic strategy (Frith, 1985).

A self-teaching model (discussed in Chapter 2) also may be used to describe Ben's reading and spelling development during this period. His phonological processing deficit severely restricted his ability to engage in successful decoding and encoding attempts. This limitation, in turn led to his persistent difficulty in acquiring knowledge of phoneme–grapheme connections and his inability to establish accurate orthographic representations of words. His remarkable lack of progress in reading and spelling from 8–10 years suggested that he was unable to engage in self-teaching of new phoneme–grapheme connections and was unable to use the skills he had been taught in the variety of remedial approaches tried at an independent level. Consistent with the self-teaching item-based (rather than stage-based) model, phoneme type and phoneme position affected Ben's performance. He was more successful in decoding and encoding initial consonants than final and medial consonants and showed significant difficulty with complex phoneme–grapheme connections.

Ben's profile of development suggested that a phonological deficit hypothesis for his reading and spelling disorder was plausible. In order to consider a causal relationship between aspects of spoken language skill development and Ben's written language disorder at least two conditions needed to be met:

1. The spoken language variable must demonstrate a stable and persistent pattern of difficulty over time (Wagner et al., 1993).
2. Training to improve the spoken language skill should lead to improvement in reading ability (Wagner & Torgesen, 1987).

Ben displayed persistent difficulty in using phonological information in decoding and encoding words, and phonological awareness intervention coincided with marked improvement in both reading and spelling. In contrast, semantic and syntactic skills in Ben's oral language improved over time to age-appropriate levels, yet reading and spelling difficulties persisted. Specific intervention to enhance semantic and syntactic skills had minimal effect on improving his reading and spelling skills.

Behavior

At the seventh assessment trial (age 13 years), Ben's teachers and school principal reported on the marked deterioration in his classroom behavior, which they described as uncooperative, impolite, and generally disrespectful of authority. His behavioral difficulties led the principal to question the continuation of his education at the school. During the assessment sessions, however, Ben always exerted concerted effort on the tasks presented, and he cooperated with the researcher and interacted in a friendly and polite manner. The learning support teacher also commented that Ben always worked well in an individual or small group withdrawal-learning situation that was focused on improving his reading and writing performance.

Other Influences on Ben's Development

This case example has emphasized Ben's linguistic skills in relation to his literacy development. However, it is recognized that a child's success in reading may be directly influenced by a range of variables. External factors, such as those related to the reading text and teacher, and internal factors, such as motivation, also may contribute to a child's success in literacy acquisition (Idol, 1988; McCormick, 1994). Children's self-perceptions of their reading ability begin to influence their reading performance early in the educational process (Chapman & Tunmer, 1997). For children with dyslexia, self-recognition of their poor reading performance may therefore have negative consequences and influence their learning and behavioral patterns as they progress through the grades. Unfortunately, Ben's classroom behavior became increasingly unacceptable over time, causing frustration for his teachers. Teachers' responses to Ben's academic needs may have been affected by the need to channel their energy toward behavior management. The brief period of phonological processing intervention, however, provided important evidence that Ben had the learning capacity necessary to significantly benefit from a program targeting phonological processing skills.

SUMMARY

This chapter defined dyslexia and summarized research that supports a phonological deficit hypothesis for reading disorder. The persistent nature of phonological awareness and other processing difficulties encountered by children with reading and spelling deficits was discussed. Following are the summary points:

- Dyslexia is a specific language based disorder.
- Children described as having developmental dyslexia have persistent word recognition and phonological processing difficulties.
- Compared to skilled readers, children with dyslexia perform poorly on a range of phonological awareness tasks; tasks at the phoneme level are particularly discriminatory between skilled and unskilled readers.
- Phonological awareness deficits restrict children's word recognition development by limiting the use of phonological decoding and orthographic analogy strategies.
- Children with dyslexia are not a homogenous group—subgroups of poor readers can be clearly identified; however nearly all poor readers will exhibit phoneme awareness difficulties.
- In addition to phoneme awareness difficulties, children with dyslexia

may have a range of other processing difficulties; speed of processing is currently attracting particular interest, and research work in this area is ongoing.

FROM RESEARCH TO PRACTICE

The case example provided an illustration of the reading and spelling difficulties that children with dyslexia encounter during their schooling. The course of Ben's development highlights many of the findings from research that has investigated the language basis for dyslexia. In addition to the case example, the following clinical implications may be drawn from research discussed in this chapter:

1. The persistent and severe nature of phonological processing and word recognition difficulties evident in older children with dyslexia underscores the importance of early identification and intervention.

2. Children with persistent reading disorder should undergo an in-depth evaluation of their spoken language abilities by a speech–language pathologist. This assessment should include evaluation of phonological awareness and other areas of linguistic processing (refer to Chapter 6).

3. Phonological awareness assessment for older children with dyslexia should include complex phonological tasks, such as phoneme deletion and spoonerism tasks, as well as assessment of their ability to use phonological information, such as non-word reading and non-word spelling tasks.

4. It is critical that intervention for children with reading disorder should aim to resolve their phonological processing deficits to enable them to use phonological information in word recognition and spelling (see Chapter 6).

Struggling to perform a task that their peers have mastered with such apparent ease must be a very frustrating experience for older children with reading disorder. The behavioral issues and poor self-concept sometimes associated with dyslexia are hardly surprising. Few of us, as adults, would persist in attempting to learn a new skill or sport if we constantly failed to experience any progress, particularly if our peers witnessed our failure on a daily basis. It is critical, therefore, that professionals who work with individuals who have reading disorder understand the nature of the disorder and adequately address areas of deficit that restrict development. The phonological deficit hypothesis for dyslexia is strongly supported by the research and demands that specific attention be directed to the child's phonological processing abilities as part of a comprehensive assessment and intervention plan.

5

Children with Spoken Language Impairment

In contrast to children with dyslexia, whose spoken language difficulties may not be identified until they begin to fail in written language, some children approach the task of reading and spelling with diagnosed spoken language impairments. Other children may display speech and oral language skills within the normal range at school entry but have a history of spoken language difficulties that required speech and language pathology services during the preschool and kindergarten years. Research has established that a large percentage of children who have diagnosed spoken language difficulties also encounter difficulty learning to read and spell (Boudreau & Hedberg, 1999; Catts, Fey, Zhang, & Tomblin, 2001; Johnson et al., 1999; Larrivee & Catts, 1999; Lewis, Freebairn, & Taylor, 2002). Indeed, children with a history of speech–language impairment are 4–5 times more likely to have reading difficulties than children from the general population (Catts et al., 2001). These difficulties are likely to be persistent in nature and not readily resolved by classroom instruction. For example, research suggests that between 50 and 70% of children with spoken language impairment present with academic difficulties throughout their school years (Felsenfeld, Broen, & McGrue, 1994; Shriberg, Tomblin, & McSweeny, 1999). Snowling, Adams, Bishop, and Stothard (2001) found that even when children's spoken language difficulties were resolved by age 5 years, 6 months at a surface level (e.g., their speech production difficulties were corrected), they exhibited some weaknesses in reading and spelling performance in adolescence. This chapter discusses the relationship between spoken and written language disorders and examines the development of phonological awareness skills in children with spoken language impairment.

SUBGROUPS OF SPOKEN LANGUAGE IMPAIRMENT

The relationship between spoken and written language disorders is not a straightforward one. Not all children who exhibit spoken language impairment experience difficulty learning to read and spell. Some show typical development in written language acquisition, whereas many fall into the high-risk category for persistent reading failure (Johnson et al., 1999). It is important to understand the nature of children's spoken language impairments and to identify the subgroups that are most likely to struggle with reading and spelling. From a clinical perspective, best practice demands that speech–language pathologists who diagnose spoken language disorders engage in in-depth assessment procedures to appropriately identify children's areas of strength and weaknesses (Bernthal & Bankson, 1998; Gillon & Schwarz, 1999; Paul, 2001). Following such assessment, a diagnosis of the nature of the child's spoken language impairment may be made. Two main subgroups of children with spoken language impairment have attracted particular interest in relation to written language ability. These are (1) children described as having *specific language impairment*, and (2) children with *speech impairment*. A discussion of each of these terms is presented, followed by a summary of the phonological awareness and literacy development typical in these populations.

Specific Language Impairment

The term "specific language impairment" (SLI) in its broadest sense refers to children who have spoken language difficulties despite a favorable language-learning environment and in the absence of lower nonverbal intellectual ability, neurological damage, sensory loss, and severe physical, emotional, or behavioral disorder. Subgroups of children with SLI are evident (Conti-Ramsden & Botting, 1999). These groups show differing profiles of strengths and weaknesses on language measures. For example, 38% of the 196 British children (age 7 years) with SLI studied in Conti-Ramsden & Botting's study (1999) had particular difficulty with expressive language tasks (e.g., a story retelling task or picture-naming task) compared to their receptive language performance (e.g., comprehending sentences spoken by the examiner). In contrast, 53% of the sample showed no discrepancy between receptive and expressive language measures. Children with SLI may have difficulty with particular grammatical aspects of language, such as marking tenses in speech (Rice & Wexler, 1996), and some children also may present with speech impairment in addition to difficulties with expressive syntax and morphology (Shriberg et al., 1999). (See Ahmed, Lombardino, & Leonard, 2001, for a review of the linguistic profiles of children with SLI and a discussion of causal factors associated with SLI.)

The broad definition for SLI is similar to the exclusionary definition of dyslexia (presented in Chapter 4). Indeed, whether the two groups can be clearly distinguished has been questioned (McArthur, Hogben, Edwards, Heath, & Mengler, 2000). Language difficulties that are apparent in spoken form at an early age may simply manifest themselves as written language disorders as the demands on the linguistic system increase with advancing academic curriculum. However, the complex interplay between spoken and written language development cautions against accepting such a linear progression from SLI to dyslexia. Differing profiles of written language competencies are evident for at least some children with SLI compared to those with dyslexia (Goulandris, Snowling, & Walker, 2000). Recent evidence also suggests that there are anatomical differences in brain structure between children with phonologically based reading disorder and children with SLI (Leonard et al., 2002). Thus the term "specific language impairment" is useful to distinguish children with particular spoken language characteristics from those whose language difficulties are more obvious in the written language context.

Speech Impairment

Articulation impairment, phonological impairment, expressive phonological disorder, and developmental verbal dyspraxia are all terms used to refer to children's speech difficulties. These terms may be used differentially to describe types of speech error patterns (Dodd, 1995). Inconsistency in the use of these terms, however, has led to confusion in the literature. For example, Catts (1993) concluded that articulation ability is unrelated to reading achievement. In contrast, Das, Mishra, and Kirby (1994) reported that articulation is a core cognitive difficulty underlying dyslexia. Such opposing conclusions can be resolved by understanding how the term *articulation* has been used by the researchers. Catts used the term in reference to speech sound errors, whereas Das et al. used it in reference to rapid naming and word repetition tasks (i.e., tasks that involve phonological processing). In considering the relationship between speech impairment and reading disorder, therefore, it is important to clarify the definition of terms used in relation to speech errors.

Articulation Impairment/Articulation Disorder

The term articulation disorder historically referred to any type of speech error and included errors that were motoric in nature, such as speech distortion errors resulting from incorrect tongue placement or facial muscle weakness, as well as phonologically based speech errors such as multiple substitutions and sound omission errors. Advances in the field of speech–

language pathology have led to discrimination between articulation and phonological speech error patterns (Grundy, 1989). This discrimination is particularly helpful in relation to written language development, because it is when emphasis is directed to the phonological rather than articulative aspects of speech production (i.e., the mechanics of actually producing the sound) that links to phonological processing involved in reading an alphabetic language can be hypothesized.

The term "articulation impairment" can be used to describe speech distortions or substitution of sounds in spoken language in all phonetic environments (Dodd, 1995). These speech errors have a physical (or motor) basis: for example, incorrect tongue placement when producing the /s/ sound, resulting in a lisp error pattern, or the use of the lips in attempting to produce a /r/ sound, resulting in a /w/ rather than an /r/ sound (e.g., *wun* for *run*) in all word positions. Articulation impairment also may result from structural abnormalities such as a cleft palate or from neurologically based motor-speech problems such as dysarthria. Many children who have phonologically based speech error patterns (discussed below) also make articulation errors. Some children, though, *only* make articulation errors, and it is important to differentiate these children from those who have other types of speech and language impairment.

Phonological Impairment

The term "phonological impairment" can be used to refer to speech errors that result from an interference with the processing of linguistic information. Phonological involvement in accurate speech production includes:

- The establishment of a phonological representation of a word in memory.
- The ability to access this representation.
- Processes that govern the ability to select and sequence speech sounds according to the language being spoken.
- The assembly of a phonological plan.
- The implementation and execution of a phonological plan.

This processing takes place at an unconscious level and is an effortless task for most people. However, the complexities involved become more apparent when breakdown occurs. The reader is referred to models of speech processing (e.g., Dodd, 1995; Stackhouse & Wells, 1997) to more fully understand where breakdown can occur within the speech processing chain.

The terms "expressive phonological impairment" and "expressive phonology disorders" have been introduced in the literature to describe phonologically based speech errors (Bird, Bishop, & Freeman, 1995;

Clarke-Klein, 1994; Larrivee & Catts, 1999; Lewis, Freebairn, & Taylor, 2000). These are useful terms because they help to distinguish phonological impairment as it refers to speech error patterns from phonological impairment as it refers to phonological awareness or phonological processing difficulties in relation to reading. "Delayed phonological acquisition" is used to describe children's speech error patterns that reflect normal phonological development but are not expected in the older child. For example, 2-year-old children often delete or simplify a cluster sound (e.g., saying *tar* for *star*) or substitute a sound that is easy to produce for a more difficult sound (e.g., *top* for *chop*). These error patterns are expected to disappear from children's speech by 4 and 5 years of age (Bernthal & Bankson, 1998). Thus a 6-year-old child who presents with these speech error patterns would be considered to have delayed phonological development.

The term "deviant phonological development" or "phonological disorder" can be used to describe children's speech error patterns that are unusual or not expected in typical phonological development (Dodd, 1995). Some children may use these unusual error patterns consistently in their speech ("consistent phonological disorder"), suggesting poor understanding of the phonological system of their native language (Dodd, 1995 p. 56). Others may show evidence of inconsistent error patterns ("inconsistent phonological disorder"), reflecting difficulty in formulating an accurate phonological plan for speech execution.

Developmental Verbal Dyspraxia

The term "developmental verbal dyspraxia" (also referred to as "developmental apraxia of speech") remains a controversial label for speech impairment. Children who have persistent speech difficulty despite therapy intervention—who (1) show inconsistency in their speech error patterns, (2) have difficulty sequencing speech sounds, and (3) show difficulty in coordinating their speech musculature and vocal tract for speech production in the absence of physical impairment, among a range of other symptoms—may be described as having developmental verbal dyspraxia (Bernthal & Bankson, 1998; Velleman & Strand, 1994). Debate exists regarding which specific features differentiate the disorder from other types of speech disorders. McCabe, Rosenthal, and McLeod (1998) found that many features considered to be characteristic of developmental verbal dyspraxia occur in the general population of children with speech impairment. However, researchers have described clusters of behaviors which, when exhibited simultaneously, may make the syndrome "developmental verbal dyspraxia" an appropriate diagnosis (Ozanne, 1995; Shriberg, Aram, & Kwiatkowski, 1997; Stackhouse, 1992; Velleman & Strand, 1994). Both Stackhouse and Ozanne describe different domains of possible deficit in developmental verbal dyspraxia: (1) knowledge of a phonological plan for the given word; (2) access to the plan for the components (sounds) of the word; and (3) ability to coordinate the vocal tract in producing the word. Ozanne's (1995) criteria for a diagnosis of developmental verbal dyspraxia necessitates a child displaying difficulty in each of the following domains:

- Phonological plan: selecting and sequencing the phonemes for a word, resulting in, for example, inconsistent speech errors and difficulty with multisyllabic words.
- Phonetic program: translating the linguistic plan for a word into a motor program, resulting in speech errors such as omissions, substitutions, and articulative groping.
- Motor program implementation: implementing the selected phonetic program, resulting in sound distortions, phonetic variability, preservation, and loss of rhythm.

Of particular relevance for understanding these children's written language acquisition is that developmental verbal dyspraxia involves breakdown in speech processing at a variety of levels and results in persistent speech difficulty that does not resolve quickly with intervention.

RELATIONSHIP TO READING AND SPELLING DIFFICULTIES

It is estimated that 7.4% of kindergarten children in the United States approach literacy instruction with a specific language impairment, and that 3.8% of 6-year-old U.S. children will be engaged in reading and spelling activities with a speech impairment (see Shriberg et al., 1999; Tomblin, Smith, & Zhang, 1997, for speech and language impairment prevalence data). In considering the relationship between speech impairment and reading, it is critical to examine the type of speech errors produced and to understand at what level in the process of producing speech that the breakdown is occurring. Children who have articulation impairment only are not at high risk for literacy difficulties (Bishop & Adams, 1990; Catts, 1993; Dodd, 1995; Kamhi, Catts, & Mauer, 1990; Stackhouse, 1982), since difficulty in processing the phonological, semantic, syntactic, or morphological information necessary for reading and writing is not implicated. However, all other subgroups of children with speech impairment and specific language impairment are potentially at risk for written language difficulties. These children exhibit impairment in one or more aspects of spoken language upon which reading and writing development draw. The extent of these children's literacy achievement will be determined, at least partially, by their pattern of linguistic weaknesses and strengths. Weakness in phonological awareness and phonological processing skills will restrict their word recognition and spelling development.

As Liberman (1991) discussed in a summary of her earlier work, an alphabetic writing system represents the same phonological segments that are used in spoken language. What differs between the two language systems is the need for conscious awareness of the phonological structure. For example, a child can recognize the spoken word *cat* and attach the word to its meaning without analyzing the word into its constituent elements. However, to deal with unfamiliar written words, children must be aware of the phonological structure the letters represent. It is plausible, therefore, that children who have poorly specified phonological representations of words in their memory store and difficulty planning and implementing a phonological plan that results in incorrect pronunciation of a word may struggle with the challenge of understanding the phonological structure of spoken words and how speech relates to print.

The merging of findings from a variety of studies that have utilized differing populations, age groups, and methodologies provides a clear picture that children with expressive phonological impairment and children described as having a specific language impairment perform poorly on phonological awareness tasks compared to children without these impairments (Bird et al., 1995; Briscoe, Bishop, & Norbury, 2001; Catts, 1993; Dodd, 1995; Fazio, 1997b; Gillon, 2000b; Larrivee & Catts, 1999; Leitao, Hogben, & Fletcher, 1997; Stothard, Snowling, Bishop, Chipchase, & Kaplan, 1998; Webster & Plante, 1992). Findings from these studies include:

1. As a group, children with expressive phonological impairment show deficits on a variety of phonological awareness tasks. For example:

- 61 New Zealand children (ages 5–7 years) performed poorly at the syllable, onset-rime, and phoneme awareness levels prior to intervention (Gillon, 2000).
- 31 British boys (ages 5–7 years) performed poorly on rhyme and phoneme identity tasks and showed a particular deficit in rhyme knowledge (Bird et al., 1995).
- 29 Australian children (age 6 years) showed delay in phoneme deletion, segmentation, and blending (Leitao et al., 1997).
- 15 American children (ages 3–4 years) showed early delay in acquiring rhyme knowledge (Webster & Plante, 1992).

2. Without specific phonological awareness intervention, the phonological awareness deficits of children with expressive phonological impairment and SLI persist over time (Bird et al., 1995; Gillon, 2002b; Snowling,

Bishop, & Stothard, 2000; Stothard et al., 1998). Particular difficulty in acquiring phoneme level skills is evident for these children (Gillon, 2002b; Webster, Plante, & Couvillion, 1997). Even when the spoken language difficulties of children with SLI are considered to have resolved during the preschool or early school years, these children display weakness on complex phonological awareness tasks (e.g., spoonerisms) in adolescence and in aspects of reading and spelling (Stothard et al., 1998).

3. The presence of phonological awareness deficits in children who have expressive phonological impairment is independent of the presence of other receptive and expressive spoken language impairment (Bird et al., 1995; Leitao et al., 1997). However, children with additional language impairment may show particular deficits on complex phoneme level tasks (Leitao et al., 1997; Lewis et al., 2000) and generally experience poorer long-term outcomes in reading and writing than children with isolated expressive phonological impairment (Lewis et al., 2000). The reading difficulties of children with both speech and language impairment may extend beyond word recognition. Factors in addition to phonological awareness deficits, such as limited vocabulary knowledge, poor oral narrative skills, oral syntactic and morphological deficits, and inference comprehension difficulties, all contribute to broad-based reading comprehension difficulties for some of these children (Catts & Kamhi, 1999b).

4. Measures of phonological awareness and rapid-naming ability are more closely related to word recognition performance in children with speech and language impairment in first grade than measures of their receptive and expressive language abilities (Catts, 1993).

5. Young children with SLI show difficulty in learning and reciting nursery rhymes (Fazio, 1997a, 1997b), a skill thought to facilitate early phonological awareness (see Chapter 3). Indeed, difficulty with early developing phonological awareness tasks at the onset-rime level was shown to persist in children with SLI who ranged in ages from 7 to 11 years (Briscoe et al., 2001). The performance in this age group was significantly below that of age-matched peers who reached ceiling levels on onset-rime tasks and did not differ from children with sensory–neural hearing loss.

6. In addition to impairment in the phonological domain, children with expressive phonological impairment display difficulties in other variables important for literacy development, such as letter-name knowledge and verbal working memory (Webster et al., 1997).

7. Children with expressive phonological impairment learning English as their second language may demonstrate phonological awareness difficulties in both languages (Martin, Colesby, & Jhamat, 1997). These difficulties may be present despite speech–language pathology that has proven successful in largely resolving their speech disorder, such as the 7-year-old case study reported in Martin et al.

8. Understanding the type of speech errors made by children with expressive phonological impairment is relevant to predicting reading outcomes. Children who show consistent use of unusual or nondevelopmental speech errors may be more at risk for severe literacy disorder than children whose speech errors indicate delayed development (Dodd et al., 1995; Leitao et al., 1997). As discussed by Catts (1993), children who show sequential speech errors such as reversing segments in multisyllabic words (e.g., *efelant* for *elephant* and assimilation errors (one sound is influenced by another sound in a word) may have more reading difficulties than children with substitution errors (Catts, 1986; Magnusson & Naucler, 1990).

9. The severity of children's speech and phonological awareness impairment influences literacy outcomes (Bird et al., 1995; Larrivee & Catts, 1999). Children who approach literacy instruction with severe speech impairment, significant phonological awareness deficit, and other language difficulties are highly likely to have persistent reading and spelling difficulties. However, these children can respond positively to phonological awareness intervention, and this instruction may prevent the pessimistic academic experience that is typical for these children (Gillon, 2000a, 2002b; see Chapter 7).

The finding of a positive relationship between speech impairment and reading difficulty appears to be sensitive to the measures of speech production used. Larivee and Catts (1999) found that a speech production task that required the children to repeat multisyllabic words accounted for more variance in their reading performance than articulation performance on a measure of single-syllable words. This factor (i.e., syllabic complexity) may help to explain previous inconsistencies in the literature. Studies that have shown a weak relationship between speech production and reading (e.g., Catts, 1993) used tests such as the Goldman–Fristoe Test of Articulation (Goldman & Fristoe, 1986). This test requires the child to articulate only a few multisyllabic words. In contrast, studies that have shown stronger evidence that children with expressive phonological impairment perform poorly on reading measures have included assessments of multisyllabic speech production. For example 13 of the 25 words from Dodd's 25-word consistency test (Dodd, 1995) and included in Gillon's (2000b) study required the articulation of multisyllabic words (e.g., *helicopter, dinosaur, ladybird, elephant*). Larivee and Catts (1999) hypothesized that multisyllabic words may be a more sensitive measure of the quality of children's phonological representations stored in memory. Imprecise phonological representations and difficulty accessing an accurate phonological representation have been strongly linked to reading disorder (see Chapter 3).

Researchers also have investigated how phonological awareness develops in relation to changes in speech production skills in children who have expressive phonological impairment (Webster & Plante, 1992, 1995; Webster et al., 1997). In this longitudinal study, 29 white middle-class children with expressive phonological impairment and 16 children without impairment, all from the United States, were followed from 3½ years to 6 years of age. At the study's outset the children with expressive phonological impairment were considered to have moderate difficulty in their speech error patterns, and all of these children were receiving speech pathology services. Six monthly assessments of their early phonological awareness development, utilizing Bradley and Bryant's (1985) rhyme oddity and alliteration detection tasks, were undertaken. Non-word segmentation was introduced at 6 years of age. The results revealed that the majority of the children with expressive phonological impairment could not detect rhyme until 6 years, and even at this age, approximately one-third of the children failed to reach criterion of 70% correct. Children showed more success on the alliteration detection tasks, and most of the children reached success by 5 years, 9 months. Rapid development in these skills was apparent between 5 and 6 years (which contrasts with the rapid development that occurs in typically developing young children at 3 and 4 years of age; see Chapter 3). The improvement in phonological awareness could be predicted from improvement in speech production measures. The authors discussed that maturation in speech development results in accompanying exponential growth in phonological awareness and that a one-way relationship between speech production and phonological awareness may be speculated (Webster & Plante, 1995).

From a clinical perspective, this finding needs to be interpreted cautiously. It could be argued that since improvement in speech production results in improved phonological awareness, speech–language pathologists and teachers need only focus on improving a child's speech output. There is strong evidence against making this clinical assumption for school-age children, however. First, many of the children with expressive phonological impairment included in studies investigating phonological awareness and reading development have received regular periods of speech pathology intervention. Given that such intervention is usually effective in improving speech intelligibility (Gierut, 1998), it may be assumed these children's speech output was improving during the course of therapy. Yet the children still displayed significant deficits in phonological awareness development. Second, even children whose expressive phonological impairment has been completely resolved perform poorly on phonological processing tasks (Stothard et al., 1998). Third, Gillon (2000b, 2002b) demonstrated that phoneme awareness must be specifically targeted in interventions with children who have spoken language impairment before gains in these skills and in reading ability are realized. Focusing solely on the remediation of speech production errors does not result in accelerated improvement in phonological awareness at the phoneme level (Gillon, 2000b; see Chapter 7).

Spelling Development

The difficulty children with speech and language impairment demonstrate in phonological awareness development is also likely to adversely affect their spelling development (Clarke-Klein, 1994; Oerlemans & Dodd, 1993). As discussed in Chapter 2, understanding the relationship between phonemes and graphemes is critical in spelling development (Treiman, 1993), and an inability to understand the sound structure of spoken words, particularly at the phoneme level, is likely to restrict knowledge of how sounds relate to letters in spelling. Indeed, early research examining the spelling attempts of children with speech impairment suggested that these children have a specific difficulty making accurate phoneme–grapheme connections when spelling (Stackhouse, 1982). Poor performance of children with speech impairment on non-words spelling tasks adds further support to this finding (Dodd et al., 1995; Gillon, 2002b)

Gillon (2002b) provided initial insights into the accuracy of phoneme–grapheme connections for children who have spoken language impairment. As part of a follow-up study, Gillon compared the phoneme–grapheme connections in the spelling attempts of 40 6-year-old children with spoken language impairment to their typically developing peers.

Each child's spelling attempt for 10 words (presented in a spelling game format) was analyzed for correct phoneme–grapheme matches. One point was awarded for each match (e.g., *fish* = 3 points; *fis* = 2 points, because the digraph *sh* was not completely represented). Additional points were awarded for knowledge of vowel changes (e.g., *cak* = 3 points, *cake* = 4 points, *teth* = 3 points, *teeth* = 4 points). The total possible score was 43 points. The average total score for the children with spoken language impairment was only 7.80 (*SD* = 8.05) compared to the significantly higher average score of 25.90 (*SD* = 8.14) for children with typically developing speech and language. Qualitative analysis prior to intervention indicated little relationship between the children's phonological production of the word and their misspellings. A phoneme analysis of speech errors compared to the spelling of the same phonemes for the children with spoken language impairment revealed that for 70% of the speech errors, there was no match with spelling; for example, *chips* pronounced as *dips* but spelled as *recs*. The spelling of the phoneme was correct in 17% of the speech errors; for example, *rain* pronounced as *wain* but spelled as *ran*. There was a match between speech and spelling errors for 13% of the spelling errors. In most instances, an *f* for *th* substitution occurred (e.g., *teeth* pronounced as *teef* and spelled as *teef*).

A lack of relationship between speech errors and spelling is consistent with previous research. Treiman (1993) reported no significant relationship between the pronunciation difficulty of a phoneme and the spelling accuracy of the phoneme for 6-year-old children with typically developing skills. Cowan and Moran (1997) also found no association for children with speech impairment on phonological awareness tasks for words that contained error phonemes. The spelling attempts of one of the participants from the Gillon (2002b) study is displayed in Figure 5.1. The sample demonstrates that Ashleigh's poor articulation of words is not influencing her spelling (i.e., she is not trying to spell words the way she articulates them). Rather, her attempts reflect poor understanding of the relationship between phonemes and graphemes and are consistent with deficits in phonological awareness development. Ashleigh (aged 6 years) had received over 12 months of formal reading and spelling instruction and had a specific impairment in expressive phonology. She had received periods of speech and

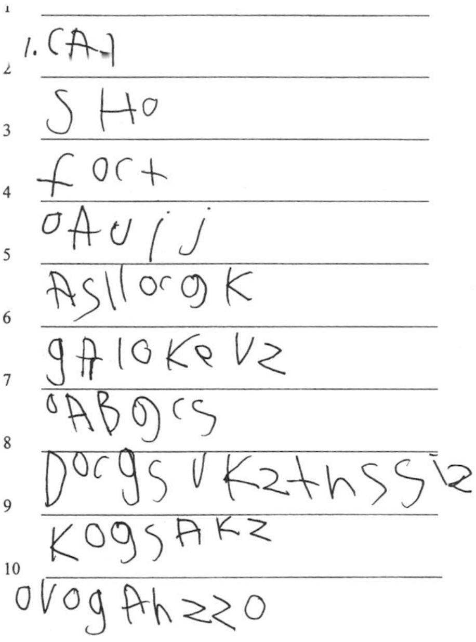

	Target word	Articulation	
1.	cake	ta	/ta/
	shark	dap	/dap/
	fish	bis	/bɪs/
	rain	run	/rʌn/
	bridge	biz	/bɪz/
	girl	dirl	/dɜl/
	chips	dips	/dɪps/
	dinosaur	sisador	/saisʌdɔ/
	kangaroo	pudroo	/pʌdru/
	teeth	teef	/tif/

FIGURE 5.1. Ashleigh's spelling and speech attempts.

language therapy intervention since 3 years of age, but this intervention had not targeted phonological awareness development.

Ashleigh's spelling responses also demonstrate some of the common characteristics found at a group level in Gillon's (2002b) investigation. These include:

1. More successes in spelling initial phonemes than final and medial phonemes.
2. Little relationship between speech errors and spelling attempts.
3. Some awareness of word length, marked by an increase in the number of letters for longer words.
4. Evidence of bizarre spellings that have no resemblance to the target word (e.g., her spelling of *teeth*).
5. More difficulty with clusters and complex consonant connections (e.g., *br* in *bridge* and *ch* in *chips*).
6. Severe difficulty representing vowel sounds (vowels often require an understanding of more complex connections, because one phoneme can be represented in more than one way—e.g., *eg, ir, er, ur*).
7. Possible use of known spellings to attempt a word (e.g., *cat* for *cake*) or use of letters that appear in the child's name (e.g., *ASH*, from the name *Ashleigh*, for *bridge*).

INTERACTIVE RELATIONSHIP BETWEEN SPOKEN AND WRITTEN LANGUAGE DIFFICULTIES

A child whose early spoken language impairment leads to delayed phonological awareness development is disadvantaged not only in written language development but also in the development of advanced spoken language. Spoken language continues to develop through the adolescent years, and this development is influenced by written language experience (see Nippold, 1998, for a review). Reading competency exposes children to more advanced vocabulary and more complex sentence structures than they would typically gain from conversational speech. Such exposure is severely compromised for children who struggle with reading. Restricted written language experiences hamper advancement in aspects of spoken language, and the positive interaction between advancing written language and development in advanced spoken language, evident for children and adolescents without impairment, is unlikely to be realized.

Figure 5.2 depicts the negative spiraling effect on later language development of early spoken language and phonological awareness impairment. Difficulty acquiring spoken language, including impairment in forming distinct phonological representations, restricts a child's awareness of the sound structure of a spoken word (among a host of other consequences). This limitation, in turn, poses a barrier for the child in understanding the alphabetic principle (particularly in the presence of poor letter-name knowledge) and restricts the use of phonological information in reading and spelling. Lack of successful early decoding and encoding experiences further restricts phoneme awareness development, which leads to inefficient word recognition performance and subsequent poor reading comprehension. In addition, semantic, syntactic and morphological impairment in spoken language and poor oral narrative language abilities further compound poor performance in word recognition and reading comprehension.

The importance of early intervention and the provision of speech–language pathology services for children with spoken language impairment is highlighted within this model. Intervention is critical to ensure that children who have spoken language impairment approach literacy instruction with the necessary phonological awareness, semantic, syntactic and morphological skills in spoken language that contribute to successful early

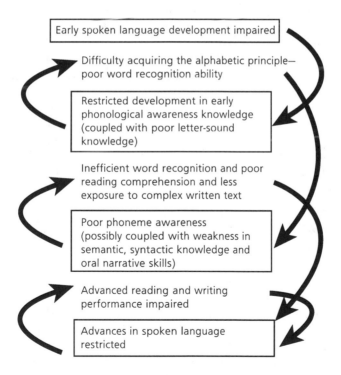

FIGURE 5.2. Negative spiraling effects from impaired early spoken language on development of phoneme awareness and word recognition performance, ultimately resulting in restricted advanced spoken and written language development.

word recognition, and reading comprehension experiences. Chapter 7 discusses interventions that can accelerate the phonological awareness and early literacy development of these children. The two case examples that follow also illustrate how the negative spiral depicted in Figure 5.2 may be interrupted to produce more positive outcomes for children with speech and language impairment.

CASE EXAMPLES

The speech, phonological awareness, and phonological decoding abilities of two girls with specific language impairment and speech disorder characteristic of developmental verbal dyspraxia are described. Their development was monitored for a 2-year period from school entry at 5 years of age. Both children attended the same language unit, which was accommodated in a regular style classroom within a junior school in New Zealand. The girls, referred to as Jane and Mary, are described in Watson and Gillon (1999), and a summary of their development is presented to provide the reader with clinical insight into the interaction between spoken and written language disorder during the early school period.

The language unit provided intensive language instruction and support with the junior school curriculum for children with specific language impairment. The unit accommodated eight children while Jane and Mary were in attendance. A full-time teacher with special needs training managed the unit with the support of a speech–language pathologist who was employed 18 hours per week to work with children in the unit. (The language unit has since been disestablished, and children with specific language impairment in New Zealand are now typically integrated into mainstream classrooms.)

Background Information

Jane

Jane presented for speech–language pathology services at the age of 2 years, 10 months. Initial evaluation indicated that her expressive language was characterized by one- and two-word utterances. Her speech was very difficult to understand (even by Jane's parents); unusual prosodic patterns, resulting in a jerky and stilted style of speech, were reported. Assessment using the Reynell Developmental Language Scales–Verbal Comprehension (Scale A) revealed that Jane's comprehension was below the mean (–0.7 SD), but within the normal range at age 2 years,

10 months. Oral motor and speech examination revealed that Jane had difficulty imitating oral movements, but no physical abnormalities of the oral cavity were apparent. Jane also displayed gross motor coordination difficulties. Jane's mother had a history of speech difficulty as a child, and she reported that she still experienced difficulty pronouncing long words. Jane's parents were monolingual speakers of standard New Zealand English.

Pure tone audiometry and tympanometry showed that Jane had normal hearing at ages 3 and 4 years, 6 months. Between the ages of 3 and 5 years Jane received regular periods of speech–language pathology intervention focused on auditory discrimination, improving speech intelligibility, and extending the length of her utterances. The speech–language pathologist reported that Jane made slow progress in therapy. An educational psychologist evaluated Jane's performance at age 4 years, 6 months and reported average performance on nonverbal tasks and receptive vocabulary measures. These findings were confirmed at school entry by her within-average range performance on the Test of Nonverbal Intelligence (Brown, Sherbenon, & Johnson, 1990).

Mary

Mary was first assessed by her local speech–language pathologist at the age of 3 years, 1 month. Her expressive language was characterized by predominantly single-word utterances and the use of gestures to make her needs known. Mary's parents were unable to understand most of her speech attempts. Mary comprehended language at an age-appropriate level, as assessed by the Reynell Developmental Language Scales—Verbal Comprehension (Scale A). A positive family history of speech disorder on Mary's father's side was noted. Mary's parents were monolingual speakers of standard New Zealand English.

Pure tone audiometry and tympanometry showed normal hearing at ages 3 years, 1 month and 4 years, 11 months. Speech–language pathology intervention prior to 5 years was irregular due to Mary's health problems that were successfully treated prior to school entry. Intervention at preschool period had broadly focused on speech production skills, auditory discrimination, and increasing verbalization. Mary made slow progress in therapy. An educational psychologist's report indicated that Mary's nonverbal skills were age appropriate, and she performed within the average range on the Test of Nonverbal Intelligence at school entry.

Both Jane and Mary attended kindergartens and child-care centers that were attached to schools rated by the government as being in mid to low socioeconomic areas.

Assessments at School Entry

Upon entry to the school language unit, the children's receptive language was measured using the Test of Auditory Comprehension of Language—Revised (Carrow-Woolfolk, 1985). Jane and Mary showed delays of approximately 14 months and 18 months in their total scores, with standard deviations of –1.9 and –1.6, respectively. Particular weaknesses in the comprehension of grammatical morphemes and understanding semantic relationships were evident. Standardized assessment, spontaneous language sampling procedures, and analysis indicated a severe expressive language delay for both girls. Spontaneous utterances analyzed were generally typical of those expected in children between 2 and 2½ years of age.

The children's speech production was assessed using the Nuffield (1994) single-word elicitation procedures and the 25-word consistency test (Dodd, 1995). Analysis from the Nuffield tasks indicated that Jane and Mary scored 89% and 50%, respectively, on imitating single sounds. Both children demonstrated poor ability in imitating oromotor movements but showed evidence of being able to produce some sounds spontaneously in words which they were unable to produce in imitation or other contexts. For example, Mary could accurately spontaneously articulate the word *buzzing* when talking about a bee buzzing, but she could not imitate /z/ in isolation or produce a /z/ in any other context.

Both children struggled to produce any multisyllabic words accurately and showed very poor diadochokinetic skill (i.e., rapid repetition of single sounds, such as saying /p/ /t/ /k/ as quickly as possible). Analysis of speech errors showed the use of nondevelopmental speech errors and inconsistency in their speech error patterns.

Comment

Based on their case histories and school entry assessments, Jane and Mary could both be described as having specific language impairment (SLI). Consistent with the definition of SLI employed in research studies, Jane and Mary demonstrated spoken language difficulties that were not associated with intellectual or cognitive impairment, neurological, emotional, or severe behavioral disorders, traumatic brain injury, or sensory and physical impairment. In addition to their oral language difficulties, they also demonstrated speech disorder that involved both phonological impairment (as evidenced by the use of delayed and unusual sound error patterns involving substitutions and omission errors) and articulative impairment (as evidenced by difficulty imitating sounds on demand that could be produced in some contexts spontaneously, difficulty in imitating oral movements, and poor ability in imitating single sounds in quick succession). They evidenced a number of the speech characteristics associated with developmental verbal dyspraxia.

These children's profiles at school entry of significant impairment in both speech and oral language, together with the nature of their speech impairment (i.e., included impairment at a phonological level and not only at an articulatory level), and the familial histories of spoken language difficulties placed these children at high risk for severe and persistent written language disorder. They approached the school curriculum with a spoken language impairment that cut across the linguistic domains that are critical for written language development: semantics, syntax, phonology, and morphology. Jane and Mary's profiles were consistent with group and case study reports in the literature of children who approached reading and writing with severe speech and language impairment and who failed to acquire age-appropriate written language skills throughout their school years.

Assessment 8 Months and 12 Months after School Entry

The children's phonological awareness and early literacy development were assessed on a range of measures following 8 months of intensive and specialist input at the language unit (time 1 data collection [T1]) and again at the beginning of year 2 when the children were 6 years of age (time 2 [T2], 12 months after school entry). Between T1 and T2 a 20-hour structured speech and language therapy intervention was implemented that focused on improving speech intelligibility (using the Nuffield Dyspraxia program) and structured activities to improve semantic and syntactic skills. The results from these assessments are reported in Table 5.1.

Data at T1 and T2 indicated very poor growth in phonological awareness development during the first year of literacy instruction. Jane demonstrated some understanding of rhyme at T1, but this was not a well-established skill. The rhyme judgment task allowed for a high element of success by guessing, and Jane's lower performance at the second assessment suggested that guessing was indeed a factor in her performance. Both girls showed a persistent inability to use phonological coding strategies in reading and spelling, with little or no growth in decoding skills and letter-name knowledge from T1 to T2.

The percentage of consonants correctly articulated from a list of 75 words, pronounced in isolation, is shown in Table 5.1. At T1 assessment, a high rate of speech-sound omissions, particularly in cluster sounds, was evident. Both children also showed inconsistent speech error patterns and the use of unusual speech error patterns. Modest improvement from T1 to T2 during the period of the Nuffield Program was noticed in speech production.

TABLE 5.1. Performance on Reading, Speech, and Phonological Awareness Tasks from 5 to 7 Years

	Jane				Mary			
	T1	T2	T3[k]	T4	T1	T2	T3[k]	T4
		(6 years)		(7 years)		(6 years)		(7 years)
Reading								
Word recognition (Burt)[a]	6	10	27	30	3	4	14	18
Word test (n = 15)[b]	7	9	15	15	1	1	10	12
Letter name[c]	29	30	100	100	54	54	98	94
Non-word Reading[d]	0	0	30	53	0	0	17	27
Phonological awareness								
LAC[e]	18	13	46	61	37	19	49	55
Syllable[f]	42	38	75	–	33	42	63	–
Rhyme[f]	83	67	67	–	50[g]	50[g]	75	–
Phoneme[f]	21	24	35	56	9	9	38	30
Speech								
PCC[h]	56	62	83	82	43	55	76	79
Cluster reduction[i]	44	41	9	3	61	60	36	19
Velar fronting[j]	100	70	9	12	95	61	0	0

Note. All assessment tasks required transfer of knowledge to untrained tasks and novel stimulus items.
[a]Burt Word Reading Test (Gilmore, Croft, ^ Reid, 1981); number of words read correctly. The average number of words expected to be read correctly by New Zealand girls at 6 years of age is 20–25.
[b]Word Test (Clay, 1993). Words tested are commonly found in early school readers.
[c]Letter identification task (Clay, 1993), percentage correct.
[d]Percentage correct.
[e]Lindamood Auditory Conceptualization Test (Lindamood & Lindamood, 1979).
[f]Syllable awareness (syllable segmentation and identification), rhyme judgment, and phoneme awareness (phoneme detection, segmentation, and deletion); percentage correct from combined tasks from the Queensland University Inventory of Literacy (Dodd et al., 1996).
[g]Rhyme performance not above chance level (responded "yes" to each question).
[h]Percentage of consonants correct from 75 single-word elicitation test.
[i]Omitting a sound from a cluster, such as saying *top* for *stop*; percentage of process usage.
[j]Producing sounds at the front of the mouth that should be produced at the back, such as saying *tar* for *car*; percentage of process usage.
[k]Post phonological awareness intervention assessment.

Comment

The poor prognosis for written language development for Jane and Mary hypothesized on the basis of the school entry profile was supported by their demonstrations of weak phonological awareness and attenuated early literacy development at T1 and T2 evaluations. The limited progress in Jane's and Mary's phonological awareness and reading development during their first 12 months at school is consistent with the research findings reported in the literature. Controlled group studies and longitudinal studies investigating children with specific language impairment have shown that these children experience persistent phonological awareness weakness and specific deficits in phonological decoding (as evidenced by non-word reading or non-word spelling), despite lengthy periods of speech and language intervention. For Jane and Mary, even the specialist environment of a language unit, which provided rich and meaningful language experiences, highly individualized language programs, and intensive therapy to improve speech production and oral language skills had little impact on these children's level of phonological awareness and early literacy development.

Phonological Awareness Intervention

Following assessment T2 an intensive phonological awareness intervention was introduced to the language unit. This program was adapted from the Gillon Phonological Awareness Training Program (Gillon, 2000c) (described in Chapter 7) and consisted of structured group and individual activities to develop knowledge at the syllable, rhyme, and phoneme level and to make explicit the links between speech and print.

Both group and individual training sessions were implemented over a 4½ month period. In the group sessions Jane and Mary participated with the other children in the language unit. The children were divided into three groups, and during the phonological awareness intervention the groups rotated around staff members (teacher, speech–language pathologist, and teacher aide) who facilitated the various intervention activities. The speech–language pathologist trained the other staff members in the program content. In the individual sessions Jane and Mary worked with the speech–language pathologist on phoneme awareness and speech-to-print knowledge activities that also integrated goals for speech production.

The data collected immediately following the phonological awareness intervention (time 3 [T3]) and at 6 months postintervention (time 4 [T4]) showed rapid and accelerated progress in all measures of speech, phonological awareness, phonological decoding, and reading. At T3 standard scores on phonological awareness subtests were within the normal range expected for their age levels. This scoring was maintained for Jane at T4 (age 7 years), but Mary's phoneme awareness skills did not continue to show accelerated development, and at 7 years of age her performance was below the average level expected for her chronological age. Consistent with Jane's now firmly established phoneme awareness skills, her reading accuracy and comprehension of connected text and her word recognition skills were all assessed as being within the average range for her age on standardized tests at T4.

Although Mary had certainly improved, elevating her nonreader status to that of a reader, her reading performance for accuracy and comprehension of connected text still showed a 9–12 month delay.

Comment

The dramatic improvement in these children's spoken and written language development coincided with a period during which 20 hours of a structured phonological awareness intervention was implemented. This pattern is consistent with findings from controlled research studies that have demonstrated accelerated performance in response to direct phonological awareness intervention for children with spoken language impairments (Gillon, 2002b). Despite being at high risk for persistent and severe reading disorder, Jane was able to demonstrate age-appropriate reading performance by 7 years of age, following phonological awareness intervention. Mary appeared to respond positively to phonological awareness intervention, but further such intervention (or another type of intervention) was necessary to ensure continued growth in her phoneme awareness and reading performance.

SUMMARY

Many young children diagnosed with a spoken language impairment struggle to acquire efficient reading and spelling skills. This chapter has reviewed research investigating the phonological awareness development in this population and discussed the implications of phonological awareness deficits in relation to these children's later spoken and written language development. The following summary points highlight key aspects from the literature.

- Not *all* children with spoken language impairment show delays in written language.
- Subgroups of children with spoken language difficulty are identified in the literature (e.g., specific language impairment, articulation impairment, expressive phonological impairment, and developmental verbal dyspraxia). In predicting literacy outcomes for these children, it is important to examine their linguistic profiles and, in particular, evaluate their phonological awareness development.
- Children who have articulation impairment *only* (and good phonological awareness skills) are not at risk for literacy difficulties, but children who approach literacy instruction with severe deficits in phonological, semantic, and syntactic aspects of spoken language are highly likely to have difficulties with written language throughout their school years.

- School-age children with specific language impairment and expressive phonological impairment frequently exhibit poor phonological awareness. This weakness is most evident at the phoneme level. Without specific phonological awareness intervention, phoneme awareness deficits are likely to persist and negatively impact reading and spelling development, despite other types of speech–language pathology intervention.

FROM RESEARCH TO PRACTICE

The case examples of Jane and Mary highlighted the interaction between spoken and written language difficulties and the potential benefits of addressing phonological awareness deficits. Other clinical implications from research investigating the literacy development of children with spoken language impairment include the following points:

1. Early intervention to strengthen children's spoken language system prior to their approaching formal literacy instruction is vital for children with speech and language impairment. For children with pervasive spoken language deficits, intervention should begin as early as possible and include activities that will enhance the emergence of phonological awareness and early print knowledge (as discussed in Chapter 3).

2. Evaluation of phonological awareness development should be included in a comprehensive assessment battery for children with spoken language impairment.

3. Speech–language pathologists and teachers who work with preschool and young school-age children with spoken language impairment should include specific activities to promote growth in phonological awareness during intervention (as appropriate to each child's assessment profile).

4. Careful monitoring of school-age children with spoken language impairment is necessary to ensure they develop phonological awareness skills at the phoneme level and that early growth in these skills in response to intervention is maintained. Importantly, practitioners need to witness that children with spoken language impairment are able to efficiently use phonological information in the reading and spelling process.

Children with spoken language impairment ultimately need to resolve any deficits in semantic, syntactic, morphological, and pragmatic areas of spoken language as well as develop knowledge of story structure and narrative to enhance reading comprehension. Many language enrichment and literature experiences will help foster both spoken and written language development for these children. Specific attention, however, must be directed toward resolving their phonological awareness deficits. This focus is particularly important in the preschool and early school years. Ensuring that children with spoken language impairment have the necessary skills and knowledge base to engage in successful early decoding and encoding experiences may allow these children to engage in the self-teaching process for reading development, as hypothesized by researchers (see Chapter 2). Access to print and stories through successful word recognition further enhances these children's spoken language development through the ongoing interaction between spoken and written language.

Although the research predicts a negative outlook for reading and spelling development in children with severe speech and language impairment, evidence is also emerging that this outlook can be altered (see Chapter 7). Strengthening these children's phonological awareness development may well prove to be a critical factor in helping children with spoken language impairment achieve literacy success.

6

Phonological Awareness Assessment

Children and adolescents who struggle with reading and writing require in-depth assessment of both their spoken and written language development. A collaborative approach to assessment that involves class teachers, reading specialists, speech-language pathologists, educational psychologists, parents, and the student (if appropriate) is necessary. Each person contributes unique knowledge about the student's performance, from which a profile of the student's strengths and weakness in language development can be developed.

In-depth language assessment should include evaluation across language domains of semantics, syntax, morphology, phonology, and pragmatics as well as assessment across modalities of listening, speaking, reading, and writing (Paul, 2001). Viewed within this context of a comprehensive language evaluation, phonological awareness assessment is a critical component of the evaluation for children who are identified as being at risk for written language difficulties and for those experiencing written language failure. It therefore warrants detailed discussion. This chapter describes assessment tools useful in the evaluation of phonological awareness development and discusses the development of a profile from which to base appropriate interventions.

It is somewhat artificial to divide assessment and intervention into separate chapters, because the two are closely interwoven from a clinical perspective. Assessment of a student's abilities is an ongoing process that serves to modify and adapt intervention procedures. Initial intervention goals for an individual, however, must be based on assessment results. This chapter focuses on assessment of children's phonological awareness to establish a need for specific intervention, to help establish intervention goals, and to monitor the effectiveness of intervention programs.

TYPES OF ASSESSMENT TASKS

A variety of differing types of assessment procedures can be used to evaluate children's phonological awareness development. Paul (2001) provided a detailed description of basic language assessment models; those that are particularly relevant to evaluating phonological awareness follow:

1. *Standardized or norm-referenced tests*. These tests allow a comparison of an individual's phonological awareness performance against a larger group of children with typically developing skills. Well-constructed, standardized phonological awareness tests are useful in identifying how an individual's performance differs significantly from a normal population.

2. *Criterion-referenced procedures*. These assessments are designed to ascertain whether children reach a defined level of performance (as opposed to determining whether they differ from a normal population) and facilitate a more in-depth assessment of specific types of phonological awareness tasks without the restriction of standardized testing procedures. They are useful in describing children's phonological awareness abilities prior to intervention, identifying intervention targets, and evaluating intervention effectiveness. Criterion-referenced assessments in phonological awareness often are designed by researchers for use in experimental studies. Many of these assessments have been adopted or modified by practitioners for use in classroom and clinical practices.

3. *Observational assessment*. These assessments are used to describe performance in a specific area. Observational recording sheets or checklists are used to collect data related to the occurrence of the target behavior. Recording the types of errors children make in an oral reading passage to ascertain whether they are using a phonological strategy in word recognition is an example of observational assessment.

Assessments also may be described as being static or dynamic (see Olswang & Bain, 1996; Paul, 2001). *Static assessments* in phonological awareness provide information related to children's current level of skills, without significant prompts or contextual support (e.g., standardized tests). *Dynamic assessments*, however, are designed to understand contexts that promote learning and change, so that children may attain their optimal performance level. Identifying each child's potential to improve phonological awareness ability, the type of phonological awareness intervention style that will promote the greatest change for him or her, the ways in which each child approaches reading or spelling an unknown word, and what strategies will assist that child in using phonological cues to aid success are examples of outcomes from dynamic assessments in phonological awareness.

Throughout this chapter these differing types of assessments are referenced in regard to the evaluation of phonological awareness in preschool children, young school-age children at risk, and older children with dyslexia.

PHONOLOGICAL AWARENESS ASSESSMENT OF PRESCHOOL CHILDREN

The focus of phonological awareness assessment at the early preschool level (i.e., when children are 3 and 4 years of age) is *not* to label children as having a phonological awareness deficit. Given the wide variability in phonological awareness performance of typically developing children in this age group, such labeling would be inappropriate. Rather, assessment should be aimed at the following tasks:

1. Observing the child's current level of phonological awareness development.
2. Determining whether the child is gaining phonological awareness skills through the home language environment, an early childhood education program, or an early intervention program that includes activities to promote phonological awareness development.

The emphasis in phonological awareness assessment at the preschool level should be on monitoring early phonological awareness development to ensure that the child is acquiring the necessary skills that will build a strong foundation for school reading and writing experiences.

Understanding typical phonological awareness development during the preschool period (described in Chapter 3) is crucial in planning assessment tasks and in interpreting assessment results. Other practical considerations that should be made in phonological awareness assessments in the preschool period include the following:

1. Assessment tasks should appear interesting and fun for the young child. The use of colorful pictures, toys, or puppets help capture the young child's attention and focus it on the assessment task, and

the provision of picture stimuli reduces demands on working memory.

2. Short assessment sessions are necessary to ensure the child's performance is not adversely affected by lack of concentration.

3. Tasks that require a nonverbal response mode should be included to compensate for young children who are very shy and reluctant to speak and for those whose speech is difficult to understand or characterized by a high number of speech errors.

4. Observational assessment during phonological awareness teaching activities in the preschool or child-care center may be particularly useful with young children. For example, a young child may enthusiastically engage in a group rhyming activity as part of the preschool routine, but be unwilling to recite a nursery rhyme to an examiner during an assessment session.

5. Typically young children's performance is variable and easily affected by fatigue, mild illnesses such as colds or stomachaches, unfamiliarity with the examiner or testing environment, and excitement regarding other ongoing events (e.g., birthday parties or preschool visits). All these factors need to be considered in interpreting assessment data. Short assessment probe tasks that evaluate the child's performance on the same task over two or three testing sessions are useful to establish a stable performance level for the child prior to intervention.

6. In the preschool level of assessment, it is important to calculate the number of items the child can score correctly on an assessment task simply by guessing. Evaluating whether the child's score is above chance level avoids overestimating his or her ability.

7. In designing criterion-referenced phonological awareness assessment tasks, it is important to vary the position of a correct response—that is, the correct response should not always be the first or last item in a series.

8. Hearing screening should be administered to all preschool children prior to any in-depth speech or language assessment and referral made for audiological assessment, as appropriate.

Assessment Tools

Standardized Tests

Two standardized tests of phonological awareness that measure a broad range of skills in young children are described. Evaluation of the psychometric properties of these tests is provided in Table 6.1.

PRESCHOOL AND PRIMARY INVENTORY OF PHONOLOGICAL AWARENESS
(PIPA; DODD, CROSBIE, MACINTOSH, TEITZEL, & OZANNE, 2000)

This test is designed for children ages 3 years to 6 years, 11 months; its administration takes about 20 minutes. The subtests measure syllable segmentation of unfamiliar words, rhyme awareness, alliteration awareness, phoneme isolation, phoneme segmentation (the child is trained to use counters to segment the words, and oral segmentation is required) and letter-sound knowledge (e.g., "What sound does this letter make?"). Normative data for both Australian and British populations are provided. All of the phonological awareness tasks provide colorful pictures for the test practice items. Rhyme and alliteration awareness and phoneme isolation also have pictures for the stimulus items. Because the rhyme and alliteration tasks require a nonverbal response (i.e., pointing), they are particularly useful for very shy children and those with speech difficulties.

PHONOLOGICAL ABILITIES TEST
(PAT; MUTER, HULME, & SNOWLING, 1997)

This test contains normative data for British children ages 4 years to 7 years, 11 months. The tasks assess rhyme detection, rhyme production, word completion (syllable and phoneme), phoneme deletion, speech rate, and letter knowledge. The complete test takes about 30 minutes to administer. Color pictures to capture young children's interest are provided; the rhyme detection task does not require a verbal response.

Chapter 1 provides examples of some of the PIPA and PAT tasks.

Criterion-Referenced Assessments

A range of tasks has been used in research studies to evaluate phonological awareness in 3- and 4-year-old children. These include:

- Asking children to complete the rhyming word in nursery rhyme line.
- Detecting the word from a series of three pictures that does not rhyme.
- Matching words that rhyme.
- Detecting the word from a series of three pictures that starts with a different sound.
- Detecting the word that starts with the same sound as a target word.
- Blending syllables to form words.
- Deleting a syllable from a word.

Examples and references for some of these assessment tasks are provided in Chapter 1. Lonigan et al. (1998, p. 310) and Maclean et al. (1987, p. 261) provide lists of stimulus items used with very young children. Colorful pictures for rhyme and phoneme detection tasks used with 3- and 4-year-old children in the Gillon study (2002a, in press) are available to download at *www.cmds.canterbury.ac.nz* (search under "people," then "Gillon").

PHONOLOGICAL AWARENESS ASSESSMENT IN THE EARLY SCHOOL YEARS (AGES 5–7 YEARS)

Phonological awareness assessment at school entry and during the early school years (usually between 5 and 7 years of age) may serve a variety of aims. These include:

1. Identifying children who are at risk for persistent reading and spelling difficulties.
2. Monitoring phonological awareness development in children who enter school with diagnosed disorders or known factors that place them at high risk for reading and spelling disorders.
3. Evaluating phonological awareness skill development in children who are not making the expected progress in early reading and writing experiences.
4. Identifying a significant phonological awareness deficit that may qualify children for special education services.
5. Profiling children's strengths and weakness in phonological awareness in relation to other phonological processing and language abilities to establish appropriate intervention goals.

A variety of assessment tools and procedures is available to address these aims. The usefulness of specific tasks to measure phonological awareness ability varies with the child's ability level. In the 5–7-year age group, tasks that require children to blend onset-rime units to make words, blend phonemes to make words and non-words, and phoneme deletion tasks are particularly accurate measures of phonological awareness ability in English-speaking children (Schatschneider et al., 1999). Most screening and standardized tests of phonological awareness include measures at the phoneme level that target blending and/or phoneme deletion skills.

Screening Tests

Phonological awareness screening tests are useful to identify children who may be at risk for reading and spelling difficulties and who therefore require in-depth assessment. Catts et al. (2001) have developed an interesting concept of a screening test formula to estimate the probability that a 5-year-old child may develop reading difficulties by second grade. The formula necessitates gathering assessment scores from four tasks: (1) a phonological awareness task involving a syllable and phoneme deletion task (e.g., "Say *seat* without the /s/," or "Say *cowboy* without the *cow*"), (2) a phonological processing task (e.g., rapid automatized naming of animals), (3) a letter identification task, and (4) a sentence imitation task. Scores from these assessments are entered into a logistic regression formula, using computer analysis, together with the number of years of education the child's biological mother received. The resulting calculation provides a reliable estimate of the child's likelihood of having reading difficulties in grade 2. Catts et al. recommend an in-depth assessment of (1) all areas of spoken language, (2) cognitive ability, (3) hearing capacity, and (4) in particular, phonological awareness and early literacy skills if the probability of a reading difficulty is greater than 30%.

Phonological Awareness Literacy Screening (PALS)

Some education districts, school areas, speech–language pathologists, and educators have developed their own phonological awareness screening tests. Justice, Invernizzi, and Meier (2002) presented suggestions for the development of screening tests by practitioners such as speech–language pathologists. An example of a phonological awareness screening test that has been a collaborative project between a state department of education and a university school of education is the Phonological Awareness Literacy Screening (PALS; see also, Dynamic Indicators of Basic Early Literacy Skills, described on pp. 123–124).

The PALS has three levels: (1) PALS 1–3 for children in grades 1–3 (Invernizzi & Meier, 2002), (2) PALS–K for children in kindergarten (5-year-old children; Invernizzi, Meier, Swank, & Juel, 2002), and (3) PALS-PreK for 4-year-old children (Invernizzi, Sullivan, & Meier, 2002). The test was developed as part of an early reading initiatives program in Virginia. It is now widely used by teachers across Virginia and in many other American states. PALS 1–3 includes measures of phoneme blending and phoneme segmentation; PALS–K and PALS-PreK include measures of children's rhyme awareness (e.g., PALS-PreK: "Point to the picture that rhymes with cat or sounds like cat" followed by pictures of a hat, whale, and a ring) and early phoneme detection (e.g., PALS-K: "Circle the picture that begins with the /b/ sound, just like you hear at the beginning of *bat*," followed by pictures of a bird, lips, and a ring). A useful student booklet, with clear black-and-white line drawings, is provided to enable the test to be administered in groups. Precise instructions for administering the screening test accompany the test, and a video on assessment training is available. The screening test also assesses letter-name and letter-sound knowledge and examines how children use phonological information by analyzing phoneme–grapheme matches in the spelling of five consonant–vowel–consonant words (e.g., *top*). Benchmark scores that a child should reach on each task and an overall benchmark score are provided, based on widescale data collection in Virginia (Justice et al., 2002) and pilot research work. Further information about PALS is available on their website at *http://curry.edschool.virginia.edu/go/pals*.

In-Depth Assessment

Following the identification of a child who is at risk for reading and spelling difficulties through screening test procedures, an in-depth assessment of the child's phonological awareness development is required. In-depth assessment serves to confirm screening test results through the identification of a phonological awareness deficit. It also provides further understanding of the child's phonological awareness abilities with the view of developing an appropriate intervention program.

A variety of phonological awareness tests is now available for school-age children. These tests can be classified as broad-spectrum standardized tests, area-specific standardized tests, and criterion-referenced tests.

Broad-Spectrum Standardized Tests

These tests measure a range of phonological awareness skills. For example, they may assess syllable, onset-rime, and phoneme level skills. They may include tasks that measure the use of phonological knowledge, such as nonword reading and spelling tasks, and measures of other areas of phonological processing, such as rapid naming and phonological memory. Letter-name knowledge skills also may be evaluated.

The PIPA and PAT described in the section for preschool children are examples of broad-spectrum standardized tests that are suitable to administer to young school-age children (the tests are designed for children up to 7 years of age). Two other broad-spectrum tests for school-age children are:

COMPREHENSIVE TEST OF PHONOLOGICAL PROCESSING
(CTOPP; WAGNER ET AL., 1999)

As its names suggests, this test measures more than phonological awareness; it includes measures of two other areas of phonological processing; phonological memory and rapid naming. The test was designed for individuals ages 5 years to 24 years, 11 months and is divided into two versions.

The core subtests for version 1, intended for 5- and 6-year-old children, consist of subtests to measure word and phoneme deletion skills (elision tasks), syllable and phoneme blending skills, and phoneme identity (sound matching task). Subtests tapping other phonological processing skills are rapid color naming, rapid object naming, digit memory, and non-word repetition tasks. In the older version, covering 7–24 years of age, a range of supplementary tasks enhance the core subtests of elision, blending, rapid naming, and phonological memory tasks. The test has been standardized on a population sample that consists of participants from 30 states across the United States.

THE QUEENSLAND UNIVERSITY INVENTORY OF LITERACY (QUIL; DODD ET AL., 1996)

This test consists of a series of tasks to measure school-age children's phonological awareness ability at three levels. Syllable identification and segmentation are assessed at the syllabic level. A spoken rhyme recognition task and a spoonerism task are presented at the onset-rime level. Phoneme detection, segmentation, and deletion skills are measured at the phoneme level. The use of phonological awareness skills is also assessed in this test by a non-word spelling and a non-word reading task. The test has been standardized on Australian children from grades 1 through 7 (6- to 12-year-old children).

Test Psychometric Properties

Practitioners need to consider the psychometric properties of standardized tests to determine the confidence they can place in the results obtained from such assessments. McCauley and Swisher (1984) developed a useful set of criteria to evaluate standardized speech and language tests. The following section applies this criterion to tests in phonological awareness. McCauley and Swisher detail the rationale for criteria selection and the implications for the clinical interpretation of the results if criteria are not met. A summary of each criterion is provided, including comments concerning the relevance of the criterion for tests in phonological awareness. Table 6.1 summarizes whether four broad-spectrum tests in phonological awareness meet the criterion discussed.

   1. A test manual should provide a description of the standardization population sample that includes details related to the geographic residence of the sample, socioeconomic status, and the basis for any exclusion of participants in the study. If children with diagnosed impairments are not excluded from the sample, details relating to the percentage of children with impairments and the types of impairment are useful.

Examining sample description is particularly critical when testing children's phonological awareness in the 4–7-year age group, where variations in the amount of formal literacy instruction is likely to occur across populations. Chapter 3 reviewed literature that suggested a bidirectional relationship between literacy experiences and phonological awareness. Thus, effects of educational practices on phonological awareness performance are expected. Knowledge of the geographic residence of the participants assists the examiner in gaining information about the educational practices within that region. This information will determine the age the participants started formal schooling and the type of literacy curriculum the participants were likely to be receiving (if not explicitly stated in the manual).

2. The standardization sample should have adequate sample size in each subgroup examined. McCauley and Swisher recommend a sample size of 100 or more in each age group. Adequate sample size is particularly important in testing the phonological awareness skills of preschool children, because research has indicated wide variability in the development of 3- and 4-year-old children. Large sample sizes help control for data instability.

3. A range of measures related to test reliability and validity should be reported in the technical manual. These include:

Test item analysis
Concurrent validity
Predictive validity
Test–retest validity
Interexaminer reliability

Measures of validity and reliability provide evidence that the test accurately measures what it is designed to measure and should give the examiner confidence in the assessment scores obtained in the process of identifying a phonological awareness deficit and planning phonological awareness intervention.

4. Information regarding the variability in the participant's performance should be reported (i.e., reporting of mean scores and standard deviations). The mean score allows the examiner to understand the average raw score received on a phonological awareness subtest by the population sample, and the standard deviation provides a measure of the variation in the scores.

5. Test administration and scoring procedures should be carefully reported in the test manual. The manner of presentation, prompts, number of repetitions allowed, and scoring procedures are all variables that can strongly influence a child's performance on phonological awareness tasks. Some tasks, such as non-word spelling, may have more than one correct response for test items. Other tasks may result in ambiguous responses from

TABLE 6.1. Criteria Met by Broad-Spectrum Tests of Phonological Awareness

Criterion	PIPA	PAT	QUIL	CTOPP
Population subgroups	Ages 3–6 years	Ages 4–7 years	Grades 1–7	Ages 5–24 years
Normative sample well described	√	√ for geographic details × for gender, socioeconomic status, impairments	√	√
Sample size 100+ in each subgroup	× U.K. norms close to 100 in most age groups Australian norms between 60 and 80	√ for ages 5–7 years × for 4-year and 7 year, 6-month to 7-year 11-month age groups	√ for five of the seven grade levels two levels close to 100	√ for ages 5–13 years 14 to 17 year age groups range from 77 to 93
Item analysis or internal consistency	√	√	√	√
Means and *SD*'s reported	×	×	√	√
Concurrent validity	√	√	√	√
Predictive validity	√	√	√	√
Test–retest reported	√ Low on one subtest	√ Low on three subtests	√	√
Interexaminer reliability = .90	√	×	√	√
Test procedures well described	√	√	√	√
Description of tester qualifications	√	Limited	√	√

√ = criterion as described by McCauley and Swisher (1984) is met; × = criterion is not met.

the child, such as orally segmenting a word correctly on a phoneme segmentation task but demonstrating the incorrect number of phonemes in the word when tapping out the phonemes. It is critical, therefore, that the test manual provide clear instructions on the details of administration and scoring. The examiner must carefully follow these procedures.

In addition to the tests reviewed in Table 6.1 generally demonstrating strong psychometric properties, all of these tests have been developed on a sound theoretical basis; indeed, some tests have evolved over many years of research and refinement of tasks. The authors of these tests include leading and experienced researchers in the fields of phonological awareness, reading disorder, and speech–language pathology. The rigorous development of these standardized tests provides the test user with confidence in evaluating a child's current level of performance compared to a normative sample (assuming that the population sample of the standardized test is similar to that of the child participating in the assessment). The well-established importance of phonological awareness to written language has led to rapid development in a range of other phonological awareness assessment tools that have also proven clinically popular (e.g., The Phonological Awareness Test, Robertson & Salter, 1997, with American normative data is suitable to administer to 5- to 9-year-old children). The next section presents a selection of area-specific tests, criterion-referenced tests, and dynamic assessments suitable for monitoring children's progress.

Area-Specific Standardized Tests

Tests that measure children's skills in one area of phonological awareness (e.g., phoneme level skills) or investigate more narrowly defined levels of operation (e.g., deletion skills) are useful adjuncts to support findings from broader-based tests. They serve to provide more in-depth investigation in one area of phonological awareness. Two well-constructed tests that may be used for a variety of testing purposes, both clinically and in research, are described.

PHONOLOGICAL AWARENESS SKILLS PROGRAM TEST (ROSNER, 1999)

This test, formerly known as the Test of Auditory Analysis Skills (TAAS), has been developed over many years. This first part of the test focuses on deletion skills at the word, syllable, and phoneme levels. Word-level example: "Say *cowboy*. Now say it again, but don't say *boy*" (response: *cow*).

Items from this section have been successfully used in a wide variety of research studies investigating phonological awareness skills of children with reading disorder as well as children with typically developing skills.

The second section of the test focuses on phoneme manipulation skills. For example: "Say *bad*. Now say it again, but instead of /b/ say /m/."

Age-equivalent scores are available, based on a field test sample of 322 children from Texas, ages 4 years to 10 years, 11 months. The test is also designed to indicate an appropriate beginning level of training in the Phonological Awareness Skills Program (PASP). Psychometric testing provides evidence that the test is a reliable and valid measure of phonological awareness skills and that test users can have confidence in the results obtained. However, see Paul's (2001) caution against using age-equivalent scores to establish whether a child has a significant deficit. If the results of other types of standardized tests that provide standard scores (e.g., CTOPP, QUIL) have indicated that the child has a significant phonological awareness deficit, then the PASP age-equivalent scores can be regarded as useful to discuss a child's current level of functioning.

TEST OF PHONOLOGICAL AWARENESS
(TOPA; TORGESEN & BRYANT, 1994)

This test measures the ability of 5–8-year-old children to isolate phonemes in spoken words. It requires respondents to draw a line through an appropriate picture in a test booklet, with no verbal responses necessary, so it may be administered individually or in groups. The test has two versions: one for kindergarten children (ages 5–6 years of age) and one for early elementary years (ages 6–8). The kindergarten version requires children to (1) identify the picture (from a choice of three pictures) that starts with the same phoneme as the stimulus picture, and (2) identify the picture that starts with a different sound from a choice of four pictures. The elementary version presents the same two activities, but the child is required to identify the final phoneme sound that is the same or different from the stimulus item. Normative data gathered from large numbers of children across the Unites States are available, and the test has strong psychometric properties.

Criterion-Referenced Test

The Lindamood Auditory Conceptualization Test (LAC) (Lindamood & Lindamood, 1979) is a well-developed criterion-referenced test that has been used successfully in a variety of research projects and in clinical work. This test was developed from the Auditory Discrimination in Depth Program (Lindamood & Lindamood, 1975) and assesses the ability to discriminate between sounds and analyze the number and order of sounds in spoken patterns, with the use of colored blocks. The test can be used with preschool children as well as adults. The test provides minimum level scores expected for children from the United States at each grade level from kindergarten to grade 6. Full mastery of the test items or near-perfect performance is expected from grade 7 to adulthood. Both English and Spanish versions of the test are available.

The first part of the LAC requires children to identify patterns of phonemes articulated in isolation—for example, "Show me /z/ /z/." Childern are expected to select two blocks (from a group of colored blocks) that are the same color to indicate that they heard two sounds that were the same. The second part requires respondents to manipulate, add, or delete phonemes in nonsense words, again through the use of colored blocks—for example, "If that says *zuz* [three blocks are placed beside each other, with the first and last block the same color] show me /ziz/." Respondents are required to change the middle block to represent a change in the medial phoneme. A particularly useful feature of the test is its pre- and posttest forms, which may be used to evaluate change in children's performance over time.

Monitoring Assessments

Some children who are identified as having poor phonological awareness skills at school entry rapidly develop these skills within a classroom program that integrates structured phonological awareness activities into rich language experiences and literacy instruction. Regular assessment of these children's phonological awareness development is necessary to ascertain whether a phonological awareness program implemented at a whole class level (in addition to wide range of reading and writing experiences) is sufficient to develop their phonological awareness skills at the phoneme level or whether more intensive instruction on a small group or individual basis is necessary.

Regular assessment procedures and classroom observational assessments provide valuable data in monitoring a child's phonological awareness development within the class program. Such monitoring assessment should include measures of whether the child is able to use phonological information in the reading and spelling processes.

Dynamic Indicators of Basic Early Literacy Skills

A useful standardized set of measures designed to monitor young children's development in phonological awareness and other early literacy skill areas is the Dynamic Indicators of Basic Early Literacy Skills (DIBELS) (Good & Kaminski, 2002). DIBELS is novel in its approach of providing a variety of 1-minute assessment measures. Measures are used to "benchmark" a child's abilities, identifying each skill area as either "at risk," "some risk," or "low risk." Assessment sets are given at regular intervals (e.g., beginning, middle, and end of the school year) to carefully monitor early literacy development and ensure that classroom instruction and specific interventions are effective in enhancing reading development for each child in a class. Assessment sets are available for children from kindergarten (e.g., 5-year-old children) to grade 3 level (e.g., 8-year-old children). For example, the following set of measures are given to first-grade children.

1. Letter naming fluency: the numbers of letters named correctly in 1 minute.
2. Phoneme segmentation fluency: the number of phonemes from 3- and 4-phoneme words that are correctly segmented in 1 minute.
3. Nonsense word fluency: the number of correct phoneme–grapheme matches read aloud or orally segmented aloud for non-words, such as *sig, rav.*
4. Oral reading fluency (the number of words accurately read aloud in 1 minute from a reading passage).

The DIBELS measures are available to download via the internet, and full details (including technical reports) are available on their website at *www.dibels.uoregon.edu.* Analyses of psychometric properties suggest that the DIBELS provide valid and reliable measures of children's progress in early literacy development (Calder, 1992; Elliott, Lee, & Tollefson, 2001; Kaminski & Good, 1996).

Case Example

Samples of children's writing attempts and examples of their spelling attempts over time provide excellent insight into whether they are developing the ability to use phonological awareness knowledge in spelling. A case example is provided to illustrate a simple monitoring procedure implemented within a class program.

The spelling attempts of a young boy, Cody, were monitored by a speech–language pathologist and class teacher over a 3-month period to ascertain whether he was beginning to use phonological information and letter-sound knowledge in the spelling process. Cody had a history of speech difficulties as a preschooler but only exhibited mild developmental speech errors at school entry and was not receiving regular speech and language therapy or any other specialist educational support. His home and school were classified as being in a low socioeconomic area in a metropolitan district. His receptive language skills were within the normal range; his teachers described Cody as a charming little boy who tried hard with his class work. Cody started primary schooling in New Zealand at 5 years, 0 months (i.e., he received the national school curriculum from 9 A.M. to 3 P.M. 5 days per week).

The first sample of Cody's spelling was taken when he was 5 years, 7 months. He had therefore received 7 months of classroom literacy instruction that exposed him to a wide range of meaningful reading and writing experiences. The spelling attempts (see Figure 6.1) at assessment 1 illustrate that Cody had no understanding of the relationship between speech and print when spelling. Not even the first grapheme of any of the target words was identified correctly. Rather, the spelling attempts show knowledge of a limited series of letters that is repeated in each spelling attempt. Many letters used are those represented in the spelling of Cody's name, which he proudly wrote correctly at the top of his response sheet.

The second spelling sample (assessment 2 in Figure 6.1) used the same words presented at assessment 1. This sample was collected after a further 3 months of classroom instruction (i.e., toward the end of his first year of school). In this sample Cody demonstrated that he could now spell some words (i.e., *I'm* and *we*). Unfortunately, these words have no relationship to the target spelling words of *teeth* and *dinosaur.* A concerning feature of the sample is the "no response" recorded by item 10. Cody had become more reluctant in his spelling attempts, perhaps indicating a realization of

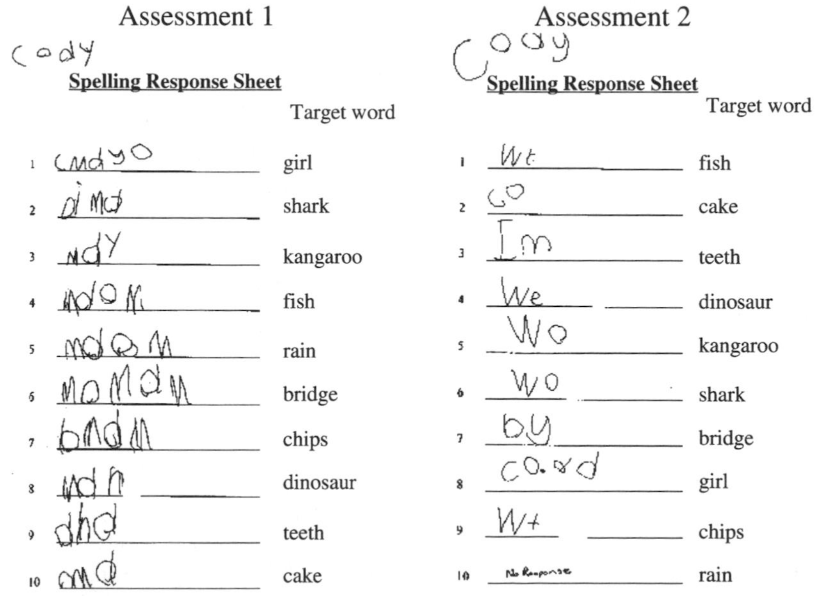
Assessment 1

Cody

Spelling Response Sheet

	Target word
1	girl
2	shark
3	kangaroo
4	fish
5	rain
6	bridge
7	chips
8	dinosaur
9	teeth
10	cake

Assessment 2

Cody

Spelling Response Sheet

		Target word
1	Wt	fish
2	CO	cake
3	Im	teeth
4	We	dinosaur
5	Wo	kangaroo
6	wo	shark
7	by	bridge
8		girl
9	Wt	chips
10	No Response	rain

FIGURE 6.1. Cody's spelling samples. The samples were collected on two occasions over a 3-month school period during the latter part of the child's first year at school.

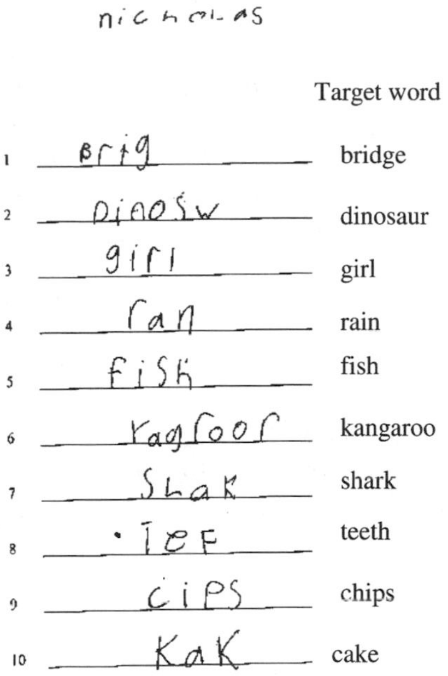

nicholas

Target word

1. _Brig_ bridge

2. _Dinosw_ dinosaur

3. _girl_ girl

4. _ran_ rain

5. _fish_ fish

6. _Ragfoor_ kangaroo

7. _Shak_ shark

8. _·Teef_ teeth

9. _Cips_ chips

10. _Kak_ cake

FIGURE 6.2. A spelling sample of one of Cody's peers who had typically developing speech and language skills. The sample was collected at the end of the child's first year at school (i.e., to match Cody's assessment 2 sample).

his limitations. An increase in the number of no responses over time is commonly seen in children who struggle with reading and writing (Gillon, 2002b). This sample provided the teacher with evidence that either Cody was not gaining phonological awareness skills, or he was not developing the ability to use phonological cues in spelling from the classroom program. Cody was referred to speech–language pathology services for in-depth phonological awareness assessment with the view to developing a structured small group phonological awareness intervention that could be integrated into his reading and writing program.

Cody's spelling attempts on the target words contrasted with the spelling attempts of many of his class peers, who clearly could demonstrate the ability to integrate a phonological strategy into spelling attempts of unfamiliar words. The spelling sample of one of Cody's peers (who had no history of speech or language difficulties) is shown in Figure 6.2. Nicholas demonstrated that he was able to use phonological information to assist him in the spelling process. Evidence of phoneme segmentation and accurate connections between graphemes to phonemes was demonstrated: *k-a-k* (*cake*) *r-a-n* (*rain*) *t-e-f* (*teeth*).

The words Cody and Nicholas were asked to spell were considered difficult words for 5- and 6-year-old children, and accurate spelling of all words was not expected. The intent in this selection was to present unfamiliar words, not words they may have learned through their class spelling program and could spell using a rote visual memory strategy. Non-word spelling tasks are used in many formal tests for this purpose. The advantage of using words that are within the child's vocabulary but are unlikely to be on early spelling word lists is that pictures of the words could be found. The pictures allowed the use of a game format rather than a spelling test format. To play this game, the children threw a counter on to an array of pictures and recorded (i.e., spelled) the name of the picture where the counter landed.

Observation and analysis of a child's reading errors when reading connected text or observing and recording strategies a child employs to attempt an unfamiliar word when reading also provide valuable information to monitor whether a child is able to integrate phonological information with other cues when reading.

Developing a Profile of Spoken to Written Language Proficiency

Integrating information from assessment measures, observations, and case history data is a critical part of the assessment process. No single test can provide the necessary information to describe children's language development in a comprehensive manner. Data collected in relation to children's phonological awareness development needs to be considered in context with other aspects of phonological processing and spoken and written language as well as related factors in the child's environment. The Speech to Print Profile (Gillon, 2000b) was designed to assist speech–language pathologists and educators in summarizing information collected and to ensure that an understanding of the relationship between spoken and written language is considered. Its use is intended as a visual aid in highlighting areas of strength and weakness in the child's language system that are directly related to the decoding of written text in early reading acquisition. It is expected that such a profile would be supported by assessment reports detailing the child's performance on individual assessment measures.

The profile is based on an interactive model of word recognition which contends that semantic, syntactic, morphological, and phonological cues are integrated when decoding text. This model also supports the theoretical view that phonological processing skills are crucial in understanding the links between speech and print. For these reasons, information related to phonological processing assessment is visually presented on the profile between aspects of spoken language and aspects of written language.

A primary purpose of the profile is to ensure that vital areas of word recognition are not overlooked and to enable information collected from different professionals to be represented on one form. For example, speech–language pathologists may collect detailed data related to the child's semantic, syntactic, and morphological knowledge in spoken language and speech production abilities (among other assessments measures). A wide variety of assessment procedures are likely to contribute to the speech–language pathologist's examination of the child's spoken language abilities: standardized tests, criterion-referenced assessment, and the collection of spontaneous language samples produced in conversational and oral narrative contexts. In recent years, the speech–language pathologist's scope of practice also involves assessment of phonological processing skills (phonological awareness, in particular), phonological decoding measures such as non-word reading and spelling assessments, and other literacy-related assessments (American Speech–Language–Hearing Association, 2001; Royal College of Speech and Language Therapists, 1996). Teachers and reading specialists frequently collect detailed information regarding the child's knowledge of print concepts, letter recognition, reading and writing performance. For children who are struggling with the task of developing word recognition abilities, it is critical that the information collected from differing professionals be shared and that the links between the various assessment findings of the child's spoken and written language system are clearly understood by all involved. It is also important to interpret assessment findings in the context of other influencing factors related to the child, family, and instructional environment.

The Speech to Print Profile, illustrated in Figure 6.3 (and available to download in a larger size on *www.cmds.canterbury.ac.nz* search under "people," then "Gillon"), is one example of how an overview of a variety of assessment measures can be achieved and how prompts to important related factors to the child's language development can be indicated. The profile can be completed in a variety of ways to reflect individual teachers' and speech–language pathologists' preferences. For example, standard scores from standardized tests can be recorded to indicate level of performance, a shading system can be used to represent a classification of mild, moderate, or severe impairment in a particular area, or the speech–language pathologist and teacher may simply checkmark areas in which a child shows relative performance strengths and circle areas of weakness (based on standardized and criterion-referenced evaluations).

To successfully complete the profile, collaboration between the speech–language pathologist, teacher, and/or reading specialist working with the child is necessary. The involvement of the child's caregivers and family (as appropriate to the child's cultural background) is also encouraged in the development of the profile. The long-term negative academic and social

SPEECH TO PRINT PROFILE

Child's Name:

Age:

Date:

Spoken language			Written language		
Underlying representation	Phonological awarenss	Phonological storage and retrieval	Print knowledge	Word level	Text level
Semantic knowledge	Syllable	Non-word repetition/ multisyllabic word repetition	Print concepts	Word recognition	Reading accuracy
Syntactic morphological knowledge	Onset rime			Non-word reading	Reading comprehension
			Letter knowledge	Spelling (regular vs. irregular words)	Fluency/rate
Expressive phonology	Phoneme	Rapid naming			
					Writing
				Non-word spelling	

RELATED FACTORS

Child
Hearing test results: Date of last hearing test:
Vision test results: Date of visual testing:
Health and behavior:
Intellect:
Early speech and language development:
Other diagnosed impairments:

Family
Family speech or literacy disorder:
Language literacy environment:
Cultural influences:

School
Instructional reading methods:
Instructional spelling methods:
Reading support:
Speech–language pathology support:

Referrals required (e.g., audiologist)   Date of referral:

FIGURE 6.3. Speech to Print Profile.

consequences of reading failure demand that a young school-age child, identified through screening procedures as being at high risk for persistent literacy difficulties, receive the full attention of appropriate professionals during an in-depth assessment process. The integration of the speech–language pathologist's expertise in language development and disorders with the teacher's knowledge of the child's curriculum performance leads to the appropriate evaluation of the child's language system on which to build well-planned interventions.

PHONOLOGICAL AWARENESS ASSESSMENT IN OLDER CHILDREN AND ADOLESCENTS

The main purpose of phonological awareness assessment of older students who have a diagnosed reading disorder such as dyslexia or have clearly identified reading and spelling difficulties is to establish whether a deficit in processing phonological information is contributing to their literacy difficulties. If a deficit is identified, assessment data should be gathered to provide sufficient information on which to plan an appropriate intervention.

Collaboration between speech–language pathologists and reading specialists is important in the assessment of older students' phonological processing abilities. As discussed in Chapter 4, some children with reading disorder do not have obvious spoken language difficulties, but in-depth assessment by a speech–language pathologist may reveal *severe* phonological processing deficits and significant delays in semantic, syntactic, or morphological processing in spoken language. Scope of practice for speech–language pathologists provides very clear indication that these professionals have an important role to play in the assessment of children with written language disorders (American Speech–Language–Hearing Association, 2001; Royal College of Speech and Language Therapists, 1996).

Phonological awareness assessment in older children may include:

- Broad-spectrum standardized tests (e.g., CTOPP or QUIL, described on pp. 116–117) to identify areas of phonological awareness strength and weakness as well as evaluating the individual's ability to use phonological information in reading and spelling (e.g., nonword reading or spelling measures).
- Area-specific phonological awareness tasks, particularly tests that involve more complex phoneme level tasks involving deletion and manipulation.
- Criterion-referenced assessments to examine whether the student can use phonological information efficiently in reading and writing; error analysis of the student's reading errors in connected text and

spelling errors in writing samples can provide important assessment information (see Masterson & Apel, 2000, for spelling sampling procedures and spelling error analysis suggestions).

As with the assessment of phonological awareness in younger children, the phonological awareness assessment of older students with reading disorder should be viewed within the broader context of their spoken and written language development and with consideration given to related factors suggested in the Speech to Print Profile. Particular attention should be directed to other processing aspects, such as rapid automatized naming (Calder, 1992; Wolf, Bowers, et al., 2000).

Some older children may not present with marked reading delays but have difficulty in spelling. Others may have superior intellectual ability that has enabled them to reach age-appropriate reading levels, but their performance remains inconsistent with their superior cognitive abilities. Some readers may expend such effort to decode words at an acceptable level that their resources for comprehending text are compromised. Still others may cope acceptably in the lower-average range in reading during their junior school years but struggle with the onset of advanced schooling, where the demands of written language steadily increase. It is plausible that weak underlying skills in processing phonological information contribute to each of these profiles. Hence, in addition to investigating the phonological processing skills of children with dyslexia, screening procedures at a class level for older students can identify students who require in-depth assessment.

Engaging students in class activities that stress their phonological system can draw the teacher's attention to those students who should receive further evaluation. Examples of class screening activities include the following:

1. *Non-word spelling test* (e.g., subtest from the QUIL). This kind of test can be presented as a fun activity rather than as a formal spelling test. The purpose in such a case is not necessarily to compare individual performances against the normative data but to examine students' attempts at phonetically plausible spellings.

2. *Spoonerism task.* Engage students in a class activity of creating spoonerisms from well-known actors, musicians, singers, or sports people's names (e.g., changing *Tom Cruise* to *Com Truise*). Alternatively, one student can present a spoken sentence that contains a spoonerism for another student to decode as quickly as possible (e.g., "They won the *mootball fatch*"; that is, "They won the football match").

3. *Phoneme deletion.* Speed games between students or teams can be introduced that require the students to press a buzzer (as on a game show) in order to complete a phoneme deletion or manipulation task (e.g., "Say

train without the *r*: *tain*," or "*Say star*, but instead of /t/, say /k/: *scar*"). Teacher prompts or team assistance may be needed to ensure that students with difficulties do not find such a task too threatening.

It is recommended that a speech–language pathologist work with a class teacher to formulate stimulus items for such class activities. Attention needs to be given to the phonological legality of novel combinations formed. That is, the spoonerisms or phoneme manipulations should create words with phoneme combinations that are found in the language of instruction.

The purpose of these activities is to identify the students who appear to have more difficulty, or rely heavily on peer assistance, with such tasks. These students should be considered for further observation of their phonological processing abilities and, if necessary, identified as in need of in-depth assessment.

SUMMARY

This chapter has raised issues for practitioners to consider in assessing phonological awareness skills in preschool and young school-age children, as well as in older children and adolescents with established literacy difficulties. A variety of available assessment tools that are useful for phonological awareness evaluation have been summarized. Following are summary points:

- In-depth phonological awareness assessment is critical for children identified as being at risk for persistent reading disorder, children who are not making the expected progress in reading and spelling development, and children with diagnosed reading and spelling disorders such as dyslexia.
- The optimum phonological awareness tasks with which to measure children's abilities differ with level of development. Phoneme deletion and manipulation tasks are particularly useful for older children.
- An in-depth assessment of a child's phonological awareness development may include broad-spectrum standardized tests, area-specific standardized tests, criterion-referenced tests, and curriculum-based observational assessments.
- Standardized tests, designed by leading researchers, are available for use in phonological awareness evaluation; these tests are theoretically based and generally have strong psychometric properties.
- Collaboration between speech–language pathologists, teachers, and reading specialists is vital when assessing children at risk or children experiencing reading disorder. Synthesis of data collected in relation to these

children's language development is necessary, and consideration must be given to factors in their spoken language system that may underlie their difficulty in reading and writing. Phonological awareness is one vital area to be evaluated in perspective with other aspects of spoken and written language.

Assessment is an ongoing process. Initial in-depth assessment provides a baseline from which appropriate intervention or monitoring of development can begin. Continued regular evaluations of a child's phonological awareness development will ascertain the effectiveness of interventions and class instruction provided. Such ongoing assessment is critical to ensure that the weaknesses identified in a child's phonological processing abilities are resolved and that newly acquired skills transfer to the ability to use phonological information in reading and spelling.

7

Phonological Awareness
Intervention

Guiding Principles

Phonological awareness intervention has a strong scientific basis. It has emerged in clinical and classroom practices as a result of research evidence that has convincingly demonstrated the significant benefits of phonological awareness training for reading and spelling development. Phonological awareness intervention is addressed in this book in two parts. This chapter discusses the clinical implications from phonological awareness intervention research and presents guiding principles for the design and implementation of phonological awareness programs. Chapter 8 focuses on three differing instructional frameworks for phonological awareness intervention and provides a range of practical suggestions to enhance phonological awareness in preschool, young school-age, and older children.

RESEARCH BASIS

Interest in whether phonological awareness could be taught to kindergarten and young school-age children began building in the 1970s (Elkonin, 1973; Wallach & Wallach, 1976). Auditory training and reading programs that included activities to promote phonological awareness skills emerged at a commercial level (e.g., Lindamood & Lindamood, 1975; Wallach & Wallach, 1976), and discussions regarding the type of phonemic awareness activities that should be included in training programs appeared in the literature (Lewkowicz, 1980). However, it was Bradley and Bryant's 1983 longitudinal and training study demonstrating a causal relationship between phonological awareness and reading development (see Chapter 3) that sparked strong research interest in phonological awareness intervention.

The goal of phonological awareness intervention is to enhance reading and writing performance. Activities that promote the explicit understanding of a word's sound structure are valuable only to the extent that they develop a child's ability to recognize printed words or to spell words. Efficiency in word recognition and spelling processes should then lead to improvements in reading comprehension and writing. Evidence from a wide variety of sources has demonstrated the successful achievement of this goal. The following populations have all demonstrated positive reading and/or spelling outcomes in response to phonological awareness intervention:

- Older children with dyslexia (Alexander, Andersen, Heilman, Voeller, & Torgesen, 1991; Gillon & Dodd, 1995, 1997; Lovett & Steinbach, 1997; Lovett et al., 1994; Truch, 1994)
- Young children at risk from low socioeconomic backgrounds (Blachman, Ball, Black, & Tangel, 1994)
- Kindergarten children and children starting school with poor phonological processing skills (Castle, Riach, & Nicholson, 1994; Torgesen et al., 1999)
- School-age children with spoken language impairments (Gillon, 2000b; Korkman & Peltomma, 1993; Warrick, Rubin, & Walsh, 1993)
- Preschool children (3 and 4 years of age) with expressive phonological impairment (Gillon, 2002a)
- Preschool and/or school-age native speakers of
    English (e.g., Ball & Blachman, 1991; Brady et al., 1994; Brennan & Ireson, 1997; Torgesen, Morgan, & Davis, 1992).
    Spanish (Defior & Tudela, 1994)
    German (Schneider, Kuspert, Roth, & Vise, 1997)
    Danish (Borstrom & Elbro, 1997; Lundberg, Frost, & Petersen, 1988; Poskiparta, Niemi, & Vauras, 1999)
    Swedish (Olofsson & Lundberg, 1983)
    Hebrew (Bentin & Leshem, 1993) and
    Dutch (Bus, 1986)

A meta-analysis of 52 controlled research studies in phonological awareness training confirmed that phonological awareness intervention has a statistically significant impact on developing word recognition, reading comprehension, and spelling (Ehri et al., 2001). Most researchers, however, caution practitioners that phonological awareness intervention should be implemented as a part of a comprehensive program in literacy instruction or in early literacy experiences. The complexities of written language development preclude the possibility that one narrowly focused type of instruction such as phonological awareness could lead to successful reading and writing for all children. Rather, phonological awareness intervention must be seen in perspective with the host of other language experiences, such as shared book reading, alphabetic instruction, storytelling, and involvement in meaningful reading and writing activities. All help to foster written language acquisition.

GUIDING PRINCIPLES FOR INTERVENTION

The immense value of phonological awareness intervention, particularly for children who are struggling to acquire efficient reading skills, necessitates that careful attention is given to the design and implementation of its procedures. Research provides clear evidence that differing conditions enhance the effectiveness of phonological awareness intervention, and guidelines on which to base phonological awareness intervention can be derived from the research findings. These guidelines follow:

• *Phonological awareness intervention should be integrated with letter-sound knowledge training and should make explicit the links between speech and print.* The phonological linkage hypothesis (Hatcher, 1994) contends that making explicit links between children's knowledge of the sound structure of words and their written representations will be more effective than teaching phonological awareness skills in isolation or providing reading instruction in isolation. Explicit instruction in teaching children the relationship between spoken and written language appears to be a critical element for successful training outcomes. In addition, Cunningham (1990) demonstrated that programs in which children are engaged in the activity of reflecting upon and discussing the phonemic awareness task and its relationship to written language resulted in significantly better progress than a skill-and-drill approach. The meta-analysis of phonological intervention studies (Ehri et al., 2001) confirmed that integrating letter-sound knowledge with phoneme awareness activities results in stronger transfer of skills from phonological awareness instruction to improved reading and spelling performance.

The use of plastic letters or letter blocks representing each grapheme (e.g., *ch* written on one block and *sh* written on another) that can be manipulated in phonological awareness tasks may be particularly useful. Defior and Tudela (1994) demonstrated that manipulating letters to form words was more effective than using written labels for words. In this study

60 Spanish-speaking 6-year-old children were assigned to one of four training groups or a no-training control group. Children who participated in phoneme categorization tasks that included the aid of letters to identify the phonemes and spell the words in the categorization set showed positive training effects on literacy development. Following training, their performance on reading and spelling tasks was significantly superior to children who had engaged in phoneme categorization tasks without letters, those who categorized words based on conceptual criteria with and without written labels provided for the words, and children who received no linguistic training.

- *Phonological awareness intervention should focus on the development of skills at the phoneme level for school-age children.* Phonological awareness activities at the sentence and word level may have little benefit for school-age children. Furthermore, incorporating activities at the sentence level in the same program as phonemic level analysis may be misleading to the child (Brady et al., 1994). Word and syllable skills require less direct instruction than phoneme analysis skills and may develop with general classroom instruction (Brennan & Ireson, 1997; Lundberg et al., 1988). In addition, training at the syllable level has little effect on phoneme analysis skills, but the reverse is apparent (Cary & Verhaeghe, 1994). Instruction in rhyming skills may have some benefit for later reading and spelling development, but instruction for children who are already experiencing reading failure should predominantly focus on developing phonological awareness skills at the phoneme level (Gillon, 2000b). Instruction in phoneme segmentation and blending skills is particularly important for reading and spelling (Ayres, 1995; Ehri et al., 2001).

- *Instruction may involve a skill mastery approach or an integrated multiple-skill approach.* Two approaches to phonological awareness intervention have been utilized in research: a skill mastery approach and a multiple-skill or integrated approach. The skill mastery approach teaches one phoneme level skill (such as phoneme blending) at a time, until children have mastered it (e.g., achieved 90% success on target stimuli). Following mastery of the first skill, a second skill such as phoneme segmentation is introduced and taught until mastery.

A multiple-skill or integrated approach involves the integration of activities with a range of phonological awareness tasks in which, for example, onset-rime and phoneme detection, blending, segmentation, and manipulation skills are addressed concurrently. Children can engage in differing levels of phonological awareness activities within the one instructional session, such as playing a game of rhyme bingo, sorting words that start with the same sound, and selecting words that are first segmented and then blended together. Ehri et al. (2001) suggested that greater gains for reading and spelling are achieved through a skill mastery approach that focuses on one or two skills only. Yet Gillon (2000b) found that, for 6-year-old children with severe phonological awareness deficits, an integrated approach proved an efficient method in gaining significant improvements in phoneme level awareness, word reading, reading comprehension, and spelling development. A range of factors may contribute to the success of each of these approaches, including the characteristics of the participants receiving the training, the length of training time, the manner in which differing tasks are presented and integrated into a program, and the motivational levels of both students and teachers.

Schneider et al. (1997) suggested that the completion of a range of activities in onset-rime and phoneme level tasks was important in gaining positive literacy outcomes. In this study children receiving training from teachers who were less consistent in program implementation and failed to complete the full range of activities made less progress than children who completed all activities. Furthermore, training in only one area of phonemic analysis skills may not generalize to other phonemic analysis skills (O'Connor, Jenkins, Leicester, & Slocum, 1993; Slocum, O'Connor, & Jenkins, 1993; Torgesen et al., 1992). Thus, from a clinical perspective, a skill mastery approach for children with pervasive phonological processing deficits may prove a laborious and lengthy process, which may adversely affect teachers' and children's motivation to complete a program that then results in less favorable literacy outcomes. An integrated approach in such circumstances may help to maintain children's interest in program content and encourage the development of a range of phoneme level skills that will contribute to literacy success. Further research is required to address these issues, and practitioners need to consider variables such as each child's abilities, learning style, and the learning environment as well as the research evidence in choosing between a skill mastery or integrated approach to phonological awareness instruction.

- *An individual or small group model of service delivery may be necessary for children with severe deficits.* Phonological awareness training programs administered by teachers at the class level have shown limited benefits for children with severe phonological awareness deficits. Individual or more intensive small-group instruction may be necessary for these children (Brady et al., 1994; Torgesen et al., 1994). Byrne and Fielding-Barnsley (1995) demonstrated less effective outcomes from phonological awareness training that employed whole-class teaching compared to more intensive small-group training that addressed individual needs.

- *Flexibility in program implementation is required.* Brady et al. (1994) discussed the need to move at the child's pace within the phonological awareness training program. Rhyme activities, for example, may be quickly acquired by children and do not need the same intensity of instruction as more difficult phoneme analysis tasks. Meeting individual needs in instructional programs is a basic premise in all special education programs.

- *Phonological awareness intervention is most effective after a period of general language instruction.* Utilizing a counterbalanced research design, Ayres (1995) investigated the effects of treatment sequence for 113 kindergarten children. Findings indicated that phonological awareness training was more effective following instruction that exposed children to a wide variety of spoken and written language experiences. Ayres's investigation also indicated that a direct instructional approach to phonological awareness training has greater benefits for literacy development than an indirect approach and that although a range of activities is necessary, particular attention should be placed on phoneme segmentation skills.

PHONOLOGICAL AWARENESS INTERVENTION FOR CHILDREN WITH SPOKEN LANGUAGE IMPAIRMENT

As a group, children with spoken language impairment are at risk for persistent literacy difficulties (see Chapter 5). It is critical that speech language pathologists and teachers work to enhance these children's underlying skills for written language development as well as improving their spoken language skills. Assessment of phonological awareness skills should be routinely administered by speech–language pathologists in their evaluation of children with spoken language impairment and structured phonological awareness interventions implemented, as appropriate to assessment findings.

Children with moderate or severe spoken language impairment frequently receive intensive periods of speech–language pathology during their preschool and early school years. Interventions to resolve speech error patterns or to improve oral language skills involve some level of phonological awareness or metalinguistic knowledge. For example, when implementing techniques to improve sound pattern errors, children's attention is drawn to initial, medial, or final phonemes in words, or children may listen to an array of words that all start with the same phoneme. Rhymes are frequently introduced into intervention as practice for the speech sounds that occur in connected speech. Semantic and syntactic awareness also are important for reading development, and many therapy programs aimed at developing oral, semantic, and syntactic skills develop children's awareness of grammatically correct and semantically plausible sentences.

However, these types of indirect phonological awareness and metalinguistic activities may not be sufficient to exert a significant impact on these children's written language development. Most studies that have reported poor phonological awareness and reading development in children with spoken language impairment have included participants that have received lengthy and frequently intensive periods of speech–language pathology services. Research suggests that some interventions that exclude structured phonological awareness activities, although effective in enhancing aspects of spoken language, may have only limited benefits for written language development (Gillon, 2002). It is recommended, therefore, that speech–language pathologists implement well-planned phonological awareness programs that directly aim to resolve phonological awareness deficits in school-age children who have spoken language impairment. It is also recommended that structured activities to enhance early phoneme level skills and letter-name knowledge be integrated into the speech–language pathology sessions for preschool children with spoken language impairment (see Gillon, in press).

Children with speech and language disorders pose unique challenges to the successful implementation of phonological awareness intervention. Unintelligible speech, limited receptive vocabulary, difficulty following instructions, difficulty formulating sentences or asking questions to seek clarification from an instructor, or difficulty listening and attending to auditory information—each limitation necessitates careful assessment and planning procedures. Benefits from phonological awareness interventions have been clearly demonstrated for children with differing types of spoken language impairment. Preschool and school-age children described as having a specific or significant language impairment (O'Connor et al., 1993; van Kleeck, Gillam, & McFadden, 1998; Warrick, Rubin, & Rowe-Walsh, 1993), 3- to 5-year-old children with phonological disorder (Gillon, 2002a; Hesketh, Adams, Nightingale, & Hall, 2000; Major & Bernhardt, 1998), and school-age children whose spoken language impairment primarily involved expressive phonological difficulties (Gillon, 2000b) have responded positively to phonological awareness intervention.

Using a controlled group design, Gillon (2000b) showed that despite being significantly delayed in phonological awareness and reading development, children with spoken language impairment can make rapid progress in acquiring these skills through structured phonological awareness intervention. This study employed 91 New Zealand children between the ages of 5 and 7 years: 61 children with spoken language impairment (all of whom had expressive phonological difficulties) and 30 children with typically developing language skills. The children with spoken language impairment participated in either 20 hours of phonological awareness intervention (n = 23), 20 hours of a control intervention targeting speech production and expressive language (n = 23), or minimal intervention focusing on speech production (n = 15). Prior to intervention, there were no group differences on a range of measures, including speech production, phoneme awareness, and reading ability.

The phonological awareness intervention was implemented by a speech–language pathologist on an individual basis and focused primarily on enhancing phonological awareness skills at the phoneme level. The program content included many of the activities described in Chapter 8 (i.e., phoneme identity, blending, segmentation, and manipulation; and tracking sound changes in words). Activities incorporated letter knowledge and made explicit for the children the link between speech and print.

The results of the study indicated that the children in the phonological awareness intervention group made accelerated progress on phoneme awareness tasks, reaching levels similar to typically developing children at the postintervention assessment (see Figure 7.1). Transfer of skills to the reading process was clearly evident. The performance of the children who received the phonological awareness intervention was significantly superior to the treatment control and minimal intervention control groups on measures of word recognition ability: reading accuracy, reading comprehension of connected text, and non-word decoding ability. The children also made significant improvement in their speech production difficulties. There was a trend for children who received the phonological awareness instruction to show more improvement in their spontaneous articulation of single words than children in other interventions that aimed predominantly at resolving speech sound errors.

Follow-up assessment 11 months following the phonological awareness intervention indicated sustained and continued growth in phoneme awareness (see Figure 7.2), speech production, reading, and spelling development (Gillon, 2002). With continued classroom instruction and reading support, the majority of children who received phonological awareness in-

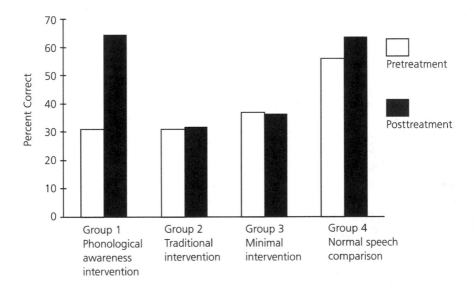

FIGURE 7.1. Group pre- and posttest performance on the Lindamood Auditory Conceptualization Test. From Gillon (2000b). Copyright 2000 by the American Speech–Language–Hearing Association. Reprinted by permission.

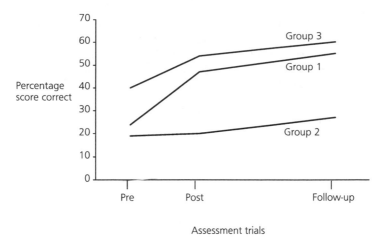

FIGURE 7.2. Group performance over time on a combined measure of phoneme awareness. Group 1, experimental group who received phonological awareness; group 2, control group; group 3, typical development. From Gillon (2002b). Copyright 2002 by the Royal College of Speech and Language Therapists. Reprinted by permission.

tervention were reading at or above the expected level for their age at the follow-up assessment.

The Gillon study (2000b, 2002b) provided evidence that children with moderate to severe expressive phonological impairments can benefit from the same type of phonological awareness instruction as presented to typically developing children and other groups of children at risk for reading disorder. The instruction, if well planned, may prevent the persistent reading and spelling difficulties these children frequently encounter and also may prove an efficient method of resolving these children's speech production errors.

BACKGROUND KNOWLEDGE OF INSTRUCTOR

In designing and implementing phonological awareness programs, the educator or clinician requires knowledge of language structure and, in particular, knowledge of the speech-sound system (readers who require professional development in this area are referred to Moats, 2000). Speech–language pathologists' expertise in normal and disordered phonological development places them in a unique position within the educational team. They have a knowledge base related to the structure of the speech-sound system, including how it develops, how it relates to orthographic symbols, and how awareness of the sound system can be promoted. Ideally, the design and implementation of phonological awareness should be a collaborative process, in which speech–language pathologists share their knowledge of language structure and phonology with teachers, who then can contribute their knowledge of the classroom language curriculum and instructional methods employed in reading and spelling.

One important area of phonology to be understood in phonological awareness instruction is the relationship between phonemes and graphemes. For example, in orally segmenting a word such as *pat* into three phonemes, it is important to articulate the actual phoneme without the addition of unnecessary phonemes. Thus /p/ is pronounced as a single voiceless phoneme, not as *puh* or *pi*, which would be two phonemes. Similarly, a sound such as /s/ is pronounced as *ss*, not as *si* or *suh*. A second area that may differ between reading or spelling instruction and phonological awareness is the treatment of cluster sounds or blends (e.g., *tr, sl, br, dr, pl, spr, spl*). Blends consist of two or three individual phonemes and are not treated as a single unit in phoneme segmentation exercises, as may be taught in some spelling approaches. Thus in segmenting a word such as *drop*, four phonemes are counted: (*d-r-o-p*). Similarly, words such as *spoon* and *spray* are comprised of four phonemes: (*s-p-oo-n*; *s-p-r-ay*). Blends at the ends of words are also separated by their individual phonemes, as is the case with desk (*d-e-s-k*) and bump (*b-u-m-p*). However, digraphs such as *sh*, *th*, *ch*, and *wh* have two letters but represent one phoneme. Thus, *shop* and *whip*, for example, would be segmented as three phonemes (*sh-o-p*; *wh-i-p*).

A further consideration in designing interventions is the type of stimulus items used during the training activities. Knowledge of word structure and phonological complexity is necessary to ensure that training items are presented in a graded order of difficulty. Teaching children to segment two-phoneme words before segmenting three-phoneme words is generally recommended. Likewise, vowel–consonant structures (e.g., *art*) are more easily segmented than consonant–vowel structures (e.g., *tar*) (Uhry & Ehri, 1999).

The phonological and orthographic constraints of the language of instruction also should be considered when using non-word stimulus items or in phoneme manipulation activities. It is recommended that target words contain combinations of letters that are found in the language of instruction. For example, the *str* combination is found in English, but *sbr* is not. Understanding the child's vocabulary knowledge is necessary for selecting stimulus items. Combining speech–language pathologists' knowledge of phonology with teachers' knowledge of the child's vocabulary and the vocabulary introduced in the curriculum ensures that training items are both phonologically and semantically appropriate for the child.

CHILDREN WITH DIFFERING LEARNING NEEDS

Children with differing learning needs who are integrated into mainstream schools can easily participate in phonological awareness training sessions alongside their peers. Minor modifications and the support of a teacher aide are necessary. Children who are blind and use Braille as their reading medium can be presented with Braille letter tiles to correspond with magnetic letters or letter blocks that teachers use on the board during phonological awareness instructional sessions. If the teacher asks the class to use differently colored blocks to represent different sounds in words, the child who is blind can be taught to use differently shaped blocks.

Children with severe physical disabilities who use alternative communication systems can be presented with materials that are appropriate to their communication abilities and devices. For example, the class teacher can ask the child closed-set questions requiring a yes or no response (using head nodding/shaking, eye blink cues, etc., if necessary) to auditory stimuli (e.g., "Does *ball* start with a /b/ sound, yes or no?"). With some advanced preparation, materials for an eye-gaze board can be prepared to match the class activities, such as having four numbers at each corner of the eye-gaze board so the child can indicate how many sounds can be heard in a word.

Tasks items can be simplified to reduce processing and memory demands for children with cognitive impairment. Using additional picture cues and verbal prompts and presenting instructions in short, simple sentences assist these children.

Teachers should ensure that children with hearing impairment have clear vision of the teacher's face and any visual stimuli presented during the training activities. In addition, teachers should consult with the children's deaf advisors regarding the inclusion of stimulus items that would be easier for the children to hear or lip read during the training activity. (See Chapter 9 for further details regarding working with children who have differing learning needs.)

CHILDREN ACQUIRING ENGLISH
AS A SECOND LANGUAGE

Presenting stimulus items from phonological awareness activities in a child's native language may help him or her develop confidence in attempting a task. Acquisition of phonological awareness skills in languages that are based on the alphabetic principle is likely to transfer to English (see Chapter 3). With the help of a native speaker, a teacher or speech–language pathologist can learn the accurate pronunciation of a limited set of appropriate stimulus words to use in some of the phonological awareness tasks, such as phoneme identity and segmentation tasks. The teacher also would need to understand the sound structure of this set of words to ensure that appropriate responses to tasks are given. Alternatively, a parent, teacher aide, or volunteer helper who is fluent in the child's native language may be available to join the phonological awareness training sessions and present some stimulus words in the child's native language, as instructed by the class teacher. These words function like non-words for other children in the class or group and challenge these children to complete a phonological awareness task for unknown words.

CLASSROOM ACOUSTIC CONSIDERATIONS

During the implementation of phonological awareness intervention, consideration must be given to the acoustics of the teaching environment. The classroom and outside environment need to be as quiet as possible; planning phonological awareness instruction times to avoid clashes with music programs or outside physical education programs of neighboring classrooms should be considered. Classroom sound-field amplification systems designed to project the teacher's voice evenly around a classroom (and ensure that children receive a clear auditory signal from the teacher's voice, no matter where they are seated) may be particularly beneficial during class phonological awareness instruction. Teachers should consult an audiologist to discuss methods of improving classroom acoustics (see Chapter 8 for further details).

SUMMARY

This chapter has focused on the practical application of phonological awareness intervention to enhance children's reading and spelling development. Guidelines for program content and implementation procedures, based on research evidence for effective training conditions, were discussed. The following points highlight areas discussed in the chapter:

- Phonological awareness instruction should be viewed within the context of a comprehensive language program to develop reading and writing. It is but one part of a range of instructional programs and language experiences a child will need in order to achieve literacy success.
- There is strong research evidence that phonological awareness intervention can enhance word recognition ability, reading comprehension, and spelling performance.

- Phonological awareness intervention may comprise a wide variety of activities and instructional methods. Research provides clear insight into conditions that enhance the effectiveness of intervention.
- Two important areas to include in phonological awareness intervention are phoneme level activities (e.g., phoneme segmentation, blending, and manipulation) and activities that strengthen children's phoneme–grapheme connections by making explicit the links between speech and print.
- Phonological awareness interventions are useful to the extent that they improve literacy development. It is important that interventions are evaluated to ensure that new skills acquired transfer to the reading and spelling processes.

    Phonological awareness intervention holds much promise for children at risk for persistent literacy difficulties and for children who have struggled to acquire efficient word recognition skills. The proven ability of such intervention to enhance reading and spelling performance for these children necessitates that practitioners carefully plan, implement, evaluate, and monitor phonological awareness programs to ensure that its potential benefits are fully realized. Chapter 8 focuses on these aspects of the intervention process.

8

Phonological Awareness Intervention

Instructional Frameworks

At a practical level, phonological awareness intervention is implemented within three general frameworks:

1. The enhancement of early reading and spelling development in all children.
2. The prevention of persistent reading disorder for children at risk or children experiencing early reading difficulties.
3. An intervention method for older children and adolescents with reading and spelling disabilities.

This chapter describes each of these frameworks. Practical suggestions for phonological awareness activities that can be included within each framework are presented.

In the following material, each of these frameworks is described individually, but there are many overlapping principles and ideas among the frameworks. A five-step structure (see Figure 8.1) can be applied to these three frameworks, with each step building upon and interacting with the previous step. This type of structure helps to ensure that phonological awareness instruction is effective in achieving the desired outcome of improved reading and spelling performance.

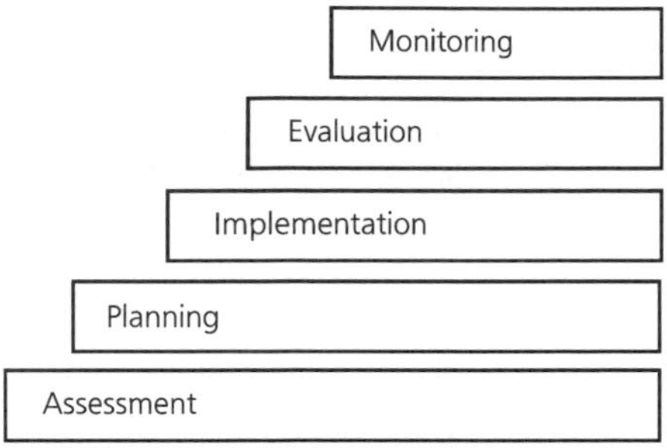

FIGURE 8.1. A 5-step structure for phonological awareness intervention frameworks.

FRAMEWORK 1: THE PROVISION OF PHONOLOGICAL AWARENESS INSTRUCTION TO ENHANCE READING AND SPELLING DEVELOPMENT IN ALL CHILDREN

The aim of the phonological awareness instruction within this framework is to enhance early ready and spelling acquisition of all children in a preschool, kindergarten, or grade 1 or 2 classroom. Phonological awareness instruction within this framework is integrated into the classroom curriculum and is usually implemented by the class teacher.

Assessment

Gathering information on all the children's phonological awareness skills prior to commencing classroom instruction is necessary to establish the benefits of the instruction provided. Assessment of all children also maps the degree of phonological awareness variability within the class and identifies class patterns of strengths and weaknesses that will help direct intervention activities. Assessment procedures such as the DIBELS, or assessments such as the PALS assessments and TOPA that can be administered in groups are useful within this framework (see Chapter 6). Gathering samplings of children's spelling and reading error analyses also provide useful data prior to class phonological awareness instruction.

Planning

In planning activities at the whole class level, developmentally appropriate phonological awareness skills for the preschool, kindergarten, or junior class level targeted need to be considered. Teachers also must have knowledge of how to increase or decrease the difficulty level of a given phonological awareness task to ensure that activities are planned that will enable less able students in the class to achieve some level of success while ensuring capable students are challenged by some tasks. Table 8.1 provides a guide to adjusting difficulty levels of a particular task.

In planning phonological awareness stimulus items from curriculum-based language work or language theme work, the teacher should consider carefully the phonological complexity of the words. Words that are phonetically regular and have simple phoneme–grapheme connections are recommended for young children. As suggested in Table 8.1 children with advanced skills can be challenged by selecting stimulus items that are phonologically more complex.

Implementation

Two approaches to implementing phonological awareness instruction at the class level can be taken. The teacher can (1) integrate phonological awareness activities into regular class activities and language programs in an informal manner, or (2) implement a structured phonological awareness program for a defined length of time. The combination of these two approaches may prove particularly useful. Informal teaching opportunities provide additional practice for children, and if the activities become part of the teacher's regular teaching practices, then phonological awareness is taught and reinforced on a daily basis. A structured program ensures that adequate attention is given to the development of phonological awareness skills for all children and more easily enables the teacher to assess and monitor children who are struggling on task activities.

In the following material, examples for both informal and structured phonological awareness programs are provided, and class activities are described for 5- and 6-year-old children who are being introduced to the alphabetic principle and early literacy instruction.

Informal Teaching

Exercises that bring young children's attention to sounds within words can be integrated into almost any classroom activity that involves spoken language. Simple classroom routines can be utilized to promote sound awareness and knowledge of how a phoneme relates to a grapheme. For example, in dismissing a group of children from class, the teacher might say, "All the children whose name begins with an /s/ sound [holding up a large letter s] may leave the class first today." When integrating phonological awareness into class activities, the important focus is to help children make the connection between speech and print and to make the activity meaningful in relation to early reading and spelling development.

TABLE 8.1. A Guide to Adjusting Phonological Awareness Task Difficulty

Task type	Easier level	⟶	More challenging level
Syllable segmentation	Segmenting two-syllable familiar words (e.g. *teddy*).	Segmenting three- and four-syllable familiar words (e.g., *elephant*, *caterpillar*).	Segmenting unfamiliar multisyllabic words (e.g., *anatomy*).
Rhyme	Rhyme recognition tasks (e.g., "Do these words rhyme: *car*, *tar*?").	Rhyme odd-one-out tasks (e.g., "Which one doesn't rhyme: *mat*, *sun*, *cat*?").	Rhyme generation tasks (e.g., "Tell me all the words that rhyme with *bat*").
Phoneme identity	Identifying phonemes in the initial position of single-syllable words.	Identifying phonemes at the end of single-syllable words.	Identifying phonemes in the middle of words.
Blending	Blending onset and rimes with picture choice (e.g., *c-at* = *cat* [pictures of a cat, hat, and car]).	Blending phonemes to form single-syllable words without blends (e.g., *d-o-g*).	Blending phonemes to form non-words and words with blends (e.g., *s-t-o-p*, *v-a-p-t*).
Segmentation	Segmenting onset-rime units.	Segmenting words with two and three phonemes at the phoneme level.	Segmenting words with four or five sounds, including words with blends.
Sound deletion tasks	Deletion at the whole word and syllable level (e.g., "Say *birthday* without the *day*").	Phoneme deletion task that results in a real word (e.g., "Say *part* without the /p/ sound" = *art*).	Phoneme deletion of non-words and words involving blends (e.g., "Say *step* without the /t/ sound" = *sep*).
Identifying and describing phoneme changes	Analysis tasks using common rhyming patterns (e.g., identifying that the first sound is changing in *cat*, *hat*, *mat*, *sat*).	Stimulus items involving two- and three-phoneme words with wide sound contrasts (e.g., identifying the last sound changes in *art* to *arm*).	Stimulus items with narrow sound contrast (e.g., *tug* to *dug*) and medial vowel changes (e.g., *sat* to *sit*); phoneme changes involving blends (e.g., *stop* to *slop*).
Matching phonological form to orthographic form	Stimulus items that involve simple one to one connections (e.g., *mat*, *top*, *bun*).	Stimulus items involving diagraphs (e.g., *shop*, *teeth*, *chip*).	Stimulus items involving complex connections, such as one phoneme to multiple graphemes (e.g., *f*, *ph*, *ff*; *er*, *ir*, *ur*).

Examples of integrating phonological awareness into class routines and the class curriculum include the following possibilities:

MORNING NEWS

Children's news items can be used as stimulus words for a phonological awareness task.

TEACHER: Grace showed us a photo of her new kitten for news today. Let's listen to the word *kitten*. It starts with a /k/ sound. Hear the /k/ at the beginning of the word *kitten*? Let's clap out the syllables [or parts] in the word *kitten*. Listen for the two parts: *kit-ten*. Let's look at the word *kitten* as I write it on the board. It starts with a /k/ sound. See the letter *k* at the beginning of the word. Thank you, Grace, for telling us about your kitten today [pointing to the word *kitten* on the board as the word *kitten* is spoken in the sentence].

WRITING WORDS ON THE CLASS BOARD

In writing the day of the week on the board the teacher might say, "Today is Monday. Hear [and feel] the /m/ sound at the beginning of *Monday* as you say the word. This is what the /m/ sound looks like when I write it on the board. See the letter *M* in *Monday*?"

HANDWRITING

TEACHER: Today in handwriting we will practice writing the letter *d*. This is what the letter *d* looks like, and this is the sound it makes—/d/. Let's think of some words that start with a /d/ sound. Does *dog* start with /d/? Does *sun* start with /d/? Now let's think of some words that end with a /d/ sound. Does *hook* end with a /d/ sound? Does *fed* end with a /d/ sound?

Let's think of all the objects or pictures we can see in the classroom that start with a /d/ sound [e.g., *door, duster, desk, dinosaur,* etc.]. Now you can practice writing the letter *d* in your handwriting book.

LANGUAGE THEME: FARM ANIMALS

Class language themes or project work are excellent areas in which to integrate phonological awareness activities. The following types of activities can be integrated into a class theme on farm animals.

Rhyme Generation. The teacher holds up a picture of a farm animal, brings the children's attention to the rime unit, and asks them to generate rhyming words. For example:

Pig: *dig, fig, wig, big*
Goat: *boat, coat*
Cow: *how, bow*

Rhyme Speech-to-Print Task. This task involves spelling and reading rhyming words displayed on a board with magnetic letters.

TEACHER: Let's spell the word *pig* with the letters *p i g*. John, can you tell me a word that rhymes with *pig*? Yes, *wig* rhymes with *pig* because they both end with the same sound. Can you please come up and help me change *pig* to *wig* by moving the letters?

Phoneme Identity. Stimulus words from a story about farm animals, for example, can be used to complete phoneme identity tasks.

TEACHER: We read an interesting story today about two children who lived on a farm. Let's talk about some of the things the children saw on the farm [Discusses the story to build vocabulary knowledge and encourage story recall.] I have some pictures from the farm story. I want you to listen carefully and tell me whether these words start with the same sound.

Do *farm* and *fence* start with the same sound?
Do *dog* and *duck* start with the same sound?
Do *cow* and *barn* start with the same sound?

Now let's work out what sound these words start with:

Does *gate* start with an /m/ sound?
Does *gate* start with a /g/ sound?

Now you tell me the first sound you hear in each word. What sound do you hear at the beginning of these words: *farm? dog? sheep?*

Relating Print to Speech. Letters and printed words also can be integrated into the language theme activity.

TEACHER: Look carefully at the word *farm*. See how it starts with the letter *f* that makes an /f/ sound. Let's think of all the words we can that start with an /f/ sound: *foot, fence, fire, phone*. I'm going to write these words on the board. *Foot* . . . *fence* . . . notice how these two words start with the letter *f* that makes the /f/ sound, but look at this word *phone*. We can hear that it starts with an /f/ sound. These two letters, *ph* also make a /f/ sound.

Phoneme Blending. Target words from the language farm theme can be selected to use in phoneme blending exercises.

TEACHER: I'm going to say a word, bit by bit, and see if you can guess the farm animal I am talking about: p - i - g, h - or - se, d - o - g, c - o - w.

Words related to the language theme that contain blends (e.g., *crop*, *spray*, *dust*, *tree*, *sky*, *land*, *stick*, *sty*, *storm*) can be introduced for 6-year-old children or children with more advanced skills.

Phoneme Segmentation. Game activities are an excellent way to practice phoneme segmentation skills.

TEACHER: Let's play a game. John, can you please put the headphones on in the listening corner, and we will practice saying some words slowly. When we've finished practicing, we'll ask you to take the headphones off and see if you can guess what words we are saying. Class, can you remember the name for where pigs live? [Holds up a picture of a pigsty so John cannot see the picture.] Let's practice saying the sounds in the word sty: /s/ - /t/- /y/ [orally segmenting the word phoneme by phoneme].

After practicing the segmentation of a few words related to the farm theme as a class, John is asked to remove the headphones, the class segments the word orally, and John guesses the word (i.e., a phoneme blending task).

Structured Approach

A second approach to classroom activities is to provide structured daily sessions on phonological awareness for a set period of time, for example, 15 minutes daily for a 10-week period. Instruction progresses from earlier developing skills to a focus on the phoneme level. If adopting a skill mastery approach, the teacher would work on one skill at a time, until the majority of the class master the skill, before introducing a second skill level activity. Rather than predetermining the number of sessions spent at each task level, the teacher should move at the pace of the class. Adequate attention in a grade 1 or 2 class program should be given to developing children's phoneme segmentation and blending skills. The program can begin by developing children's general awareness of speech sounds through nursery rhymes, syllable clapping, and discriminating between similar sounds. At the same time, it is important to build children's knowledge of relevant vocabulary and concepts, such as understanding the concepts of a word, a syllable (or part), a speech sound, and a letter, as well as the semantic vocabulary/knowledge required to describe sounds in words, such as *same, different, first, middle, last*. Once appropriate background knowledge and skills are established, the phonological awareness class sessions should follow a structured, sequenced program aimed at developing the phonological skills necessary for reading and spelling, such as onset-rime level skills and phoneme identity, blending, segmentation, and manipulation.

Activities and stimulus items for each class session should be carefully planned to suit the age and ability level of the class. The teacher needs to remember to plan easier as well as harder stimulus items in each activity to cater to the wide range of phonological awareness abilities that may be evident in the class. Speech-to-print tasks (e.g., letter-name and letter-sound matching tasks, segmenting and blending words with letter blocks) also should be incorporated into every session, as appropriate to the children's abilities.

Commercially available resources can serve as useful stimulus items and activity ideas. The teacher should modify resources as necessary to ensure that the activities make explicit the link between speech and print. Using magnetic letters on a white board during the phonological awareness activity and discussing how the activity helps develop reading and spelling skills ensures that the phonological awareness task is meaningful. For example, the purpose of teaching rhyme in a phonological awareness program is not simply for the children to be able to rhyme words, but to help them recognize and hear rhyming patterns in words so that they then can generate a new spelling or read a new word from a known word (i.e., reading or spelling by analogy). Even from a very young age, children's attention can be drawn to the orthographic similarity in regular rhyming patterns (e.g., "*Hat, mat,* and *cat* are rhyming words; they look the same at the end and they sound the same at the end"). For 5- and 6-year-old children, rhyming games can be integrated with manipulating letter blocks to read and spell rhyming word chains, such as changing *cat* to *mat* by changing the first letter block.

Examples of activities that can be included in a structured class program are provided in the following material.

PHONEME SEGMENTATION ACTIVITY

In this adaptation of the "Say it and move it" activity, from Ball and Blachman (1991), the children receive a light cardboard, which they place on their desks. A large box is drawn on the top of the page and four small boxes appear underneath, as illustrated in Figure 8.2. A small group of

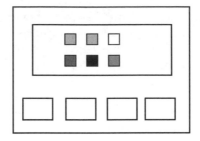

FIGURE 8.2. Phoneme segmentation board for a class activity.

different-colored blocks or counters is placed in the large box. For each phoneme heard in the stimulus word, the children bring down one block from the top box to the smaller boxes below. They articulate the phoneme as they bring down the block. For example:

TEACHER: How many sounds in the word *feet*?

CHILDREN: *f* [bringing down one block to the small box on the left of the page], *ee* [bringing down one block to the second box], and *t* [bringing down one block to the third box].

The children are then encouraged to articulate the word *feet* slowly, touching the colored blocks in the boxes as each sound in the word is spoken. The teacher can demonstrate the activity with an overhead projector and small squares of color overlay, or with the use of a large felt board and colored felt squares.

PHONEME MANIPULATION WITH LETTER BLOCKS

The children sit around a large white board with magnetic letter blocks, or a large felt board with felt letter squares. One grapheme is written on each letter block or felt square (e.g., *sh* is written on one letter block, *ee* on another). Graphemes written on sturdy cards with magnets glued to the back of the cards also can be used for this activity. The teacher carefully selects a small group of consonants and two or three vowels that can be used to make a variety of words to display on the board. The children identify sound changes in words and demonstrate the changes by coming up to the board and changing the appropriate letter square or reading the newly formed word. For example:

TEACHER: This word says *at*. Lewis, can you make it say *mat*? If that says *mat*, Georgia, can you change it to *map*? If that word says *map*, and I change the first letter to an /s/, what word have I made?

The teacher demonstrates the activity, describes the sound change occurring, and provides plenty of prompts until the children develop skills in identifying the sound change and manipulating the phonemes. (This activity is described in detail in the next section for structured small-group activities.)

Materials

Materials used in class phonological awareness training activities for young children need to capture their interests. Having a class hand puppet that "helps" the teacher during phonological awareness activities can serve as a painless, even fun, method for correcting children's responses. For example, the puppet can whisper in the teacher's ear that an answer is incorrect and ask the child to try again. The puppet can demonstrate activities such as phoneme segmentation by clapping out the phonemes or nodding its head the correct number of times.

Letters used during phonological awareness activities need to be clearly presented and of a reasonably large size for young children. For example, graphemes used in phoneme manipulation, phoneme segmentation, and other speech-to-print tasks in the Gillon (2000b) intervention study were created in PowerPoint using lower-case 96-point Century Gothic font (font example). In addition to teaching connections between graphemes and phonemes during phonological awareness training, most kindergarten and grade 1 teachers promote the learning of letter names and/or letter sounds as part of their class program. Many interesting programs for developing children's letter knowledge are currently available. Animated Literacy (Stone, 2002) is one example of a well-structured program that captures young children's attention in learning letter names and sounds through rhymes, songs, gestures, and a variety of literature experiences.

In this program English phonemes are associated with alphabet characters and introduced to the children through (1) stories about the characters, (2) chanting of rhymes about the characters to tunes of familiar songs, and (3) accompanying gestures for the alphabet characters. The complexities of English, such as one phoneme represented by more than one grapheme, are also introduced in this manner: For *oi, oy* phonemes, the sentence example "*Joy oils her noisy toy*" is provided. Once the children have mastered a few letters, they are introduced to decoding words using these letters for reading and writing (e.g., once they know *u* and *p*, the words *up* and *pup* are introduced into reading and writing language activities).

A range of commercial materials specifically designed to promote children's phonological awareness development are also readily available. Useful websites for teachers are rapidly increasing, and searching under the term "phonological awareness" will direct the reader to many commercial resources. The following materials are examples of resources and programs that provide useful ideas and stimulus activities for regular class phonological awareness training sessions:

- *Road to the Code: A Phonological Awareness Program for Young Children* (Blachman, Ball, Black, & Tangel, 2000)
- *Phonemic Awareness in Young Children: A Classroom Curriculum* (Adams, Foorman, Lundberg, & Beeler, 1997)
- *Sounds Abound: Listening, Rhyming and Reading* (Catts & Vartianen, 1993)
- *A Sound Way: Phonological Awareness—Activities for Early Literacy* (Love & Reilly, 1995)
- *Ladders to Literacy: A Preschool Activity Book* (NotariSyverson, O'Connor, & Vadasy, 1998)
- *Sourcebook of Phonological Awareness Activities: Children's Classic Literature* (Goldsworthy, 1998)

(Refer to publishing company websites or search under program names for full details, activity examples, and ordering procedures for these resources.)

It is important to remember that readily available resources should be carefully evaluated in relation to whether they provide the optimum training in phonological awareness (refer to Chapter 7), and whether they are suitable for the developmental level of the children receiving the training. Some of the materials listed have been developed by leading researchers in phonological awareness and include training activities that have proven successful in research intervention studies. For example, *Road to the Code* by Blachman et al. (2000) was developed based on the findings of a variety of phonological awareness intervention studies, in which the activities included in the program were demonstrated to successfully enhance reading development in young children. Similarly, *Phonemic Awareness in Young Children* (Adams, Foorman, Lundberg, & Beeler, 1997) has developed on the foundation of a successful research intervention project.

Evaluation and Monitoring

Teachers can monitor children's progress in class phonological awareness instructional frameworks by testing their skills prior to the start of the program (e.g., beginning of a school term) and retesting these same skills after a defined period of time (e.g., at end of a school term or a 10-week period). Teachers also should note any transfer of skills to the reading and spelling process, whereby children use phonological strategies to help them decode words in print and to spell words. DIBELS monitoring assessment (described in Chapter 6) may be particularly useful for tracking class progress over time.

It is useful during whole class structured programs to have a teacher aide or parent helper assisting those children who are struggling with phonological awareness activities. Children who experience persistent difficulty in the class-structured program should be referred to a speech–language pathologist for assessment of their phonological processing abilities. These children also should be referred for audiological assessment if a recent hearing assessment has not been administered. Children who do not develop age-appropriate phonological awareness skills from a class instructional framework must receive small-group instruction to ensure that these vital skills are developed during the early school years.

FRAMEWORK 2: PREVENTATIVE MODEL FOR CHILDREN AT RISK OR CHILDREN EXPERIENCING EARLY READING DIFFICULTIES

The aim of phonological awareness intervention within this framework is to contribute towards the prevention of reading disorder in "at risk" children. The intervention is implemented in a small group or individual sessions and ideally involves a collaborative approach that includes a speech–language pathologist.Children can be identified as being at risk for persistent reading difficulties for a variety of reasons. They may have:

- Diagnosed impairments that are frequently associated with reading disorder, such as spoken language impairment.
- A familial history of reading disorder.
- A high probability of reading difficulty identified through assessment procedures at 5 years of age, such as those described by Catts et al. (2001; see Chapter 6).
- Delayed development compared to their peers during the first 12 months of literacy instruction.

Educational systems differ in their procedures for identifying children at risk and in their philosophies of what is an appropriate age to introduce literacy instruction or begin preventative programs. Some countries consider a 6-year-old child who has limited reading ability to be in need of intensive reading intervention (e.g., New Zealand's Reading Recovery program). In other countries children are only beginning to be exposed to literacy experiences at 6 years of age. Differences in educational systems and cultural influences must be considered in the provision of preventative programs.

Assessment

Assessment should establish preintervention abilities in phonological awareness, in letter-name knowledge, and in early reading and spelling skills (if the child is in grade 1 or 2). These data can be used to evaluate the effectiveness of the phonological awareness intervention. Assessment of children's other language skills, particularly receptive language and speech production, is necessary to establish what type of instruction the child can be expected to comprehend, the type of vocabulary that will be familiar to the child, or the type of speech errors the child is likely to make on tasks that require verbal responses. Information related to the child's abilities to attend to task, to interact with peers, and his or her motivational levels will assist in planning session delivery models. Chapter 6 discusses further issues related to assessment and presents suitable assessment tools for preschool and young school-age children.

Planning

The content of structured phonological awareness programs aimed at preventing persistent reading difficulties should be carefully planned in relation to the child's assessment profile. Research findings related to factors that enhance the effectiveness of training (as described in Chapter 7) also must be considered when planning content and implementation procedures. Because these children are at high risk for literacy problems, it is critical that they receive phonological awareness intervention that supports optimal learning conditions. If a phonological awareness program is poorly planned and the child makes little or no gains, there is the risk that an instructional method that potentially *could* be very effective in enhancing the child's reading development will be discarded by teachers.

Many activities fall under the umbrella of phonological awareness instruction. Teachers, speech–language pathologists, and reading specialists who are involved in planning structured programs must select program content carefully. Commercial products in phonological awareness should be reviewed before use in regard to their appropriateness to an individual's assessment profile and recommendations from the research findings. Teachers and clinicians should modify or supplement these resources with additional activities to ensure that each child's needs are met. Programs that have proven effective in controlled research studies may be particularly useful to consider as a basis for instructional planning.

Implementation

Following the planning of program content, the phonological awareness intervention should be implemented in small groups (e.g., two to five children) or on an individualized basis. Children with severe phonological awareness deficits require greater intensity in instruction than can be afforded by large group or whole class activities. The program must be implemented for a sufficient length of time to ensure that program content is acquired and, importantly, that transfer of skills to the reading and spelling process is realized. The Gillon (2000b) study demonstrated the successful transfer of phonological awareness skills to reading and spelling tasks by 6-year-old children with spoken language impairments following 20 hours of intervention. The meta-analysis of phonological awareness intervention studies (Ehri et al., 2001) suggested between 5 and 18 hours of instruction may be sufficient, but cautioned practitioners that training time should be tailored to the individual needs of the children. Clinical and teaching experience gained from successful training programs should guide practitioners' decisions regarding training length.

Phonological awareness intervention for children at risk of reading failure needs to be intensive (e.g., 2 hours per week for 10-week period). These children have not developed phonological awareness skills through incidental learning or more informal procedures. They therefore need an intensive period of training to ensure that these skills develop. Infrequent periods of training (e.g., 30 minutes in 2 weeks) are unlikely to produce any rapid change in performance for these children and may disillusion parents and teachers as to the benefits of phonological awareness intervention.

A variety of service delivery models may prove useful for phonological awareness instruction within a preventative framework. For example, a speech–language pathologist may implement the instruction with a small group of children within the classroom setting. This instruction is best provided during a language activity in which all the children are working in small groups, such as reading group time. An in-class small group model allows the children to feel part of a class activity and allows the teacher to view some of the activities the clinician is implementing. Alternatively, a speech–language pathologist or reading specialist may work with individual children or small groups of children on a withdrawal model, either in the school environment (e.g., in a library or interview room), in a reading specialist clinic or center, or in a speech–language pathology clinic. The clinic environment has the advantage of providing a quiet, noise-controlled setting, allows children from neighboring schools to attend the one group session, and allows the specialist to work with greater numbers of children per day (since travel time to schools is unnecessary).

Experienced teacher aides may help implement small group or individual phonological awareness training sessions under the supervision of teachers or speech–language pathologists. The teacher aides must be thoroughly trained in implementation techniques, in particular, the importance of linking speech to print, to ensure that the relevance of the activity for the reading and spelling process is made clear to the children. It is advisable that the teacher aide receives professional development in phonological awareness to gain a broad understanding of its importance for reading and spelling and to build knowledge of the speech-sound system.

Further research is needed to investigate the effectiveness of differing models of service delivery, teaching styles, and interactions to optimize phonological awareness intervention. Current research indicates success for children with severe phonological processing deficits from small group and individual models of service delivery implemented by speech–language pathologists, researchers, special education teachers, and class teachers (the latter have been well trained on the intervention techniques by the researcher).

Evaluation

The phonological awareness instruction provided must be evaluated to ensure that (1) children have acquired program content, (2) the phonological awareness skills have transferred to novel stimulus items not included in the instructional program, and (3) newly acquired phonological awareness skills are transferring to the reading and spelling process. A comparison of postintervention assessment data with preintervention data is necessary to demonstrate both quantitative and qualitative changes in performance.

Other aspects of the instructional program also may be evaluated to assist in the enhancement of future intervention. Such evaluations may include teachers' observations of transfer of skills to curriculum materials, teachers' and parents' perceptions of the value of the instruction provided, teachers' and parents' feedback related to the model of service delivery (i.e., withdrawal vs. in-class) and children's evaluations of which activities they liked in the program.

Monitoring

Monitoring the ongoing development of children at risk of persistent reading disorder in the areas of phonological awareness, reading, and spelling is important. It is critical to establish that any accelerated gains that are evident immediately following intervention are maintained over time and further development is made. Informal monitoring of skills should be ongoing through the class curriculum activities and the phonological awareness activities that are integrated into the class program. Periodic formal evaluation of phonological processing abilities by the speech–language pathologist and in-depth evaluation of reading and writing development by a reading specialist are recommended.

Research indicates that although phonological awareness intervention is effective for many children at risk for persistent reading disorder, there is often a small percentage of the participants in research studies who do not transfer skills acquired in phonological training to the reading and spelling process (Gillon, 2002b). Careful evaluation and ongoing monitoring of written language development can be employed to identify these children and help ensure that other types of intervention are implemented, as appropriate to each child's needs.

Intervention Suggestions for 5- to 7-Year-Old Children

Examples of activities that can be included in the implementation step of a structured phonological awareness program are presented in this section. The activities are designed for 5- to 7-year-old children who are at risk for persistent literacy difficulties or who are already struggling in early reading and spelling acquisition. A variety of commercial programs are also available. Some of these commercial resources have resulted from research projects that have investigated the efficacy of phonological awareness for children with reading disorder. For example, *Sound Linkage: An Integrated Program for Overcoming Reading Difficulties* (Hatcher, 1994) was developed from activities used in the Hatcher et al. (1994) intervention study for children with reading delay. The package contains the phonological training items implemented in the study as part of a combined reading and phonology intervention. Instructions for phonological awareness exercises at the syllable, rhyme, and phoneme levels are included.

The Phonological Awareness Skills Program Test (Rosner, 1999) is another example of curriculum designed for children with identified phonological awareness deficits. The PASP test provides an indication of where a child should start in the curriculum. Training activities to develop the phonological awareness skills expected of 4- to 10-year-old children are presented in the PASP curriculum.

Examples of Activities

Specific examples of phonological awareness activities are described in the following material to provide readers with ideas for developing their own training activities. Some of these activities described are from the *Gillon Phonological Awareness Training Program* (2000c). This program proved successful in rapidly accelerating the phonological awareness skills of children with spoken language impairment who were delayed in reading development. The activity is briefly described and examples of how the activity can be simplified or extended are discussed.

ONSET-RIME LEVEL

Picture Rhyme Bingo. Each child in the group has a "bingo board" illustrating six or eight pictures. Each child selects a card from a deck of picture cards, articulates the name of the picture, and finds a rhyming match on his or her bingo board. A counter is placed over a picture if a match is found.

• *Materials for rhyme bingo.* Commercial rhyme bingo games are available, or practitioners can make up their own boards using clip-art pictures. The following are examples of commonly found pictures in clip-art packages that have a visual as well as an auditory rhyme pattern.

Bingo board picture	Matching card
boat	goat
bat	mat
tie	pie
fan	pan
hose	nose
house	mouse
fish	dish
man	pan
coat	goat
nail	mail
bear	pear
cat	hat
clock	block
rose	nose
ring	king
van	pan
sun	gun
rat	hat
snake	rake

• *Activity simplification.* The instructor moves the picture card along each picture on the bingo board to help the child find the rhyming pair: "Does *pie* rhyme with *boat*? Does *pie* rhyme with *bat*? Does *pie* rhyme with *tie*?"

• *Activity extension.* Once the child has found a rhyming pair, the instructor asks him or her to generate other rhyming words or non-words that rhyme with the bingo board target word.

• *Speech-to-Print Activity* (i.e., making the task relevant for reading and spelling). Letter knowledge can be integrated into the rhyme bingo activity by matching the printed word with its picture and observing the visual rhyme pattern in the words.

TEACHER: This word says *mat* [placing the word *mat* under the picture on the bingo board], and this word says *bat* [placing it next to the matched picture of the baseball bat]. See how the words both look the same at the end. They both end in *at*, but they start with a different sound. See how *mat* starts with an /m/ sound, and *bat* starts with a /b/ sound?

Applying Rhyming Knowledge to a Novel Task. The teacher places a "human bag" of words and an "alien spaceship" of words (non-words) in front of the children and tells them that the alien words are like human words but look different at the beginning. The children are asked to help the teacher read the alien words from the spaceship. The words should be printed in a plain, large font (e.g., 48-point type).

First a child selects a word from the human bag. The instructor and children read the word together.

TEACHER: This word says *cat*. Now here is a word from the Alien spaceship [the instructor carefully selects a rhyming non-word from the alien ship to match the real word, such as *dat* or *vat*]. Can anyone work out how to read the alien word?

The instructor provides prompts as necessary and places the alien word underneath the word *cat* so that the orthographic similarities are obvious.

Other Rhyme Activities. Numerous activities can be used to bring children's attention to sounds within words at the onset-rime level. Additional game suggestions include:

- *Odd-one-out games with rhyming pictures.*

  TEACHER: Throw the beanbag onto the picture that does not rhyme: *ring, king, sing, soap.*

- *Rhyme snap (played like the children's card game Snap).* Picture cards are slowly turned over from a pile of cards and placed, face up, on top of each other. When a rhyming card is placed on top, the children snap their hands down on the pile, calling out "Snap!"
- *Rhyme picture wheel.* Create a spinning wheel of picture cards. Spin the wheel and make up a rhyming word for the picture on which the wheel lands.
- *Rhyming cards.* Create picture cards with one word written underneath each picture. On the back of each card is a list of rhyming words written in clear print; for example, a picture of a king, with the word *king* written underneath, has these words on the back:

ring
sing
wing

The children read the words on the back by using an analogy strategy based on the word *king*.

• *Rhyming chains with letter blocks.* Using letter blocks, the instructor changes the initial consonant of a word to form a new rhyming word and asks the child to read the new word. Alternatively, the instructor calls out a new rhyming word, and the child is required to change the letter blocks to match the change.

Many commercial resources are available to teach rhyming words. Simply entering "rhyming pictures" into a Web search produces a variety of sites for commercial rhyming products, rhyme activities, and rhyming words (e.g., *www.rhymezone.com*). Teachers and clinicians should focus on integrating speech-to-print activities into the rhyme task, remembering that phonological awareness programs for school-age children should focus predominantly on teaching skills at the phoneme level. Although teaching young children to recognize and produce rhyming words is often a useful first step in a structured phonological awareness program, teaching rhyming skills should not be the major focus of the preventative program. Rather, the program must progress to activities that improve the child's phonological awareness skills at the phoneme level.

PHONEME LEVEL

A range of phonological awareness activities at the phoneme level is necessary to develop children's skills in identifying sounds in words (i.e., phoneme identity), blending sounds to form words (i.e., phoneme blending), segmenting words into individual phonemes (i.e., phoneme segmentation), and identifying and describing sound changes in words (i.e., phoneme manipulation). Examples of activities that can be included in structured small group or individual sessions for children at risk are presented in the following material.

Phoneme Identity. Suggestions for games to teach children to identify phonemes in words are:

• Games that involve the identification of sounds at the beginning and end of words.

> TEACHER: Find all the pictures that start with a /b/ sound. Roll a ball over the picture that ends with an /s/ sound.

• Games that require the selection of odd-word-out based on initial and final phonemes.

> TEACHER: The toy crocodile wants to munch the food that starts with a different sound: *pea, pear, pie, soup*.

• Activities that involve the grouping of pictures based on a target initial or final sound.
• Initial phoneme bingo games (played in the same way as rhyme bingo, but pictures are matched if they start with the same sound).
• Picture card games, such as word pairs, memory, or snap, that involve finding pictures that start with the same sound.

Table 8.2 provides examples of single-syllable stimulus words that can be easily illustrated for phoneme identity games. For children who are at risk of developing reading difficulties because of global language delay, words are grouped in semantic categories to enable the integration of phoneme identity activities into language theme work or vocabulary extension work. Letter-name knowledge should be integrated into the phoneme identity games. For example:

> TEACHER: This is the letter *d*, and it makes a /d/ sound. Find all the animals that start with a /d/ sound.
> What sound does *fox* and *fawn* start with? (*Placing out a small group of letters*: f, s, m, sh) Can you find the letter block that makes that sound?

TABLE 8.2. Examples of Stimulus Words for Phoneme Identity Games

Animals	Food	Transport	Sport
Initial phoneme			
dog deer duck	corn cake	bus bike	ball boot bat
cat cow	pea pear pie	train truck	dart dive
fox fawn	salt soup		
goat goose			
Final phoneme			
mouse/horse		bike/truck	net bat dart
cat/goat		van /train	
dog/pig			
Odd one out			
dog deer cat	corn cake pie	bike van bus	ball surf boot
cow cat mouse	soup pea pear	car train truck	bat ball cup (trophy)
fox goat fawn			
goat pig goose			

Phoneme Segmentation and Blending. Segmenting single-syllable words into phonemes using colored blocks to represent differing phonemes is the goal of this task. For example, using a picture with a horse and four carrots, place the colored blocks at the top of one side of the picture, as shown in Figure 8.3.

TEACHER: Here is a picture of a horse. He'd like some carrots to eat. I'll say a word, and I want you to show me how many sounds are in the word. We'll give the horse one carrot for each sound we hear. This horse lives in a barn. How many sounds can you hear in the word *barn*?

CHILD: *B-ar-n* [orally segmenting the word].

TEACHER: [Brings down one block at a time as each phoneme is articulated and places it on a carrot below the horse to represent each sound.] Yes, that's right, *barn* has three sounds: *b-ar-n* [blending the word together but touching each block separately to match the phonemes in the word]. The horse got three carrots to eat.

At the completion of each turn, the teacher clears the blocks from the carrots and replaces them on the other side of the board.

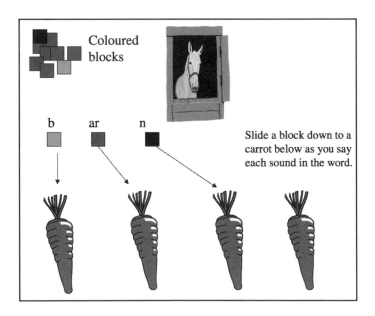

FIGURE 8.3. Illustration for a phoneme segmentation activity.

Additional Suggestions. Talk about what horses like to do and eat and consider related words to segment: for example, *eat, nose, barn, horse, food, hay, run, trot, track, grass, reins.* If necessary, employ a simplification of this exercise: Select two- and three-phoneme words only and prompt by saying the phonemes with the children as you help them move the blocks to the carrots below the horse. Gradually fade out the prompts.

Extension Activity. Choose words with blends to segment, such as:

trot: *t-r-o-t*
grass: *g-r-a-ss*

Speech-to-Print. Segment the phonetically regular words used in the activity by replacing the colored blocks with letter blocks. Make available a small selection of letter blocks and prompt the child with the vowel blocks, as necessary

TEACHER: Let's bring down the letter blocks for the word *barn: b-ar-n* [articulating the phonemes as he or she brings down the letter blocks or helps the child bring down the letter blocks to place on the carrots below the horse]. Now let's slide the letter blocks together and articulate the word together: *barn.*

Phoneme Blending. This activity can be included in the above task by segmenting the word and asking the child to blend the sounds together and say the word.

TEACHER: Now it's my turn to say the word slowly and you can guess what it is: *f–oo–d* [bringing down the colored blocks or letter blocks onto the carrots below the horse and articulating each phoneme].

Other Phoneme Segmentation and Blending Activities

- Segment two-, three-, and four-phoneme words from a storybook.
- Segment words in a picture bingo game. First, the teacher creates bingo boards with single-syllable words that have two, three, or four phonemes, depending on the child's ability level. Then bingo is played in the same manner as described for rhyme bingo, but when the child finds a match, the teacher segments the words into phonemes, using different colored blocks to represent each phoneme.
- The Auditory Discrimination in Depth program (Lindamood & Lindamood, 1973; updated to the Lindamood Phoneme Sequencing Program for Reading, Spelling, and Speech [Lindamood & Lindamood, 1998]

described later in this section) is a comprehensive program for children with reading difficulties that includes a component that teaches children to track sound changes in syllables using colored blocks and small letter tiles. Children are taught to consciously reflect upon the sound changes in each non-word or syllable presented. A modified version of this activity proved very useful with older children with specific reading disability (Gillon & Dodd, 1995, 1997) and is reviewed in the next section. Gillon (2000b) further modified this activity of tracking sound changes in words for 5- to 7-year-old children by introducing large letter blocks (12.5 cm by 12.5 cm, Century Gothic 90-point type) and using predominantly regular real words in the chain sequence.

In tracking sound changes in words, graphemes rather than a letter are written on the blocks (e.g., *sh* is written on one block, *ee* is written on another block). The children are required to identify and reflect upon sound changes in two-, three-, and four-phoneme words with the use of both colored blocks and letter blocks. For example, if the word *see* changes to *say*, the child is required to recognize and articulate that the last sound changed in the word. The child demonstrates the change in the sound of the word first with colored blocks and then with letter blocks. Figure 8.4 is an example of using colored blocks to identify sound changes in words.

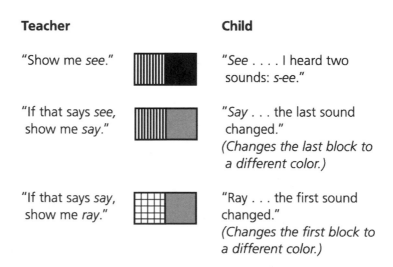

Teacher

"Show me *see*."

"If that says *see*, show me *say*."

"If that says *say*, show me *ray*."

Child

"*See* . . . . I heard two sounds: *s-ee*."

"*Say* . . . the last sound changed."
(Changes the last block to a different color.)

"Ray . . . the first sound changed."
(Changes the first block to a different color.)

FIGURE 8.4. Use of colored blocks to identify sound changes in words.

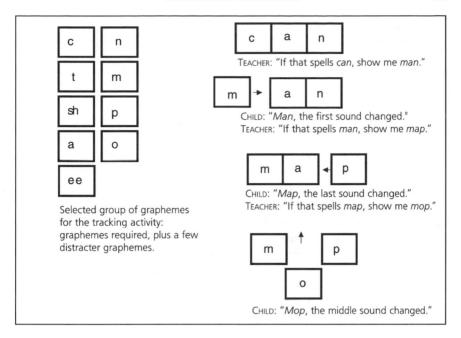

FIGURE 8.5. An example of using letter blocks to identify sound changes in words.

The instructor should demonstrate the activity and give plenty of prompts until the child begins to recognize where the sound change is occurring in the word and can represent this change with a different colored block. When letter blocks are used to make these changes, the teacher presents the child with the appropriate vowel block while explaining: "This says *ay* (*presenting the letter block* ay). Show me how to change *see* to *say*." Once the child understands the process of changing one letter block each turn and can identify where the sound change occurs, display the correct vowel block and a distracter vowel block and begin letting the child select the correct vowel. Figure 8.5 illustrates the use of letter blocks to identify sound changes in words.

Most 5- and 6-year-old children can achieve competency tracking changes in words with two and three phonemes. Four-phoneme words are appropriate only after competency at the two- and three-phoneme level has been achieved. For children who are not ready to make the changes with the letter blocks and then read the new word, the instructor can make the changes with the letter blocks and help each child read the new word at each change. For example:

TEACHER: This word says *can*. I'm going to take away the /k/ sound and put an /m/ sound in its place [changes the letter *c* to an *m*]. Now what word have I made? [Prompt:] *Mmmaaannn* [drawing out the articulation of the word and pointing to each grapheme as the phoneme is articulated].

Table 8.3 contains examples of words and non-words that can be used in the tracking sound changes at the two-, three-, and four-phoneme level. The instructor moves down each list with the child, identifying and describing the sound change that occurs at each entry.

Identifying sound changes in words can be modified for children with speech impairment to help cue their speech errors. Children can be encouraged to ensure that they have a "match" between the spoken and written form of a word. For example, in tracking sounds with letter blocks, if a child made a speech substitution error by responding "*tar*" to the presentation of a printed word with letter blocks spelling *car*, the instructor may respond in the following manner:

TABLE 8.3. Stimulus Item Suggestions for Tracking Changes in Words

Two phonemes	Two phonemes	Three phonemes	Three phonemes	Four phonemes
at	car	can	chop	slip
it	coo	man	cheep	slop
ip (as in *sip*)	boo	map	keep	stop
up	bee	mop	sheep	stock
us	bar	top	ship	stick
uck (as in *truck*)	tar	tap	dip	stack
ock (as in *sock*)	far	sap	dish	slack
ack (as in *back*)	for	cap	fish	snack
ick (as in *lick*)	foo (as in *food*)	hap (as in *happy*)	fig	sneak
if	moo	hop	big	speak
eef (as in beef)	too	hot	pig	spok (as in *Star Trek!*)
eep (as in *beep*)	tie	pot	pog	spot
een (as in *seen*)	pie	pat	posh	slot
an	paw	sat	dosh	slat
in	saw	cat	dish	sleet
on	say	hat	wish	sleep
un (as in *under*)	may	hit	with	bleep
um	day	sit	tith	blop
am	die	sip	teeth	blot

TEACHER: When you say *tar*, I hear a /t/ sound at the beginning. But I'm looking at the letter *c*, which makes a /k/ sound, so I know we haven't got a match. *Car*, hear the /k/ sound at the beginning? Let's try saying *car* with a /k/ sound [pointing to the letter block *c*].

CHILD: Car.

TEACHER: Great, now I hear the /k/ sound [pointing to the letter *c*].

Second example:

> Speech error: sound deletion
> Target word: *bus*
> Child: *bu*

TEACHER: When you say *bu*, I can't hear this last sound [pointing to the letter *s*]. *Bus* has three sounds: *b-u-s* [segmenting the word and pointing to each letter block as it is sounded]. Try saying *bus* with three sounds . . . *b-u-s* [touching each letter block to correspond with each sound in the word].

Third example:

> Reading error: substitution
> Target: written word *cap*
> Child: reads the word as *cat*

TEACHER: Good try. The word starts with a /k/ sound, but let's see if we've got a match. When you say *cat*, I hear a /t/ sound at the end, but I can see the letter *p* [pointing to the final letter], and *p* makes a /p/ sound, so I know it can't be *cat*. Let's see if we can work it out: *ca-p* . . . *cap* [working together with the child].

Intervention Suggestions for 3- and 4-Year-Old Children

Children whose spoken language difficulty is diagnosed at a young age often receive speech–language pathology services well before they enter the school system. This early intervention provides an excellent opportunity for the clinician to help stimulate phonological awareness development and letter-name knowledge in addition to enhancing the child's spoken communication skills (Gillon, 2002a, in press).

Activities that can be introduced in speech–language therapy sessions for very young children include the following:

COMPUTER-MEDIATED ACTIVITIES

Computer software that teaches the alphabet letters and speech-to-print concepts can provide a novel activity for young children. The "word shop" activity from *Winnie the Pooh Kindergarten* (Disney, 1999) teaches children to identity words that start with a target grapheme and phoneme. With the use of a small data projector in a group therapy session, the speech–language pathologist can project the Winnie the Pooh characters in this activity onto a wall and have children run up and touch the target words. Dimming the lights in the therapy room to ensure a strong projected image on the wall helps to capture young children's attention and keeps them focused on the activity being presented. The speech–language pathologist can use the mute sound button on the computer to teach an activity at a slower pace or reinforce ideas presented by the computer image.

PHONEME IDENTITY GAMES

Phoneme Categorization. Sort toys and animal friends by their initial phoneme, choosing toys with wide initial phoneme contrasts. For example:

PATHOLOGIST: This is my friend, *turtle*. *Turtle* starts with a /t/ sound. *Turtle* wants to find a friend that starts with /t/. Let's name other soft toys [such as teddy, mouse, seal] and find the toy that starts with /t/.

Mystery Bag. Into a mystery bag place toys or picture cards of objects that start with one of two phonemes that are represented by letters that are visually different (e.g., *m* and *c*). Select toys that are appropriate to the child's speech production goals. Ask the child to select a word from a mystery bag, identify the initial phoneme, and place beside it a large, poster-size corresponding letter. For example:

PATHOLOGIST: You've found a car in the mystery bag. Can you say *car*? *Car* starts with a /k/ sound, and this letter can make a /k/ sound [pointing to a large, poster-size letter *c*]. Can you drive the car to the letter *c* [child has the choice of *c* or *m*]?

Odd One Out.

PATHOLOGIST: Here is the letter *p*. It makes a /p/ sound. Can you help me make the /p/ sound? [The teacher encourages the child to articulate the sound correctly.] My friend "munching crocodile" is going to eat up all the pictures that don't start with a /p/ sound. Let's listen carefully and be ready to make crocodile eat the pictures that don't start with a /p/ sound.

It is best to choose words with wide initial phoneme contrasts: *pie, pea, pear, scone.* (Here the speech–language pathologist would help the child make the crocodile "eat up" the picture of the scone. When the odd-one-out activity is finished, the teacher asks the child to articulate all the words that started with a /p/ sound (i.e., the words the crocodile didn't eat) and place the pictures on the letter *p.*

The Speech Train. The train stops at each train station but only picks up pictures of words that start with a target speech sound (e.g., /k/). Ensure that pictures with wide sound contrasts are placed at each station.

PATHOLOGIST: Does *mouse* start with a /k/ sound? Does *sun* start with a /k/ sound? Does *key* start with a /k/ sound? Say *k-e-y* [encouraging the child to articulate the word correctly]. Hear the /k/ sound at the beginning?

LETTER-SOUND GAMES

Use large, poster-size pieces of cardboard with one target grapheme written on each piece of card. Place the large letter cards in a line on the floor. Choose three or four target letters that are visually different.

1. The speech–language pathologist tells the child the letter name and sound of each target phoneme (selected in relation to the child's speech production goals), asks the child to repeat the phoneme, and tosses a beanbag onto the corresponding grapheme. ("Talking" beanbags are great devices for holding a young child's attention.) The pathologist repeats the activity, asking the child to drive a car to the target grapheme, push a teddy in a trolley to the target phoneme, fly Superman to the target grapheme—or any other activity that involves the child physically moving him- or herself or an object to the target grapheme. The child should articulate the phoneme at each turn.

2. The speech–language pathologist gives the child a target picture with the word written (in a large point size) underneath the picture, brings the child's attention to the print under the word, and asks him or her to look carefully at the first letter, say the word, and listen to the sound with which the word starts. Next the pathologist asks the child to take the picture (in a trolley, on a skateboard, or via some other such novel means) to the poster-size letter with which the word begins (placed out on the floor). If a target is /k/, for example, the pathologist places large, poster-size letters of *c* and *k* on the floor and explains to the child that both of these letters can make the /k/ sound.

3. Once children have acquired the names of a few letters, these letters

can be linked to printed words. For example, using a white board and marker, the speech–language pathologist writes a word on the board using segmentation squares (i.e., one grapheme in each square), orally segmenting the word in the process and encouraging the children to join in articulating each sound in the word.

> PATHOLOGIST: This word says *mat—m-a-t* (*pointing to each letter as the phoneme is pronounced and asking the children to join in articulating the phonemes*).

> Now I want to make a new word. Connell, can you come up and wipe off the letter *m* for me. [If the child is unsure, the speech–language pathologist helps him or her find the *m* and then lets the child wipe it off the board] Now I'm going to write the letter *b* that makes a /b/ sound. I've made a new word. This word say *bat*. Let's say it slowly—*b-a-t* (*pointing to each letter as the phoneme is pronounced and encouraging the children to join in articulating each phoneme correctly*). Let's say the word together—*bat*.

If a child deletes the final consonants in words, the speech–language pathologist brings his or her attention to the final letter and explains that he or she needs to make a sound for that letter when saying the word.

> PATHOLOGIST: When you say *ba*, I didn't hear this sound at the end of the word (*pointing to the /t/ sound*). Let's try saying the word together with this final /t/ sound.

RHYME ACTIVITIES

A range of activities that brings children's attention to the rhyme unit in words and helps them to make a link between speech and print, using simple rhyming spelling patterns (e.g., *hat, mat, bat, cat, sat*), can be incorporated into therapy sessions.

Teaching Tips

In the phonological awareness activities, select target words based on the child's speech production targets, vocabulary knowledge, and the phonological complexity of the word.

When working in small group sessions with 3- and 4-year-old children, the speech–language pathologist can arrange the children in a semicircle on the floor, sitting on their own mats (e.g., a small carpet mat). The mats help in several ways: They (1) organize the children's positioning in the room, (2) help structure the activities and focus the children's attention (e.g., a new stimulus item is presented only when all children are back on their mats), and (3) helps curb the tendency of some young children to wander around the room during a therapy session. When children are required to stand up and engage in an activity, they should be encouraged to return to their mat after each turn. The mats can be rearranged in a line for games in which the children stand up and throw a beanbag onto letters or picture cards and then are rewarded for returning to their mat.

If possible, a sound-field amplification system should be used for a group session. The teacher should pay careful attention to the acoustic properties of the room, and any distracting noises should be minimized. Young children may have frequent ear infections and fluctuating hearing ability that will affect performance on listening tasks.

It is advisable to avoid spending too long on one activity; rather, changing the activities regularly keeps children's attention and interest in the session. The same goal can be targeted, with different toys and games. Careful observation of children's behavior provides cues signaling the need for a change of activity is required. Discovering what type of toys the children particularly like and, if possible, use these toys in the therapy session is particularly helpful in sustaining participants' attention and motivation.

FRAMEWORK 3: INTERVENTION FOR OLDER CHILDREN WITH DYSLEXIA

Phonological awareness intervention for older children and adolescents with dyslexia must include the same structured approach described for children at risk for reading disorder. Assessment, planning, implementation, evaluation, and monitoring of phonological awareness instruction are all essential. The very nature of these children's reading disorder suggests that they have a specific deficit in processing phonological information that is not resolved by classroom instruction and is resistant to many forms of remedial reading intervention. An informal approach to phonological awareness intervention that is not carefully planned is unlikely to impact significantly the reading and spelling development of children with dyslexia.

Research investigating the benefits of phonological awareness training for children with dyslexia has produced very encouraging results. The severe phonological processing deficit that many children and adolescents with dyslexia exhibit is amenable to treatment (e.g., Gillon & Dodd, 1995, 1997; Lovett et al., 1994). However, the treatment provided must focus directly on resolving the phonological deficit. Working from a deficit model may be uncomfortable for many educators, given that fostering children's strengths (in this context, e.g., visual whole word recognition) and teaching compensatory or supporting strategies are encouraged in the field of education. The research evidence, however, is very clear. *A phonological processing deficit will persist into adulthood, unless it is directly targeted in intervention.* Furthermore, the resolution of a phonological deficit will lead to accelerated growth in reading and spelling for many children with dyslexia.

Assessment

An in-depth assessment of phonological awareness skills that includes the use of well-constructed standardized assessment tools (described in Chapter 6) should be incorporated into a comprehensive assessment battery for children with dyslexia. A collaborative approach to assessment is advocated when working with children who have dyslexia: Professionals such as speech–language pathologists, class teachers, reading specialists, and educational psychologists must combine their efforts and communicate freely with one another. In addition to phonological awareness skills, other phonological processing skills, such as rapid naming and phonological memory skills, also must be assessed. Researchers hypothesize that children with difficulty in both rapid naming and phonological awareness require additional programs, either following phonological awareness training or integrated with it, to build accuracy and fluency when reading (Wolf, Miller, & Donnelly, 2000). In-depth assessment assists clinicians and educators alike in identifying such children and ensuring that they receive appropriate intervention.

Assessment also should establish preintervention baseline performance in phonological awareness, phonological processing, and in the child's ability to use phonological information in the reading and spelling process in order to evaluate the effects of the intervention provided. Assessment probes using qualitative analysis as well as quantitative data are useful in measuring the benefits of the intervention provided.

Planning

Phonological awareness instruction for older children should be seen as one part of a comprehensive intervention program that may take many months to implement. Obviously, a 13-year-old adolescent reading at a 7-year-old level will not dramatically progress to an age-appropriate reading level after a few months of phonological awareness intervention (as has been witnessed in much younger poor readers). Rather, phonological awareness intervention for older children and adolescents should be seen as a *starting point* in their intervention program. The aim of such intervention is to resolve their phonological processing deficit in order to provide a strong foundation on which to build and enhance reading and writing skills. Some remedial reading approaches may have been unsuccessful with these children because they fail to resolve underlying phonological processing problems. Although the program may improve the children's ability to read and write, to some extent (there are very few adolescents who cannot read at all), the children never develop speed and efficiency in reading, and the decoding of print remains an effortful task requiring much of their cognitive resources. This imbalance, in turn, negatively impacts their ability to comprehend text.

Phonological awareness intervention for these children should therefore be designed to develop speed and efficiency in word recognition skills. Activities should target phoneme segmentation, blending, and manipulation skills that require children to hold phonological information in working memory and to efficiently retrieve this information. Such a program must make explicit the link between speech and print and involve the analysis of orthographic patterns in relation to phonological patterns (i.e., develop accurate phoneme–grapheme connections). Older children are likely to know letter names but struggle with the more complex connections, such as one phoneme represented by more than one grapheme (e.g., *ir, er, ur; ee, ea*—Dodd & Gillon, 1996).

Program content needs to address these issues by first teaching children to rapidly and accurately hear and identify phonemes within words, and then to develop fluency in recognizing these patterns in their orthographic forms. Repetition is required to develop children's speed and efficiency in these tasks, and careful planning is required to balance the need for adequate repetition with enough novel stimulation to maintain children's interest and motivation to improve their processing abilities. Children need to be actively engaged in reflecting on and discussing phoneme changes in words and how speech relates to print. It is important to develop their metacognitive strategies, which will enable them to apply phonological processing skills to the reading and spelling process. Thus, more than just drill practice on a phoneme or orthographic analysis task is required. Children need to understand the skills involved and how the new skills will assist them in recognizing words in print or will help them spell a new word.

Practitioners should seek programs or program activities that are strongly based on research or have proven effective in controlled intervention studies. The field of reading disorder has been fraught with many interventions that lack a research basis and frequently result in a failure to develop fluent and efficient reading skills in children.

Implementation

Phonological awareness intervention for older children requires small group or individual work on a withdrawal basis. The persistent nature and severity of these children's phonological processing deficits demand an intensive intervention model, such as two 1-hour sessions per week or daily practice. Older children and adolescents with learning difficulties may have a poor self-concept and appear resistant to further intervention, given their history of difficulty with, and failure in, acquiring written language. Unfortunately, some older poor readers may engage in school truancy or exhibit associated delinquency problems that will hamper intervention attempts (see Maughan, 1994, for an overview of behavioral issues in relation to reading disability). Therefore, the speech–language pathologist or reading specialist must create a positive and motivating environment in which to implement phonological processing intervention.

A combination of small group work and individual work has proven effective in developing phonological processing skills in older children. The children and adolescents with reading disorder who made significant gains in reading accuracy and comprehension following intervention in the Gillon and Dodd studies (1995, 1997) received 2 hours of phonological processing intervention each week for a 10-week period. Some of the participants spent 1 hour per week in a group session with five children of a similar age; they spent the second session each week in an individual session. These children attended the sessions after school at a university literacy clinic in a speech–pathology department. Group sessions involved the children in group game activities and capitalize on the competitive nature that older children and young adolescents often display. Individual sessions focused on individual needs and allowed students intense practice in the skills required for the group game activities.

Other researchers also have proposed intensive models of small group service, delivery for developing phonological processing skills in children with dyslexia. Wolf et al. (2000) proposed an intensive pull-out program wherein the children and the teacher work to create a positive classroom-type atmosphere for a small group of children who receive a daily curriculum in phonological and orthographic processing. The curriculum, referred to as RAVE-O (Retrieval, Automaticity, Vocabulary Elaboration, Orthography), includes 70 1-hour classes. The Lovett et al. study (1994) demonstrated significant benefits from phonological awareness intervention for children with dyslexia between the ages of 7 and 13. The intervention was implemented over 35 training sessions, with each session lasting 1 hour. The children attended the session in pairs, four times a week, at a pediatric hospital or in satellite classrooms at local schools.

Evaluation and Monitoring

Evaluating and monitoring children's phonological processing skill development (as well as other aspects of spoken and written language development) are essential program components when working with children who have dyslexia. The phonological awareness program implemented must be of sufficient length and rigor to resolve the children's deficit in phonological processing. Follow-up assessments are required to ensure that the skills developed during intervention are maintained over time and have transferred to reading and spelling.

As the child's word decoding abilities improve and he or she advances in grade levels, more complex written text will become the challenge. Such text places additional demands on the phonological system due to the need for rapid and efficient decoding of less familiar vocabulary and of words that are phonologically more complex. Monitoring children's development ensures that their phonological abilities are sufficiently well established to accommodate these increasing demands. Class teachers or reading specialists can implement ongoing monitoring at the school level. When regression in phonological processing ability is suspected, further in-depth assessment of these abilities by a speech–language pathologist is warranted.

Programs and Their Content

Comprehensive programs to enhance children's phonological processing skills, as well as their reading and spelling performance, have been developed for children with dyslexia. One such program, the Lindamood Phoneme Sequencing Program (LIPS; Lindamood & Lindamood, 1998), formerly known as the Auditory Discrimination in Depth program [ADD; Lindamood & Lindamood, 1973], has been successfully used in clinical and research studies for a number of years (Alexander et al., 1991; Torgesen et al., 1997). This program uses a multisensory approach to teach children with severe reading disorder the relationship between phonemes and graphemes as well as intensive training in phonological processing skills and training to improve decoding and encoding of syllables within words. The complex nature of the program necessitates a lengthy period of intervention (the participants in the Alexander et al. study received, on average, 110 hours of training), and instructors require intensive training before implementing the program with children.

The Gillon and Dodd series of experiments adapted the tracking of speech sounds section of the ADD program that specifically addresses phoneme blending, segmentation, and manipulation skills. In these experiments the focus of intervention was to resolve phonological processing deficits of 8- to 14-year-old children with reading disorder. When implementing the complete ADD program, children are taught to identify and classify speech sounds according to the auditory, visual, and tactile characteristics of the phoneme, such as labeling *p* a "lip popper" and *t* a "quiet tip tapper." However, the Gillon and Dodd studies utilized the tracking of syllables section of the ADD program without introducing this alternate classification for letter names. The children were taught to represent sound changes in syllable (non-words) with the use of colored blocks and letter blocks. A problem-solving approach was adopted, and the children were required to alter the block pattern according to the changes they heard in the speech pattern and to describe the sound change. The children were encouraged to reflect upon their responses to ensure that their spoken pattern matched the written pattern (or when spelling, to check that the written pattern matched the spoken pattern). That is, the connections between phonological and orthographic forms of the word were strongly emphasized in the training. Speed and accuracy in decoding and encoding, using letter blocks, was encouraged. Game activities were introduced to improve the children's efficiency in using a phonological strategy. In one such game, speed was the focus; "personal best times" were recorded, with points awarded for accuracy in the decoding or encoding of a given set of non-words.

As children gained confidence in reading and spelling the non-words, transfer of skills to real words was introduced. The real words were phonetically spelled words at a similar level of difficulty as the non-words and were selected from the schools' spelling lists. Simple game activities were introduced to give the program variety. This approach proved valuable, and after only 20 hours of training, the children's phonological awareness deficits were resolved. Transfer effects in reading accuracy and comprehension of connected text were clearly evident (Gillon & Dodd, 1995, 1997).

In the Lovett et al. study (1994), the researchers adapted materials from a direct instruction approach and implemented a program they referred to as Phonological Analysis and Blending (PHAB). The 35-hour program consisted of intensive training in phoneme segmentation and blending. In the first part (e.g., for the first 7 or 8 hours), the children were engaged in activities in which they were required to say each sound in a word one at a time (left to right order) and to blend phonemes to form words without the use of the printed form of the words. Following successful learning at this stage, printed words were introduced with the segmentation and blending activities. Children also were instructed in letter-sound correspondences; a skill mastery approach was used to introduce each letter-sound correspondence in a systematic sequence. Children trained in this approach made significant improvement in their ability to use a phonological strategy to decode words: They showed significant improvement in word recognition skills and transfer effects to the reading of phonetically regular real words and to the decoding of non-words.

Further developments in this training approach by the researchers have resulted in a more integrated program referred to as PHAST (Phonological and Strategy Training; Lovett, Lacerenza, & Borden, 2000). This program aims to resolve the phonological awareness deficits of poor readers, strengthen phoneme–grapheme knowledge, and to train students on word identification strategies that they can apply to text reading activities. The intervention is implemented over 70 hours.

The research provides evidence, then, that even though phonological awareness deficits in older children with dyslexia have proven resistant to other types of remedial reading approaches, they can be resolved for many children. What appears to be required is a direct approach that specifically targets phoneme level skills and explicitly integrates the strengthening of phoneme–grapheme connections in relationship to word decoding and encoding.

Treatment Resisters

One type of treatment approach is unlikely to resolve reading and writing difficulties for all children at risk or all children who experience reading failure. Group studies that have investigated the benefits of phonological awareness intervention for poor readers have reported that a small number of children in the study failed to show the gains in reading or spelling demonstrated by the group average (Gillon, 2002b; Schneider, Ennemoser, Roth, & Kuspert, 1999). Research is beginning to identify factors that may contribute to lack of success for some children, such as their competence levels in other linguistic and phonological processing areas (Lovett, Steinbach, & Frijters, 2000). Other variables such as length of training time, type of instructional procedures, program content, service delivery model, teaching and learning styles, motivational levels of the instructors and students, environmental and cultural influences, and any emotional, behavioral, or health issues relevant to the child are all factors that need to be considered when evaluating program effectiveness. Regular monitoring of a child's progress in phonological awareness interventions is important to ensure that adjustments to meet individual needs are made, as appropriate.

SUMMARY

Phonological awareness instruction may range from simple activities to stimulate early phonological awareness development in very young children to complex programs designed for adolescents with severe reading or spelling disorder. This chapter has presented three instructional frameworks that reflect differing aims and populations that phonological awareness instruction may target. Within each framework attention has focused on:

1. The importance of assessment to guide intervention and to establish a child's preintervention performance to enable evaluation of programme effectiveness.
2. The need for careful planning and implementation of program content.
3. The evaluation and monitoring of children's phonological awareness to ensure enhanced skills transfer to the reading and spelling process.

A variety of practical suggestions for phonological awareness activities within the differing frameworks have been presented.

9

Phonological Awareness Development in Children with Physical, Sensory, or Intellectual Impairment

*with Sally Clendon, Linda Cupples, Mark Flynn,
Teresa Iacono, Traci Schmidtke, David Yoder,
and Audrey Young*

Children with physical, sensory, or intellectual impairment frequently struggle with written language acquisition. The child's primary area of impairment undoubtedly contributes to any literacy difficulties experienced. Weak phonological awareness skill development, however, may further constrain word recognition and spelling performance. Consistent with the importance of phonological awareness to reading and writing in children with normal development, consideration must be given to the phonological awareness development of children with diagnosed impairments. It is critical to (1) include measures of phonological awareness in a comprehensive assessment of the spoken and written language development of children with special needs, and (2) integrate phonological awareness into intervention plans as appropriate to the individual's abilities.

   This chapter examines the phonological awareness skills of children who have severe speech and physical impairment, children who are blind

183

and use Braille as their reading medium, children with significant hearing loss, and children with Down syndrome. Issues related to the unique features of phonological awareness assessment and intervention procedures for these children are discussed.

CHILDREN WITH SEVERE SPEECH AND PHYSICAL IMPAIRMENTS

It is well documented that children with severe speech and physical impairments (SSPI) experience literacy difficulties (Berninger & Gans, 1986a, 1986b; Dahlgren Sandberg, 2001; Dahlgren Sandberg & Hjelmquist, 1996a, 1996b; Koppenhaver, Evans, & Yoder, 1991; Koppenhaver & Yoder, 1992a; Vandervelden & Siegel, 1999). These children have, at best, a 30% chance of being able to read and write as well as their peers (Koppenhaver, 1991). The difficulties that children with SSPI have in learning to read and spell have been attributed to a myriad of factors, including quantity and quality of literacy-related experiences (Koppenhaver & Yoder, 1993; Light & Kelford Smith, 1993), parent, teacher, and learner expectations (Light & McNaughton, 1993), degree of physical or speech impairment (Barsch & Rudell, 1962; Schonell, 1956), and individual cognitive and perceptual capabilities (Danilova, 1983; Dorman, 1985, 1987; Jones et al., 1996). Knowledge of the importance of phonological awareness skills to reading development has led researchers to examine the phonological awareness skills of children with SSPI and to consider the possibility that poor phonological awareness may be contributing to these children's reading difficulties.

This section (1) provides an overview of literature that has investigated phonological awareness skills in children with SSPI, (2) recommends factors to consider in phonological awareness assessment for these children, and (3) presents a case example that highlights the challenges and potential benefits of phonological awareness intervention for children with severe physical disabilities.

Initial investigations into the phonological awareness skills of children with SSPI focused on evaluating rhyme or homophony judgment ability. Bishop (1985) examined the homophony judgment skills of seven adolescents with SSPI and compared their performance to seven children (matched for vocabulary age) who had physical disabilities but normal speech production. The participants were required to judge whether pairs of printed words (e.g., *won, one*) or non-words (e.g., *cobe, koab*) would sound the same if spoken. No significant group differences were found.

In extending their earlier work, Bishop and Robson (1989) compared the rhyme judgment abilities of two groups of children with cerebral palsy.

One group consisted of 24 children with anarthria (i.e., no speech production) or dysarthria (i.e., severely distorted speech production) between the ages of 10 and 18 years. The control group consisted of 24 children with normal speech production. The groups were matched according to chronological age, nonverbal intelligence, and receptive vocabulary. Participants were presented with a series of 40 cards, each card showing two nameable pictures. The task required the participants to think of the names of the pictured items and to indicate whether the words rhymed. No group difference was found in task performance. The authors concluded that phonological coding is not dependent on articulatory coding and can occur in the absence of speech.

Dahlgren Sandberg and Hjelmquist (1996a, 1997) conducted a more in-depth examination of the phonological awareness performance of children with SSPI. Rhyme recognition, phoneme blending and identity, and word length tasks were used to assess the phonological awareness skills of two groups of children with SSPI, one group aged 5–7 years (Dahlgren Sandberg & Hjelmquist, 1996a), and the other aged 7–10 years (Dahlgren Sandberg & Hjelmquist, 1997). These authors also found no significant differences between the performance of children with SSPI and their matched controls on any of the phonological awareness tasks. However, the children with SSPI had difficulty in the use of phonological knowledge, as evidenced by their poor performance on a non-word spelling task. This difficulty persisted over time (Dahlgren Sandberg, 2001).

In contrast to other research, Vandervelden and Siegel (1999) identified significant phonological awareness deficits in two groups of children with cerebral palsy. The first group included 32 children with anarthria or dysarthria who were reliant on alternative and augmentative communication (AAC) techniques for communication (a communication board is an example of an AAC device). The second group included 32 children who had impaired but intelligible speech. Both groups exhibited decreased performance on eight measures of phonological awareness (rhyme judgment, initial and final phoneme recognition, complex phoneme recognition, phoneme deletion and substitution, speech-to-print matching, non-word spelling, and alliteration) compared to two reading-age-matched control groups of children with no disabilities. The speech-impaired group also scored poorly on the psuedo-homophone judgment and pseudo-word rhyme judgment tasks.

Careful examination of the methodologies and scores reported helps to explain these apparent inconsistencies in research findings. Some studies that reported no statistically significant group differences between children with SSPI and children with normal speech production did report a trend of lower performance and less efficient processing in children with SSPI, particularly on phoneme level tasks (e.g., Dahlgren Sandberg & Hjelmquist,

1996a, 1997). The lack of statistical group difference may be related to ceiling and priming effects. On the nine assessment tasks used by Dahlgren Sandberg (2001), the children with normal speech achieved at or near ceiling (greater than 90% accuracy) on five tasks: rhyme identification, sound identification, word length, phoneme blending, and phoneme segmentation. This ceiling effect may have prevented a significant difference between the performance levels of children with SSPI and their matched controls. Priming effects may also have influenced results. Dahlgren Sandberg and Hjelmquist (1996a, 2001) conducted pretest labeling of picture material immediately prior to assessment tasks. This pretest activity may have simplified tasks for children with SSPI by providing them with more direct access to phonological representations in their memory store. Vandervelden and Siegel (1999) implemented a 24-hour delay to control for such effects.

In addition to controlling for priming effects, Vandervelden and Siegel (1999) incorporated a reading-level-matched control group into the design of their study. This addition provided strong evidence that children with SSPI have underlying phonological awareness deficits that cannot be attributed to a lack of exposure to print. These authors found that the AAC user group demonstrated more severe difficulty with tasks requiring whole word recognition (i.e., access to, and retrieval of, phonological representations). However, within-group comparisons of the AAC user-group data revealed no correlation between speech intelligibility ratings and levels of phonological awareness achievement. Indeed, "even complete lack of speech did not prevent relatively exceptional performance" (p. 207).

The reason some children with SSPI acquire competent phonological awareness skills when many do not requires further investigation. Blischak (1994) proposed that voice output communication aids might be influential in determining success. Researchers have observed that the phonological awareness and literacy skills of children with SSPI are superior in children who have received regular exposure to auditory feedback. This feedback may be conveyed via some form of voice output device or an adult bringing the child's attention to speech–print connections by pointing to each word as it is read aloud (Foley, 1993; Koke & Neilson, 1987; Smith, 1989; Vandervelden & Siegel, 1999). Continued research is needed to more fully explicate the phonological awareness development in children with SSPI and to identify possible factors that may enhance this development.

Phonological Awareness Assessment

Children with SSPI are unique in that the extent of their speech and physical impairments significantly influences the methods available for the accurate assessment of phonological awareness. Some phonological awareness assessment tasks (e.g., rhyme awareness and phoneme identity and segmentation) can be easily adapted for children with SSPI. Tasks that do not require a spoken response have already been developed and used successfully with preschool children (e.g., selected subtests of the Preschool and Primary Inventory of Phonological Awareness [PIPA; Dodd et al., 2000]).

Other phonological awareness assessment tasks, such as spoonerisms or rhyme generation, frequently require considerable adaptation. Unfortunately, this adaptation tends to either increase or decrease the cognitive, linguistic, and motor demands placed on the child, making it difficult for the examiner to distinguish the demonstration of the particular skill being assessed from the impact of other extraneous variables (Blischak, 1994; Vandervelden & Siegel, 1999). Various strategies have been employed to counteract this problem. Some researchers have selected test materials that are appropriate to the motor abilities of children with SSPI but that require as few adaptations as possible (Dahlgren Sandberg, 2001; Foley & Pollatsek, 1999).

Factors to consider in assessing the phonological awareness skills of children with SSPI include the following:

1. Before commencing a phonological awareness assessment, the assessment team must ensure that the child has a reliable and reasonably efficient motor response (Beukelman & Mirenda, 1998). Ideally, this response is assessed using a direct selection technique. Research has shown that scanning techniques introduce additional cognitive and linguistic loading to tasks (Mizuko, Reichle, Ratcliffe, & Esser, 1994). Such demands may negatively impact task performance. Sometimes it is not possible to establish a direct selection method. In these circumstances, the child should be evaluated to see whether he or she is able to answer questions using a reliable and accurate yes/no response system (Beukelman & Mirenda, 1998; Glennan, 1992).

2. Children with SSPI are likely to participate in a longer assessment period than that which is normally required for children. Physical impairments are likely to significantly increase response times; for example, waiting for the child to view all four corners of an eye-gaze board before selecting a response. An extended assessment period has the potential to influence motivation levels, which in turn may negatively impact performance. Vandervelden and Siegel (2001) recognized that children with SSPI frequently need repeated presentation of test stimuli and that testing sessions should be halted and resumed at a later time if children show signs of fatigue.

3. Many of the adapted assessment tasks require yes/no responses. Of course, this means that children who do not know the answer to a set of

questions can still achieve a reasonable score through guessing. For these tasks, it is imperative to check that scores obtained are above chance level so as to avoid overestimating a child's phonological awareness abilities.

4. As in assessment procedures for any child, it is important to provide conditions that allow children with SSPI to demonstrate their best performance. Comfortable and correct positioning of the child, adequate light, minimal surrounding distractions, and a quiet environment are particularly important when assessing children who may be more vulnerable to fatigue.

5. Establishing a stable baseline of phonological awareness performance prior to intervention also may be particularly important for children with SSPI. Related to fatigue and motivational factors, these children's performances may vary from day to day. Thus designing short assessment probe tasks that can be repeated on two or three occasions to confirm whether a skill is indeed a weakness and therefore requires specific intervention is important in evaluating the effectiveness of the intervention provided.

6. When adapting a task from a standardized phonological awareness test, additional training items to those provided in the test may be necessary. It is important to ensure that the child understands the task and that his or her response mode is reliable.

Issues discussed in the evaluation of children's phonological awareness development (see Chapter 6) are also relevant for children with SSPI. Additional considerations and suggestions for adapting assessment tasks are provided in this section.

Word Decoding and Encoding Assessment

To establish the need for phonological awareness for school-age children, evaluation of the children's word decoding and encoding abilities is recommended. A number of published reading tests are available to evaluate word identification skills. Many require a simple pointing response or can be adapted easily to allow for alternative response modes (Beukelman & Mirenda, 1998). The Burt Word Reading Test (Gilmore et al., 1981) is a word identification assessment that consists of a series of words graded in order of difficulty. The test requires the child to read words across a test sheet until 10 consecutive errors are made. The test can be adapted using a strategy suggested by Erikson and Koppenhaver (2001): For each target word, three distracter words that begin with the same letter and are of similar length can be provided. For example, "Show me the word that says *for*: *fun, for, fox, far.*" Vandervelden and Seigel (1999) also have assessed nonword reading in this manner: "Show me the word that says *gop*: *gop, saf, mot.*"

The performance of children with SSPI on such an adapted version of the word identification task should be interpreted with caution, however. The task requires children to match speech to print but does not require them to access their own phonological representation. The adult provides the speech, and the child links it to the print. This process is the exact opposite of what occurs when children with typical development read.

Spelling skills can be assessed through the use of published spelling tests or the collection of written language samples. Spelling responses should be analyzed at the sub-word level rather than scored only as correct or incorrect. The examiner should evaluate the accuracy of specific phoneme–grapheme connections. Such analysis is important for AAC users. Some children may be unable to correctly spell entire words, but they may be able to identify the first letter in words. This skill would make them appropriate candidates for word prediction or word menu selection techniques (Beukelman & Mirenda, 1998).

Non-word reading and spelling tasks provide insights into whether children with SSPI are relying solely on visual information in word recognition or whether they can use phonological information to decode novel or unfamiliar words. Vandervelden and Siegel (2001) found that the ability of children with SSPI to match spoken non-words to print is a strong predictor of reading ability.

Letter-Name and Letter-Sound Knowledge Assessment

In evaluating letter–name and letter–sound knowledge in children with SSPI the examiner should ask the child to look at, or point to, specific letters by name (e.g., "Show me the letter s") and to identify them by sound (e.g., "Show me the letter that makes the /s/ sound"). Children with limited physical abilities can be asked to select the correct letter from a limited number of choices (Glennan, 1997). The literacy screening tool developed by the Kennedy Krieger Institute limits the assessment set to the following letters: A, D, E, I, P, R, S, and T. They recommend a selection of letters that can be combined to form a variety of words. The same letters also can be used to evaluate spelling skills (Glennan, 1992, 1997).

Phonological Awareness Tasks

A variety of subtests from standardized tests of phonological awareness that require yes/no responses or pointing responses may be used in assessing the phonological awareness development in children with SSPI (see Chapter 6 for test descriptions). Examples of tasks that may be useful to include in an assessment battery for children with SSPI include the following:

1. Identifying the number of syllables or phonemes in words by pointing to a choice of four appropriate numbers on an eye-gaze board.
2. Identifying with a yes/no response whether word pairs presented verbally rhyme.
3. Selecting from a choice of three or four words (represented by pictures):
   - "Which word doesn't rhyme: *cat, bag, mat, hat*?"
   - "Which word starts with a /b/ sound: *dog, man, boat*?"
   - "Which word starts with a different sound: *sun, fork, soap*?"
4. Selecting the picture that matches a word when sounds are blended together. For example: "Which word am I saying: *b . . . a . . . t* [pictures of a bat, ball, bag are presented]."
5. Identifying sound changes in words. For example, identifying that the last sound changes from /r/ to /t/ in *man* and *mat* (see case example on p. 193).

Intervention

Little is known about the effectiveness of phonological awareness intervention for children with SSPI, but it is generally considered that these children benefit from the same type of literacy instruction that is provided to children without disabilities (Erikson & Koppenhaver, 1995). It is therefore plausible that phonological awareness intervention that has proven successful for children with reading disorder also will be useful for children with SSPI who have poor word decoding abilities. Foley (1993) and Nelson (1992) have cautioned educators against assuming that children with SSPI will absorb phoneme awareness skills through informal exposure. Often, these children have not acquired the rich experiential language base that is a necessary foundation for the literacy learning process (Foley, 1993). They also have had little or no experience of producing speech patterns orally and therefore may need more explicit instruction and focused practice in order to recognize the links between speech and print (Nelson, 1992).

The integration of structured and systematic phonological awareness intervention (based on an individual's assessment profile) into literacy programs for children with SSPI addresses some of the concerns raised in the literature regarding literacy instruction. Observational studies conducted in classroom settings have indicated that children with SSPI receive reading and writing instruction that is quantitatively and qualitatively different from that which is received by their peers with typical development (Koppenhaver & Yoder, 1993). Unfortunately, for children with SSPI, the "provision of consistent instruction based on an appropriate theoretical framework has probably been the exception rather than the rule" (Foley, 1993, p. 30).

Four case studies have contributed valuable information to our understanding of successful literacy programs that improve the reading and writing outcomes for children with SSPI (Blischak, 1994; Erikson & Koppenhaver, 1995; Erikson, Koppenhaver, Yoder, & Namce, 1997). The authors identified key principles that underlie effective instructional programs. These principles include (1) communicating high expectations of the children's ability to succeed in reading and writing, (2) demonstrating team commitment and collaboration, (3) offering child-directed and child-centered instruction, (4) promoting peer interaction, (5) incorporating technology, and (6) providing purposeful age-appropriate literacy experiences. Phonological awareness intervention for children with SSPI should be one part of a comprehensive literacy program that adopts these principles.

Case Example

The case of Anna, a 10-year-old girl with cerebral palsy, is presented to provide initial insights into the possible efficacy of phonological awareness training for children with SSPI . The purpose of this intervention was to determine whether phoneme segmentation and manipulation skills could be successfully trained in a child with SSPI.

Anna attended a Conductive Education Unit attached to a public school in New Zealand. She received the majority of her education in a unit but was integrated into mainstream classes for a variety of activities. She used a wheelchair and required substantial assistance with daily personal care activities.

Anna's hearing and vision were normal, and she utilized a low-tech communication book with picture communication symbols (Mayer-Johnson, Inc.) in the classroom environment. This book contained starter phrases (e.g., "I like . . . ") and vocabulary organized into various semantic categories. Anna selected a phrase or vocabulary item by indicating the page containing the item was on. Once the correct page was determined, she indicated the appropriate line, then finally identified the item within that line. Using this system, Anna was able to make simple comments and requests.

Anna's educational team regularly presented her with closed or yes/no questions. She was able to indicate *yes* by smiling and nodding or *no* by shaking her head. She was able to use eye gaze to indicate a choice among up to four items presented on an eye-gaze board. She also utilized a Macintosh computer with Discover: Switch software (Don Johnston, Inc.) to complete a variety of educational and communication activities. She accessed the computer using a Jelly Bean switch (Ablenet, Inc.) that she activated with her left knee. Anna used the computer for most of her written language work. Predominantly she wrote using a whole word approach.

She accessed vocabulary from a computer-based replica of her communication book. When a vocabulary item was unavailable, she was encouraged to attempt to spell the word using an alphabet set-up in which the letters were arranged according to frequency of use.

Preintervention Performance

Anna's receptive vocabulary was estimated at a 5- to 6-year-old level (PPVT-III, adapted with permission), and her word recognition ability was estimated at a 6-year-old level (Burt Word Reading Test, adapted). Her teacher reported that although Anna recognized initial sounds in words when reading, she had difficulty with vowels and final phonemes, and she frequently confused words that started with the same letter (e.g., *look, like*). This weakness was confirmed by her below-average performance on non-word reading and spelling tasks. However, Anna scored 100% accuracy on a letter-name and letter-sound recognition task.

Assessment indicated that Anna could accurately identify phonemes in the initial position of words but had difficulty with phoneme segmentation and manipulation tasks. The assessment probes clearly established that her performance was below chance levels on these tasks.

Intervention Activities

Based on the assessment findings, observational data, and teacher reports, Anna's intervention program was designed to improve her phoneme segmentation and manipulation skills and to increase her awareness of the relationship between speech and print. Intervention activities required Anna to identify phoneme manipulations in words and non-words and to identify the number of sounds in words. These tasks were adapted from phoneme segmentation and manipulation activities that have proven useful for children with reading disorder (Gillon, 2000c). Anna received 11 hours of intervention over a period of 8 weeks. Each session was approximately 30 minutes in length, varying between two to four sessions weekly. The researcher (a speech–language pathologist) implemented the intervention program in the speech–language clinic in the Conductive Education Unit. Anna's teacher aide observed and assisted in the sessions. Examples of intervention activities used with Anna follow.

PHONEME SEGMENTATION BINGO

The researcher selected a picture card from the pile placed face down on the table and clearly articulated the name of the picture. Anna was instructed to say the name of the picture in her mind and to think about how many sounds were in the word. She was then asked to indicate the number of sounds in the word using an eye-gaze display with the numbers *1*, *2*, *3*, or *4* in each corner.

PHONEME MANIPULATION WITH LETTERS

Activities were developed using the Hyperstudio (Roger Wagner Publishing, Inc.) computer software package.

Activity A: Identifying Position of Sound Change.

TEACHER: On the computer screen we can see the word *pin*. I want you to change it to make the word *pit*.

CHILD: [Anna activated a switch that moved an arrow horizontally across the computer screen (see Figure 9.1). She waited until the arrow moved across the letter *n* and activated the switch again. The computer program then replaced letter *n* with letter *t*.]

TEACHER: Great work. You changed the last sound, and now the word says *pit*. Now show me *bit*. Which sound are you going to change?

Activity B: Identifying Sound Changes in Words.

TEACHER: That word says *hut*. Now show me *hot*. [Prompt:] Which vowel sound are you going to put in the middle . . . the /ɛ/, the /ɑ/, or the /i/ (short *e*, *o*, and *i* vowel sounds)?

CHILD: [Anna activated a switch that moved an arrow horizontally across the computer screen (see Figure 9.2). until it reached the letter *o*. She activated the switch again, and the computer program replaced letter *u* with letter *o*.]

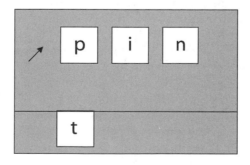

FIGURE 9.1. Activity A example: Identifying the position of a sound change in a word.

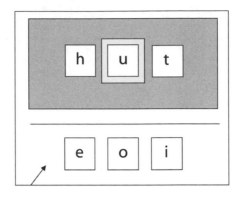

FIGURE 9.2. Activity B example: Identifying sound changes in words.

TEACHER: Great listening. You chose the /ɑ/ sound, and now the word says *hot*. Now show me *hop*. Which sound are you going to put at the end . . . the /p/, the /d/, or the /f/?

Findings

At each intervention session data were collected through assessment probes to document progress in Anna's phoneme manipulation ability. Figure 9.3 illustrates the progress she made. Activity A required Anna to identify the position of a sound change. Prior to intervention, her performance was below chance levels with a recording of only 20% correct on the first assessment probe (see Figure 9.3). Toward the completion of intervention, her performance was consistently above chance levels. Similar improvements were evident for Activity B, in which Anna was required to select the phoneme to make a sound change within a word, as shown in Figure 9.2.

Improvement in phoneme segmentation ability was also evident, and Figure 9.3 demonstrates performance on pre- and postassessment probes that utilized novel stimulus items not trained during intervention. Analysis revealed that post-test performance reflected a high accuracy rate on the ability to segment two-, three-, and four-phoneme words, but she failed items with five phonemes. (Anna did not reach a five-phoneme level in phoneme segmentation training.)

A control measure (utilizing a semantic awareness task of identifying whether a sentence was semantically plausible) was introduced pre- and postintervention to demonstrate that improvement was specific to the phonological awareness activities and not due to general language improvement over the course of the intervention period. No change in the control measure was evident.

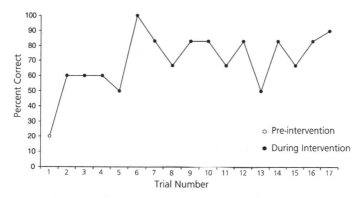

Identifying position of sound change: Intervention Activity A

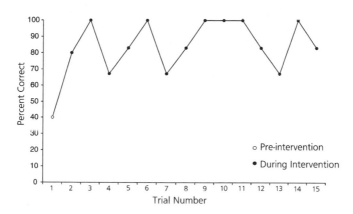

Identifying phoneme changes in words. Intervention Activity B

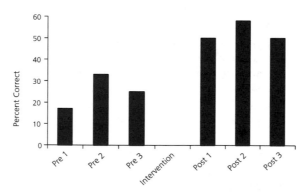

Pre- and post-test segmentation performance

FIGURE 9.3. Anna's performance on phonological awareness tasks.

Discussion

This case example demonstrates that phoneme segmentation and manipulation skills can be trained in a child with SSPI. The results are encouraging. Adapted versions of phoneme awareness intervention activities that have proven useful with children who have a reading disorder also are beneficial for children with SSPI. Following 11 hours of intervention, Anna demonstrated improved ability to manipulate sounds in word, to link speech to print, and to segment words into individual phonemes. Indeed, even after a few hours of intervention, above-chance level performance on assessment probes was evident.

The goal of phonological awareness intervention is to improve reading comprehension and writing ability (via improved word recognition and spelling performance). The transfer effects to the reading and writing processes were not specifically examined in Anna's case, but this question of transferability requires investigation. Gillon (2000b) demonstrated transfer effects to word recognition, reading comprehension, and spelling from 20 hours of phonological awareness training for children with spoken language impairment. It is expected that a similar length of intervention may be necessary for children with SSPI, before strong transfer effects to reading and writing (using computer devices) would be realized.

Challenges

In this case example, the design of appropriate and accessible assessment tasks and intervention activities using computer software was a lengthy process. Each task or activity required careful planning, testing, and modifying to ensure (1) that it was targeting the appropriate skill level, (2) that it could be administered efficiently (e.g., the computer-based activities were checked to ensure they worked reliably and were error free), and (3) that Anna was able to clearly indicate her chosen response. The luxury of choosing readily available, well-designed assessment and intervention programs for children without physical disabilities is currently not afforded to educators working with children who have SSPI. However, many available tasks can be adapted and, with thought and imagination, new activities designed for children with SSPI. Foley (1993) and Paul (1997) discussed further ideas for adapting phonological awareness intervention activities. The importance of phonological awareness to efficient reading and writing performance and the likely benefits of such intervention for children with SSPI demand that continued efforts and resources are devoted to developing this area of assessment and instruction as part of a comprehensive literacy program these children.

CHILDREN WHO ARE BLIND AND USE BRAILLE AS THEIR READING MEDIUM

Braille is a universal tactile reading system frequently taught to children who are blind or who have severe visual impairments. This system is based on the alphabetic principle, wherein a cell of six raised dots is presented in various combinations to represent letters. At Braille grade 1 level, an individual cell represents each letter of the alphabet. At Grade II level the system employs contractions—that is, one symbol is used to represented common letter combinations or high-frequency words. For example, *ing* is represented by one symbol in grade 2 Braille, rather than being spelled out, letter by letter, as it would be presented in grade 1 Braille (see Pring, 1994, for examples of words in contracted and uncontracted Braille cells).

Debate has arisen regarding the appropriateness of teaching Braille to children who are integrated into mainstream education and its use in an age of technological wizardry (Green, 1996). New technology, such as talking computers and speech recognition devices, has allowed children to access information without the use of written language. However, Braille is still viewed by many as an "educational priority" for children with severe visual impairment (Swenson, 1991, p. 217), and its continued use as a reading medium is strongly supported in the literature (Johnson, 1996; Wittenstein & Pardee, 1996). Integrating whole language literacy principles into Braille has been encouraged (Lamb, 1996), and the advantages and pleasures afforded by meaningful literacy experiences are made available to many children with severe visual impairments through competency in Braille.

As with any reading system, some children struggle to learn Braille despite favorable learning conditions and adequate exposure to instruction. Given that Braille is based on the alphabetic system and has many similarities to the sighted reading process, differing primarily at the sensory and stimulus input level (Sowell & Sledge, 1986), it is plausible to consider that weak phonological processing skills would contribute to a child's difficulty in acquiring Braille literacy. Poor readers with severe visual impairments may have a linguistic basis for their lack of reading progress, in addition to any obstacles posed to accessing print by their limited vision or lack of vision (Gillon & Young, 2002). Pring (1982) suggested that the main information-processing tasks in reading are essentially the same, irrespective of whether the input stimulus is visual or tactile (Pring, 1982). Pring demonstrated that Braille reading is influenced, at least to some extent, by the reader's ability to generate a phonological representation of the word from the tactile stimulus. That is, a level of phonological mediation may occur between the child feeling the Braille cells and accessing the meaning of the word. Just as phonological awareness skills have been shown to help facilitate this phonological mediation process in sighted children, so too may phonological awareness knowledge serve as a bridge between the tactile stimulus for a word and its spoken representation for children who are blind.

It is important, therefore, to understand the relationship between phonological awareness and Braille literacy and to investigate assessment and intervention practices that are appropriate for users of Braille. This section discusses the phonological awareness development of children who are blind, suggests how phonological awareness assessment tasks can be adapted for this population, and presents a case example of an 11-year-old boy struggling to acquire Braille literacy who was helped by phonological awareness intervention.

In a case study report, Pring (1994) tested a 5-year-old British child, Becky, on measures of rhyme, syllable, and phoneme segmentation, phoneme identity, and non-word repetition ability. Becky had congenital blindness but no other physical, cognitive, or sensory difficulties. The child performed well on early developing phonological awareness tasks such as rhyme production and syllable segmentation and showed developing knowledge at the phoneme level. With the exception of her difficulty in rhyme recognition, this child showed good knowledge of phonological awareness for her age. Becky was successful in learning Braille to read and spell, and at 7 years of age, her literacy skills were similar to children with normal vision.

In contrast, Dodd and Conn (2000) demonstrated that the performance of British children who were blind was inferior to their peers with normal vision on reading and some phonological awareness tasks. In this study the abilities of 15 children who were blind (ages 7–12 years) were compared with 15 chronologically age-matched children with normal vision on phonological awareness, reading, and spelling tasks. The children who were blind performed below their peers on reading measures and showed difficulty on complex phoneme awareness and phonological use tasks. They did, however, perform at an age-appropriate level on a phoneme deletion task (e.g., "Say hill without the /h/ sound") and were competent spellers of real words. Dodd and Conn (2000) hypothesized that the use of Braille contractions influences children's ability to segment words into phonemes. The children were better at segmenting words and non-words into phonemes that did not involve contractions.

Gillon and Young (2002) investigated the phonological awareness skills of 19 New Zealand children who are blind and used Braille as their reading medium. These children were between 7 and 15 years of age, and most of the participants were mainstreamed into regular classes at schools in their hometown. They received intensive teacher aide support and regular support from their visual resource teacher.

The participants typically acquired knowledge of Braille through the following process: The children received Braille tactile training using the Mangold Development Program of Tactile Perception and Braille Letter Recognition (Mangold, 1977) and were taught to read and write the Braille alphabet code. The participants received one of two approaches to the introduction of grade 2 Braille, depending on their teacher's experience and beliefs. In the first approach the children were taught grade 1 Braille until they reached a reading age of around 7 years and were then introduced to grade 2 Braille. In the second approach the children were introduced to grade 2 Braille directly following the tactile and alphabet training. A structured spelling program was emphasized in the teaching of Braille. The children worked through the list from the Essential Words for Spelling and Reading (a list of high-frequency words) produced by the New Zealand Council for Educational Research. The primary school children (7–12 years old) in the study were exposed to a "whole language" approach to reading and writing in the classroom context. The visual resource teachers or, in some instances, the teacher aides translated class and group stories into Braille as appropriate to the child's learning.

Using the Braille standardized version of the Neale Analysis of Reading Ability (NARA), reading assessments indicated that seven participants were reading at a level well above their chronological age when compared to the normative data for Braille users (Greaney, Hill, & Tobin, 1998). The remaining 12 participants showed delayed reading accuracy and comprehension development. A strong relationship between phonological awareness ability and Braille reading accuracy and reading comprehension performance was evident. The children who read well below age expectation levels also were delayed in their ability to understand the sound structure of spoken language at the phoneme level and in their ability to use phonological knowledge in the reading process.

At a group level, the participants showed a pattern of strength and weakness in their phonological awareness development that could be predicted from developmental patterns of children with normal vision. Consistent with typical development, children who are blind showed proficiency in rhyme and syllable awareness tasks and more difficulty with tasks at the phoneme level, particularly complex phoneme analysis tasks.

The second part of the Gillon and Young (2002) study employed a reading-age-matched design to control for the effects of reading experience on phonological awareness development. The 12 children who were blind and reading below age expectation were individually matched for gender and the number of words correctly read on the Burt Word Reading Test to sighted children with typically developing language skills. The children who were blind were, on average, 3 years older than the children with normal vision. Statistical analysis revealed no significant differences ($p < .05$)

between groups on tasks tapping phonological awareness at the phoneme, syllable, and phonological use levels. There was a significant group difference, however, on the rhyme task, with the children who were blind performing significantly better at recognizing whether spoken word pairs rhymed.

These results suggest that the reciprocal relationship between phonological awareness and reading acquisition reported for children with normal vision (discussed in Chapter 3) is also evident in Braille reading. The reading match design demonstrated that phoneme awareness skills of the children who are blind were consistent with their abilities to decode Braille. Developing competencies in Braille word naming may facilitate later developing skills, such as phoneme segmentation and manipulation. The good Braille readers achieved standard scores within or above the average range for their age, when compared to sighted children on complex phonological tasks. A reciprocal relationship, however, also would suggest that training to strengthen young Braille readers' phonological awareness skills would significantly enhance their Braille reading development. Further research is needed to investigate this possibility.

Phonological Awareness Assessment

Many phonological awareness tasks rely on auditory rather than visual input and therefore can be easily administered to children who are blind (see Chapter 6 for a description of useful phonological awareness tests). In the Gillon and Young study (2002), the syllable segmentation, rhyme recognition, phoneme detection and segmentation, and spoonerism tasks were administered from the QUIL (described in Chapter 6) without adaptation. The reading non-word subtest was adapted to a grade 1 Braille format, and the children were asked to orally spell the non-words in the spelling non-word task.

As a further measure of participants phoneme awareness and auditory discrimination abilities, Gillon and Young (2002) adapted the Lindamood Auditory Conceptualization Test (Lindamood & Lindamood, 1979). This test was adapted by using large-shaped blocks instead of colored blocks to identify whether the sounds heard were the same or different and to identify the sound changes in syllable patterns. The children were trained in the use of the blocks prior to the administration of the test (e.g., the children were trained to identify the different shapes of circle, square, triangle, rectangle, and hexagon), place the shapes in a row from left to right, and identify whether the shapes were the same or different.

Educators also may consider adapting or devising assessment tasks that utilize objects of the target stimulus rather than pictures. For example, an assessment probe for phoneme identity ability may include the child feeling three toy objects such as a ball, box, and car, as the examiner names the toys. The examiner could then ask the child to identify which word starts with a different sound. The use of additional sensory information through touching the objects may assist younger children in completing a task.

Intervention

Very little is known about the benefits of phonological awareness intervention for children using Braille. Well-controlled intervention studies have yet to be conducted to provide strong evidence of the usefulness of phonological awareness for this population. A case study, however, undertaken by Young and Gillon (2002), provides initial insights into the potential benefits of phonological awareness intervention for children who are blind. The case study aimed to measure the phonological awareness abilities of a child who had failed to learn to read using Braille and to examine whether any identified deficits were amenable to treatment.

Case Example

James (a pseudonym) was a 12 year-old boy who had had a significant visual impairment from the age of 4 years due to retinal dystrophy. His hearing was normal, and he had no physical impairments. James had a history of delayed speech and language development and had received periodic speech and language therapy from the age of 3 years, 6 months. His receptive language and expressive phonological impairments were largely resolved by 6 years of age, but he received further speech–language pathology intervention at 9 years to address pragmatic language difficulties and persisting minor speech errors. He showed pronunciation difficulties on multisyllable words and *f* for *th* substitution.

Educational History

James attended kindergarten and a mainstream school during his early school years. At this tage he was able to see very large print (print size N80) and was able to follow the classroom literacy program. He enrolled in a visual resource unit in his hometown at the age of 8 years. Braille was introduced at the unit, and the instruction was based on the Mangold (1977) approach. Further deterioration in his vision occurred, and he became unable to read print. His literacy program therefore focused solely on Braille.

Commencement of the Study

At 11 years of age, James failed to read any connected text using Braille. From a list of 26 high-frequency words used in his Braille program, he read only two words correctly. Assessment of his phonological awareness skills indicated significant deficits, particularly in phoneme analysis and manipulation tasks. Weakness in syllable segmentation was apparent, but his knowledge of spoken rhyme was age appropriate.

Assessment of his decoding skills showed severe deficits, and he was unable to read any Braille non-words. Examples of his non-word reading attempts included: *zug* read as *bat*; *sep* read as *light*; *hud* read as *yook*; *gluff* read as *kick*. From a list of 30 non-words, only four of his responses started with the same sound as the stimulus non-word, and 61% of his responses contained none of the sounds or letters of the stimulus items.

Intervention

A phonological processing skills intervention program was planned for James to resolve his deficits and examine the effects of this type of intervention on Braille literacy. The implemented program (Young & Gillon, 2002) drew heavily on activities from the Gillon and Dodd (1997) phonological processing skills intervention program for older children with specific reading disability and the Gillon Phonological Awareness Training Program (Gillon, 2000c). The intervention consisted of two main components: intensive training in phoneme awareness (analysis, phoneme synthesis and manipulation) and explicit teaching in linking speech to the Braille cells. Games typically played with colored pictures were replaced with toy objects that James could easily recognize by touch, or an auditory presentation of the stimulus was given. Tracking sound changes with colored blocks, as occurred in other programs (Lindamood & Lindamood 1998; Gillon, 2000c), was adapted to tracking sounds with shaped blocks. For example:

> "Show me how many sounds in *slip*": James was required to place four different shapes beside each other to represent the four phonemes.
> "That says *slip*, now show me *slit*": James was required to recognize that the last sound changed by changing the last shape.

Tracking sound changes in reading and spelling was completed in the same manner, except Braille phoneme cards replaced the shaped blocks. Individual Braille cell cards using grade 1 Braille were used (e.g., *sh* on one card, *s* on another; Young & Gillon, 2002).

James received 25 hours of phonological processing skills training over a 4-month time period. Each session was 1 hour in length and, when possible, were given twice weekly. The therapy was administered at the speech–language clinic on an individual basis. James continued to receive his regular class program but did not receive any other type of specialist intervention or additional reading assistance during the phonological awareness intervention period. Following the intervention James was reassessed on two occasions: at 2 weeks postintervention and 6 months postintervention. Between these two postintervention assessments, James suffered from glandular fever. He therefore did not receive any schooling for 4 months, including the summer break.

The same literacy and phonological awareness measures administered prior to intervention were given. None of the test stimulus items had been practiced in the training sessions. His performance on the three assessment trials (preintervention, immediately following intervention, and 6 months postintervention) is shown in Table 9.1.

TABLE 9.1. James's Phonological Awareness Performance (Percentage Correct) and Reading Performance

Task	Pre-intervention assessment	2 weeks post-intervention	6 months post-intervention
Phoneme awareness[a]	32.4	53	53
Phonological use	4	37.5	29.2
Spoonerism	0	65	85
LAC test (adapted)[b]	39	82	64
Syllable awareness (untrained)	41.6	41.6	50
CVC non-word reading (e.g., *vab*)	0	100	100
CCVC (e.g., *plob*)	0	60	90
Vowel rule (e.g., *pute*)	0	40	60
High-frequency word list	1	100	100
Burt word reading	5 words read correctly	27 words read correctly	28 words read correctly
Connected text reading (Neale)	Nonreader	6-year level	7-year level

Note. All stimulus items used during assessment were untrained novel items.
[a]Combined score from phoneme identity, phoneme segmentation, and phoneme deletion tasks.
[b]The LAC test was adapted by using shaped blocks instead of colored blocks and James was trained to identify and manipulate the shapes prior to testing (similar to precheck described in the LAC).

Discussion

James, who had a significant visual impairment from the age of 4 years, presented at 11 years as a nonreader. Despite the expertise of classroom and specialist teachers, he continued to struggle at the alphabetic phase. He failed to read any connected text using Braille and could read only a few words in isolation. Assessment revealed severe phonological processing skills deficits at a variety of levels. As with sighted children who have persisting spoken language impairment, James's history of delayed phonological development and language impairment placed him at risk for reading difficulties.

Following a course of 25 hours of phonological processing skills training, dramatic improvement in his phonological processing and reading skills were observed. Follow-up assessment indicated that skills acquired during training had generally been maintained and had accelerated his growth in literacy development (despite no further educational input). Inspection of postassessment treatment data indicated that the training effects appeared specific to the phonological skill areas targeted in training. Phonological awareness ability at the syllable level, which was not trained, showed no improvement during the treatment period. In contrast, awareness skills at the phoneme level showed accelerated growth.

James's improved phoneme analysis and decoding skills transferred to the reading process, and reading growth was evident at both the single-word and connected-text reading levels. Discussion with James and his teachers at the follow-up assessment revealed that he had become confident in his literacy abilities, and he now engaged in Braille reading and writing activities during his leisure time.

Because Braille is based on the alphabetic principal, particularly in the early stages of its acquisition (grade 1 Braille), it is apparent that a phonological processing deficit also may restrict Braille reading development. However, it is encouraging to discover that strategies successfully used to resolve phonological processing deficits of sighted children with reading disorders can be adapted for children with severe visual impairments.

Summary

The desire for children who are blind to acquire reading and writing abilities through Braille has been strongly supported in recent literature (Johnson, 1996; Wittenstein & Pardee, 1996). Despite the rapid advancement of technology, the acquisition of written language is still a vital component for effective participation in a literate society. Understanding possible causes that may restrict a child's acquisition of Braille literacy and working to resolve these difficulties must therefore be a priority for teachers and specialists working with children who are blind. The difficulties some children who are blind have acquiring Braille literacy may not be attributed solely to their sensory loss, nor can they be accounted for by their learning environment. Rather, an in-depth assessment of their spoken language abilities, particularly their phonological awareness skills, is recommended to ensure that they acquire the necessary knowledge of spoken language on which to build knowledge of a written language system. Further investigation of assessment tasks to appropriately identify phonological awareness deficits in children who are blind is warranted. In addition, determining the efficacy of phonological awareness training for these children requires further investigation. Such research efforts will help to ensure that an area of spoken language considered crucial for literacy development in children with normal vision is not overlooked for children acquiring literacy through Braille.

CHILDREN WITH DOWN SYNDROME

Children with Down syndrome exhibit literacy skills of varying degrees. Despite their well-documented cognitive impairments, many of these children can at least read some words at an independent level (Kay-Raining Bird, Cleave, & McConnell, 2000). Significant changes in educational practices for children with severe cognitive impairment has led to increased attention and value being placed on teaching children with Down syndrome to read and write. It is important, therefore, to understand written language acquisition in this population and to investigate variables that may influence successful reading and spelling outcomes. This section reviews literature on the relationship between phonological awareness and word recognition in children with Down syndrome and discusses important issues in the assessment of phonological awareness in this population.

Particular weakness in auditory-phonological processes, including phonological short-term memory, has been observed in children with Down syndrome (Kay-Raining Bird & Chapman, 1994; Marcell & Armstrong, 1982). Difficulty remembering phonological segments severely restrict these children's ability to use a phonological strategy in reading and spelling. Severe phonological memory deficits may hamper these children's abilities to benefit from phonological awareness interventions; redirecting the focus to other instructional methods in reading and spelling may be more appropriate. Consistent with this view Cossu, Rossini, and Marshall (1993) asserted that children with Down syndrome could learn to read without developing phonological awareness. They reported on a group of 10 Italian children with Down syndrome who were matched on reading measures with 7-year-old children with typical development. The reading tasks contained regular words (conforming to spelling–sound rules), exception words, and pronounceable non-words. The results indicated that despite the children's equivalent levels of performance on the reading and decoding measures, the children with Down syndrome performed significantly worse on four tests of phonological awareness. The researchers concluded that children with Down syndrome show evidence of dissociation between phonological awareness and alphabetic reading, in that word decoding can be acquired in the absence of phonological awareness.

However, Cupples and Iacono (2000) discussed methodological problems and interpretative difficulties with Cossu et al.'s (1993) study. The phonological awareness measures used in this study were not designed for children with the cognitive and short-term memory deficits that are characteristic of children with Down syndrome. The children's lack of success may have been influenced by the task type rather than indicating an absence of phonological awareness knowledge (see also, Bertelson, 1993; Byrne, 1993). Furthermore, Cossu et al. did not report directly on the relationship between reading and phonological awareness. Rather, they inferred that phonological awareness and reading were unrelated in children with Down syndrome based on group performance. The possibility remains, however, that within their sample of participants with Down syndrome, superior levels of phonological awareness were associated with stronger reading performance.

To provide clearer evidence of the relationship between phonological awareness and reading in children with Down syndrome, Cupples and Iacono (2000) conducted a correlational longitudinal study. Participants were 22 Australian children with Down syndrome, between the ages of 7 and 10 years at the initial assessment. Contrary to Cossu et al.'s (1993) conclusions, Cupples and Iacono demonstrated a positive association between phoneme segmentation and word recognition. A partial correlation of $r = .52$ ($p < .02$) was obtained on initial assessment (after controlling for the variance associated with phonological memory, chronological age, and listening comprehension), and a partial correlation of $r = .73$ ($p < .001$) was obtained on follow-up assessment 7–12 months later. The finding of a positive and stable association between reading and phonological awareness suggests that phonological awareness does contribute to literacy development in children with Down syndrome.

Subsequent research has provided further support for this position:

1. Cardoso-Martins, Michalick, and Pollo (2002) demonstrated that phoneme detection scores were associated with reading ability in Brazilian children with Down syndrome, after controlling for variation in chronological age, letter knowledge, and intellectual ability.
2. Snowling, Hulme, and Mercer (2002) reported significant correla-

tions between syllable segmentation, phoneme identity, and reading performance in British children with Down syndrome between the ages of 6 and 17 years.
3. Boudreau (2002) found that onset-rime and phoneme blending skills, as well as phoneme alliteration performance, were predictive of word recognition ability in children from the United States with Down syndrome.
4. Gombert's (2002) analysis revealed a significant correlation between a metalingusitic composite score (i.e., phoneme spelling, segmentation, and deletion task performances) and reading ability for 11 French children and adolescents with Down syndrome.

It may be concluded, therefore, the phonological awareness skills of children with Down syndrome can predict, in general terms, their reading ability.

Of particular interest is the pattern of phonological awareness development evident in children with Down syndrome. A specific deficit in phonological awareness at the onset-rime level has been suggested by recent findings (Cardoso-Martins et al., 2002; Gombert, 2002; Snowling et al., 2002). A careful inspection of the task types employed in research studies provides insights into the differing phonological awareness abilities of children with Down syndrome. Snowling et al.'s (2002) data anal yses revealed the following in relation to their participants with Down syndrome:

1. They demonstrated knowledge of nursery rhymes similar to children with typical development matched for reading ability.
2. Consistent with typical development, they showed more success on a syllable segmentation task (segmenting two-syllable words) than on a phoneme detection task.
3. They exhibited particular difficulty with rhyme. For example:
   • "Which word rhymes with cat: *fish, gun, hat?*" (picture stimuli used): Only one of 29 participants with Down syndrome scored above chance level.
   • "Do these words rhyme: *fox, box?*" (picture stimuli used): Only two of the 23 participants scored above chance level in the first trial of this task and only 5 of 30 participants on a repeat of this task with different stimulus items.
5. They showed more success on phoneme identity type tasks. For example:
   • "Do these words start with the same sound: *cat, cow?*" (picture stimuli used): 14 of the 30 participants scored above chance level.

- "Which word begins with /b/: *bike, car, deer*?" (picture stimuli used): 24 of 29 participants scored above chance.

An important finding from this series of experiments was that, as a group, the children with typical development (matched to the children with Down syndrome for reading ability) performed above chance levels on both the rhyme judgment and phoneme judgment tasks. In contrast, the children with Down syndrome performed above chance level only on the phoneme judgment tasks, suggesting a specific weakness in rhyme knowledge. Gombert (2002) also demonstrated that, relative to the performance of reading-age-matched controls, participants with Down syndrome showed greater impairment in tasks requiring rhyming knowledge than on tasks requiring phoneme segmentation and deletion skills. However, unlike Snowling's findings, the individuals with Down syndrome in Gombert's experiment did perform significantly better on rhyme judgment and rhyme oddity tasks than they did on tasks requiring phoneme segmentation, sequencing, and deletion ability, as would be predicted by typical development (discussed in Chapter 3).

Continued research is required to more fully understand phonological awareness development in children with Down syndrome and its influence on these children's reading and spelling development. Careful consideration of research methodology and phonological awareness tasks and stimulus items employed is essential. The differing results between studies involving children with Down syndrome highlight the influence of the type of phonological awareness measures used on both the overall level of performance of these children and also on the nature of the relationship between phonological awareness and reading performance. The following section discusses issues that are important to consider, from both research and clinical perspectives, in the phonological awareness assessment of children with Down syndrome.

Assessment

Procedures for assessing phonological awareness skills in children with Down syndrome need to be designed with the particular cognitive and linguistic characteristics of the children in mind. Limitations in short-term phonological memory capacity and receptive language skills and possible difficulties in phonological output are among the important characteristics of children with Down syndrome that need to be considered. In addition, these children may perform inconsistently from one testing session to another: Wishart and Duffy (1990) and Wishart (1993) observed that instability and lack of consistency are characteristic of the performance of young children with Down syndrome. Attention to the following issues is therefore recommended:

Phonological Short-Term Memory

Most children with Down syndrome have a digit span of two to three, on average (Cupples & Iacono, 2000; Kay-Raining Bird & Chapman, 1994). This limitation in phonological short-term memory could clearly impact children's ability to perform phoneme blending and segmentation tasks, especially when the target words or non-words contain four phonemes or more. Support for this possibility is provided by Cupples and Iacono's (2000) reanalysis of the phoneme blending data cited by Cossu et al. (1993). In Cossu et al.'s study, children with Down syndrome were required to blend four or six individual phonemes on each trial. Children with a digit span of four achieved significantly better phoneme blending scores than children with a span of three or below (Cupples & Iacono, 2000). To obtain an accurate measure of children's phoneme blending and segmentation abilities, it is recommended that the examiner use word and non-word stimuli that do not overload the children's limited working memory capacity. A maximum of three or four phonemes per target word or non-word would seem appropriate.

Receptive Language Abilities

Children with Down syndrome are impaired in their ability to understand spoken language. As a result of their limited receptive language skills, these children may find it difficult to follow task instructions. It is important, therefore, to ensure that instructions used to introduce and explain phonological awareness tasks are kept as simple as possible. Numerous practice items are required, with explanatory feedback provided for all errors. In addition, a flexible approach to test administration is required to accommodate the needs of individual children with Down syndrome who may differ markedly in their cognitive and linguistic abilities. For example, it may be necessary to repeat practice items for children who require further training to understand a task, and to provide regular reminders of task requirements for children who apparently lose track of these requirements during the test items.

Phonological Output

Many children with Down syndrome exhibit speech that is difficult to understand. Some children are unable to produce particular phonemes. Iacono (1998) reported on the phonetic inventories of five children with Down syndrome: One child failed to produce the phonemes /tʃ/, /dʒ/, /θ/ /ð/, another failed to produce the phonemes /ŋ/, /v/, /θ/ /ð/, /tʃ/, and a third child failed to produce /tʃ/. In addition to these missing phonemes, the speech of children with Down syndrome often shows evidence of phonological error patterns. Iacono (1998) noted that cluster reduction (e.g., st →s) and devoicing (e.g., b → p) occurred in the speech of all five children with Down syndrome studied. Given the frequency with which difficulties in phonological output occur in children with Down syndrome, words and non-words need to be chosen carefully to minimize the likelihood that a child will fail to respond correctly because of a difficulty in producing the required sounds, which in turn may result in avoiding certain words (Iacono, 1998). An assessment of each child's phonological skills is recommended to assist in interpreting performance on phonological awareness tasks. As a general measure, however, the number of target words and non-words containing potentially problematic sounds, such as /tʃ/, /dʒ/, and /θ/ /ð/, and clusters (e.g., /str/, /sk/, /fl/) should be kept to a minimum. It is also best to avoid including word pairs that have minimal phonological contrast, such as *sip* and *zip*, which may be produced identically by a child who demonstrates a voicing process, or words such as *take* and *dog*, which are often affected by errors of assimilation (see also, assessment of children with speech impairment in Chapter 6).

Performance Instability

Wishart and Duffy (1990) and Wishart (1993) have provided evidence suggesting that infants and young children with Down syndrome demonstrate unstable patterns of cognitive performance from one testing session to another, often failing to respond correctly to particular items or tasks on which they have succeeded previously. If such instability in performance is a reflection of the extent to which a child's level of engagement with the task varies from one testing session to the next, then it is likely that a single measure of performance will not provide a true measure of competence for a child with Down syndrome. One way of guarding against this potential problem and determine test–retest reliability is to engage in selective reassessment of some of the same skills.

Motivation, Attention, and Avoidance Behavior

Wishart (1998) noted that children with Down syndrome tend to engage in avoidance behavior when they are faced with problems or tasks that are well beyond their abilities. They may refuse to engage in a difficult task or attempt to divert attention away from the task. In order to minimize the likelihood of avoidance behavior and problems with lack of motivation, assessment tasks should not be too difficult for these children. It is a good idea to intermix easier tasks with more difficult ones, and to avoid persisting with a task or item to the point at which the child becomes frustrated and/or loses motivation.

Assessment Summary

Children with Down syndrome have particular cognitive/linguistic characteristics that need to be taken into account when designing and administering phonological awareness assessment procedures. Limitations in phonological short-term memory and difficulties with phonological output are best addressed by careful selection of items. Use short (three- or four-phoneme) words and/or non-words that do not overload phonological short-term memory. Avoid use of (1) words or non-words that contain "difficult" phonemes, and (2) word pairs that are likely to be difficult to distinguish from one another, should a phonological error pattern occur. Problems with receptive language, performance instability, and test behavior (e.g., lack of motivation and inattention) need to be addressed at a procedural level. Tasks themselves need to be straightforward, with simple, clear instructions and abundant use of examples. It is recommended that selected assessment tasks be repeated to evaluate reliability of measurement. Finally, a positive attitude toward the testing needs to be fostered by using a mix of easier and more difficult tasks and by pacing assessment so that children's interest will be maintained.

Intervention

Research establishing the contribution of phonological awareness to reading and spelling for children with Down syndrome has laid the foundation for future research to investigate the effectiveness of phonological awareness interventions in this population. Cupples and Iacono's (2002) intervention study provides promising results. They demonstrated that Australian children with Down syndrome can respond positively to analytic reading instruction that encompasses explicit training in onset-rime blending to form monosyllabic words. In a series of experimental case studies, the researchers compared a whole word ("look-and-say") approach with a word analysis approach, in which children were taught to read monosyllabic words by combining the phonological units of onset and rime. Seven children with Down syndrome participated in the 6-week intervention. The results indicated that only children who received the analytical training showed significant improvement in reading untrained words at postintervention.

Continued research utilizing well-designed intervention methodologies is necessary to provide further insight into the causal relationship between differing levels of phonological awareness and reading and spelling performance in children with Down syndrome. Further intervention research is also required to guide practitioners in the implementation of phonological awareness intervention as part of a comprehensive language program for this perspective.

Summary

The research evidence provides support for the view that phonological awareness is associated with learning to read in children with Down syndrome. The way in which phonological awareness is assessed, however, can have a substantial influence on these children's overall performance levels and on the observed relationship between phonological awareness and reading. It is crucial, therefore, that phonological awareness assessments and interventions are designed with the cognitive/linguistic characteristics of children with Down syndrome in mind. If this aim can be fulfilled, research findings will have important implications for literacy instruction in this population.

CHILDREN WITH HEARING IMPAIRMENT

Hearing impairment in early childhood has a significant impact on the development of speech and language skills. Individuals with a hearing loss frequently present with marked delays in spoken and written language development compared to peers with normal hearing, particularly if intervention is delayed (Davis, Elfinbein, Schum, & Bentler, 1986; Dawson et al., 1992; Levitt, McGarr, & Geffner, 1987; Miyamoto, Kirk, Svirsky, & Sehgal, 1999; Moog & Geers, 1999; Moores, 1997; Ramkalawan & Davis, 1992; Svirsky, Robbins, Kirk, Pisoni, & Miyamoto, 2000). Historically, these delays have led many children with severe to profound hearing impairment to finish high school with reading ability below that of children in fourth grade (Allen, 1986; Trybus & Karchmer, 1977). Even a mild degree of sensorineural hearing loss can present a significant barrier to social and academic achievement (Bess, Dodd-Murphy, & Parker, 1998; Quigley & Kretschmer, 1978). It is plausible to suggest that at least part of the literacy difficulties faced by children with hearing impairment are caused by restricted development of phonological awareness and phonological processing abilities as a result of the hearing loss (Sterne & Goswami, 2000). This section discusses the phonological awareness skills of children with hearing impairment and provides suggestions for practitioners to consider in the assessment and treatment of phonological awareness for this population.

Influences on Phonological Awareness Development

Within mainstream schools the incidence of hearing impairment is estimated at 11.3% (Bess et al., 1998). Many factors including etiology, time of onset, severity, progression, configuration, and type of hearing loss all interact to produce large differences in these children's spoken language performance. The development of phonological awareness, reading and spelling skills in children with hearing impairment will be influenced by their underlying spoken language abilities and by the different educational approaches children with hearing impairment receive (e.g., auditory based, total communication, and sign language approaches). Each system differs in the emphasis placed on auditory input.

Significant advances in technology have made available a wide range of advanced hearing instruments. Both means of amplification—hearing aids and cochlear implants—provide advantages over previous instruments in terms of digital signal processing, directional microphones, feedback cancellation systems, and speech enhancement strategies. This improved technology provides the child with a hearing impairment greater access to the speech cues (Allen, Nikolopoulos, & O'Donoghue, 1998; Blamey et al., 2001; Boothroyd & Eran, 1994; Meyer, Svirsky, Kirk, & Miyamoto, 1998; Svirsky & Meyer, 1999; Svirsky et al., 2000). Such advancements may positively influence children's phonological awareness and literacy development, although these evaluations await future research.

A further important influence on the language development of children with hearing impairment is the age at which the hearing loss was detected and the intervention received. Coupled with improvements in hearing instrument design are improved technologies for the early detection of deafness. Using Auditory Brainstem Response (ABR) or Otoacoustic Emissions (OAE), it is now possible to detect hearing impairment within a universal newborn hearing screening program. The outcome of such programs is that infants are screened for hearing impairment and those with hearing loss are confirmed before the age of 6 months and fitted with advanced hearing instruments. Early detection of hearing loss is crucial to maximize the critical developmental period for language development and to facilitate cognitive, emotional, and social development (Mauk & Behrens, 1993; Yoshinaga-Itano, 1995). Research has demonstrated that early diagnosis and intervention (before 6 months of age) of severe to profound hearing impairment to be effective in allowing children with congenital hearing loss to acquire age-appropriate cognitive and spoken language skills (Carney & Moeller, 1998; Robinshaw, 1995; Yoshinaga-Itano & Appuzzo, 1998; Yoshinaga-Itano, Sedey, Coulter, & Mehl, 1998). Early detection of hearing impairment followed by appropriate early intervention result in the mainstreaming of a greater proportion of children with hearing loss into regular schools and a greater exposure of this population to regular preschool and school curriculum.

Thus, in examining the phonological awareness development of children with hearing impairment, the wide diversity in early speech and language experiences, educational approaches, and curriculum exposure that individuals with hearing impairment have received must be considered.

Phonological Awareness in Children with a Sensorineural Hearing Impairment

Research interest in the phonological awareness and phonological coding skills of children who are deaf began in the late 1970s. Results from Dodd and Hermelin (1977) and Dodd's (1980) experiments suggested that children who are deaf are able to make use of phonological information in generating spelling patterns and reading words. The few subsequent studies of the phonological awareness skills of children with hearing loss, conducted in the 1980s to the late 1990s, have produced mixed findings. For example, Hanson and McGarr (1989) and Hanson and Fowler (1987) demonstrated that children who are deaf can produce rhyming words and make accurate judgments about rhyming words pairs. In contrast, Campbell and Wright (1988, 1990) concluded that children who are deaf have poor rhyme awareness and are unable to use phonological information in rhyme judgment tasks. Methodological problems, limited information regarding participant details, and subject selection procedures used in the studies hampered the interpretation and generalization of some of these earlier findings.

Sterne and Goswami's (2000) series of experiments examining the phonological awareness skills of children with congenital deafness addressed many of the difficulties in data interpretation inherent in earlier investigations. Inspection of Sterne and Goswami's findings provide clear insights into the phonological awareness abilities at the syllable, onset-rime, and phoneme level of children with hearing impairment. Details from these experiments are therefore summarized.

In Sterne and Goswmai's (2000) first experiment, participants included 15 British children with profound hearing loss between the ages of 9 and 14 years with an average reading age of 7 years. Eleven of these children attended a specialist school for the deaf and received an oral educational approach. The other four participants were in a deaf unit that offered a total communication approach. The participants' syllable awareness knowledge was evaluated using a word length task. The children were required to decide whether two words (displayed in picture form on a page, e.g., a strawberry and a car) were the same length (i.e., whether they contained the same number of syllables). Careful pretesting for picture naming and explicit task instruction was given prior to testing. No significant differences in accuracy and reaction times between the children with profound hearing loss, chronologically-aged matched children, and reading-age-matched children were found. All participant groups performed above chance levels, and the researchers concluded that children who are deaf have good phonological representations of syllables.

The researchers also examined phonological decoding ability through the use of non-words. The children were required to select a homophone of a pictured item from four non-words. For example, in response to seeing a picture of two boys, the children were required to select one of the following four printed non-words that would sound the same as the word *boys* if spoken: *boiz* (correct homophone) *boin*, *beiz*, *roiz*. The results indicated that the children's performance was significantly above chance level, with an average score of 63% correct. A group comparison with reading-age-matched controls, however, showed that the performance of the children with hearing loss was significantly inferior. Error analysis indicated that the children who were deaf were more likely to select a word that started with the same phoneme as the stimulus word than they were to select a word that ended with the same phoneme.

In another experiment the researchers (Sterne & Goswani, 2000) examined the rhyme judgment abilities of 14 British children with profound hearing loss. The children attended integrated deaf units or a residential school for the deaf. The children's ages ranged from 7 to 13 years, with an average reading age range from 6 to 10 years. The participants were required to decide which picture, from a choice of two pictures, rhymed with the target picture. Pretest practice and training was given to ensure that the participants understood the concept of rhyme and what was required in the task. The children with hearing loss performed significantly above chance level, but their performance was inferior to the reading-age-matched control group. The performance of the children with hearing loss varied with type of stimulus items and distracter items used. They appeared to use lip-shape information to help them make a rhyme judgment and were faster at identifying words whose spellings are orthographically similar (e.g., *sock*, *clock*) than words whose spellings are orthographically different (e.g., *fly*, *eye*). However, further analysis revealed that children who were deaf were not exclusively using visual cues and orthographic knowledge of the words' spelling to make rhyme judgments. They were able to use phonological information on at least some of their successful rhyme judgments.

These experiments suggested that school-age children with profound hearing loss can demonstrate phonological awareness skills above chance levels at the syllable, onset-rime, and phoneme levels. However, only knowledge at the syllable level was consistent with their reading and chronological ages. Deficits in rhyme and phoneme level knowledge were evident.

Briscoe et al. (2001) provided further evidence for an onset-rime deficit in British children with hearing impairment. In this study the performance of 19 children with mild to moderate bilateral sensorineural hearing loss, ages 5–10 years, was compared to children with specific language impairment and age-matched peers with typical language development. The performance of the children with hearing impairment was significantly inferior to their peers with normal hearing in their ability to match rhyming words and match words with the same initial phoneme. They also showed difficulty on a non-word repetition task, and their performance on phonological tasks did not differ from children diagnosed with specific language impairment. The interesting finding from this study was that, unlike the children with specific language impairment, the children with hearing loss performed at a similar level to children with typical development on a range of language and reading tasks. However, wide variation within the group of children with hearing impairment was evident, and there was a trend for children with lower performance on phonological measures to perform lower on language measures.

Continued research investigating the relationship between differing levels of phonological awareness, particularly at the phoneme level, and reading and spelling development in children with sensorineural hearing loss is required. Deficits in phoneme level awareness severely restrict reading development in many children with normal hearing; if these skills are poorly developed in children with hearing impairment, it is likely that they will underachieve in reading and spelling.

Phonological Awareness in Children with a Conductive Hearing Impairment

Otitis media with effusion is one of the most common childhood diseases (Freil-Patti, 1990). Approximately 10% of preschool and school-age children have a persistent version of this condition (Downs, 1981). The etiology is typically an inflammation of the middle ear, where there is a build-up of fluid behind the tympanic membrane, most often caused by the inability of the immature Eustachian tube to drain the middle ear space or to impede the flow of fluid from the nasopharynx into the middle ear cavity. This build-up of fluid can lead to hearing losses of up to 50 dBHL and is often fluctuating in nature (Fria, Cantekin, & Eicher, 1985).

There is a large body of literature indicating a link between otitis media and deficits in speech, language, and educational performance (Roberts, Wallace, & Henderson, 1997; Silva, Chalmers, & Stewart, 1986; Walker & Wigglesworth, 2002; Zinkus, Gottlieb, & Schapiro, 1978). Similarly, a number of studies has demonstrated that children with a significant history of conductive hearing loss show impeded auditory development (Gravel & Wallace, 1992, 2000; Groenen, Crul, Maassen, & van Bon, 1996). Recent studies have proposed that conductive hearing loss may have the greatest impact when it occurs with other social or health risk factors (Nittrouer, 1996; Peters, Grievink, van Bon, Vab den Bercken, & Schilder, 1997). Such factors are not favorable for the development of phonological awareness and thus place children with otitis media at risk for written language difficulties.

In addition, children with significant histories of otitis media may have underlying phonological representations of spoken words that are distorted (Shriberg, Friel-Patti, Flipsen, & Brown, 2000). Given the hypothesis that under-specified or indistinct phonological representation may be a causal factor in weak phonological awareness and reading development (Elbro et al., 1998), it may be further hypothesized that children with a significant history of conductive hearing loss will perform poorly on phoneme awareness and word recognition tasks. Kindig and Richards (2000) demonstrated a link between literacy achievement and history of conductive hearing loss; however, few studies have directly investigated the phonological awareness development in children with conductive hearing impairment. A small study by Walker and Wigglesworth (2002) found that in their cohort of nine matched Aboriginal children with significant history of otitis media, there was a strong correlation ($p < .01$) between phonological awareness skills and significant history of conductive hearing impairment. Significant differences between the participants and the matched control group were found on measures of rhyme, alliteration, blending, and segmentation.

It is important that children who are suspected of conductive hearing loss receive audiological assessment, with possible medical intervention, in as timely a manner as possible. The reality is that there is often no "quick fix" for conductive hearing loss, and the condition may persist. In these cases it is imperative that the child is not further disadvantaged; ensuring maximum audibility of the speech signal in the classroom and other learning environments is essential on a continuing basis. Good classroom acoustics (i.e., low background noise and reverberation) and sound-field amplification systems are recommended. Additionally, in a small number of children with persistent conductive hearing loss hearing, aids may be recommended by the audiologist to further improve their access to the auditory signal.

Assessment

Unfortunately, there are very few published assessment activities or procedures specifically designed for children with a hearing impairment. In the absence of such tools, crucial adaptations, along with sensible precautions, should be made when measuring phonological awareness in children with a hearing impairment. The following suggestions for practitioners are offered:

• Ensure maximum audibility by checking that the child's hearing aids or cochlear implants are appropriately set. FM systems or other assistive devices should be used to further enhance the speech signal. Performing the Ling "six sound check" (Estabrooks, 1998; Ling, 1989), which gives the clinician information on which frequencies the child can access and also ensures correct functioning of hearing instruments on a daily basis, is recommended prior to assessment administration.

- As in the assessment of all children, background noise and reverberation should be reduced and controlled to create the best possible listening environment.
- The clinician should be aware of the acoustic frequencies of the sounds tested to ensure that the child with hearing impairment can actually hear these sounds. Discussion with an audiologist and reference to the child's aided audiogram are essential to determine what the child can hear. If the child cannot hear the stimulus item, a visual cue (e.g., a sign or picture) should be added.
- It is important to gain the child's attention and make sure he or she is ready to listen prior to beginning the stimulus item. Cueing the child to "listen" may be a useful strategy.
- If the child has adequate speech production skills, asking him or her to repeat the stimulus word (e.g., a word to be segmented in a phoneme segmentation task) will ensure correct perception.
- Children with a hearing impairment often have reduced auditory short-term memory skills. If this particular form of memory is a concern, then visual cues should be used to supplement the auditory information (Briscoe et al., 2001 p. 338).
- The vocabulary level of the stimulus items in the phonological awareness tasks should be appropriate to the child's level of receptive vocabulary development.
- The examiner needs to understand the child's phonological production system to determine the effects of speech impairment on responses to phonological awareness items.
- Careful interpretation of data is necessary to evaluate whether the child has used a phonological or an orthographic strategy (when this is possible) to complete the task (Sterne & Goswami, 2000). For example, does the child recognize a rhyming word pair based on knowledge of similar spelling patterns in the words rather than the phonological similarities of the word?
- Caution should be exercised when interpreting performance on a non-word spelling task. Perception of words is often distorted for children with profound hearing loss. In effect, these individuals are frequently hearing "non-words." As a result, educational instruction encourages students to employ a top-down processing approach. Students are taught to make inferences about the likely value of the speech signal and then to apply the closest lexicon (Kess, 1992). Asking participants to orthographically produce non-words may be in direct opposition to their internalized methods of perception, wherein they have been taught to approximate the speech signal they hear to a known word. Findings on non-word spelling tasks

may therefore reflect discrepancies between their understanding of task requirements and their speech perception and discrimination skills.

• Selecting tests or subtests that require nonverbal responses is recommended for those children with hearing impairment who have poor speech intelligibility. Non-word reading selection tasks (as opposed to reading non-words aloud) and the rhyme selection tasks with pictures used in Sterne and Goswami (2000) experiments are examples of nonverbal tasks. Standardized phonological awareness tests designed for younger children, such as the Preschool and Primary Inventory of Phonological Awareness PIPA (Dodd et al., 2000; described in Chapter 6), also include tasks with picture stimuli and nonverbal responses.

Assessment Findings for Children with a Cochlear Implant

As part of an ongoing larger study investigating phonological awareness and word recognition in children with cochlear implants (CI) and children with hearing aids, 14 children with CI were assessed on the PIPA (Dodd et al., 2000). Data were analyzed to establish the suitability of this test with the population and to investigate how the children performed in relation to the normative data provided in the test.

The children with CI were between the ages of 5 year, 8 months and 10 years, 11 months. They had a profound sensorineural hearing loss in the best ear, spoke English at home as their first language, and at the time of the assessments, were enrolled in a mainstream educational program in New Zealand. They generally used spoken language without a signing supplement. Some of the children had used signing in previous educational settings, and they used signing with their advisor for the deaf. The children had no other diagnosed physical or intellectual impairments. All children used the Nucleau 22 or 24 cochlear implant, with either the SPEAK, ACE, or CIS speech processing strategy, and had at least 14 active electrodes. The children had received their cochlear implant prior to beginning formal literacy instruction or within the first few months of school (i.e., prior to 5 years, 4 months of age). Indeed, eight of the 14 children had received cochlear implants before the age of 3 years, 2 months.

The *Hearing in Noise Test—Children (HINT-C) speech perception test* was used to assess speech perception of phonemes in words (mean = 81.3% accuracy; SD = 9.97). The children's expressive phonology was evaluated using the *Phonological Profile for the Hearing Impaired* (Vardi, 1991). A percentage of correct consonants and phonological process usage was calculated using Computerized Profiling (Long, Fey, & Channell, 2002). Analysis indicated that 11 children exhibited a mild phonological impairment (mean Percentage Consonants Correct score 85.04; SD = 11.43), and three children exhibited speech impairment in the moderately delayed range. All of the children exhibited delayed receptive and expressive language skills, as measured by standard score performance on the *Oral and Written Language Scales* (*OWLS*; the average composite standard score was mean = 59.9; *SD* = 14.19) (Carrow-Woolfolk, 1991). The results from the Burt Word Recognition test revealed 50% of the group was significantly delayed in word reading, whereas the other 50% performed within the average range expected for hearing children.

The subtests from the PIPA were administered according to the manual instructions, with the following exception. In some instances the examiner asked the child to repeat the stimulus word before completing the task. For example, in processing how many sounds are heard in a word on the phoneme segmentation task, the examiner presented the target word, asked the child to repeat the word to confirm correct perception, and then identify the number of phonemes in the word. The examiner ensured that the child understood the task instructions for each subtest, and ample feedback and discussion were provided during the practice items. Children also were cued to listen (and look at the examiner) prior to the production of each stimulus word. The examiner was careful to give a clear presentation to ensure that lip-reading cues were clear to the child.

The raw scores on the PIPA subtests for the six children between the ages of 5 and 6 years, 11 months (younger group) were transformed into standard scores, according to the PIPA manual. From this group only one child (a good reader) achieved a standard score within the average range on any of the subtests. This child scored the mean standard expected for hearing children on the rhyme oddity task. All other children showed significant delays compared to the normative data, and none of the younger group could accurately segment any word into phonemes on the phoneme segmentation task. The older children's raw scores were compared to the normative data for children of the same age. One child, 10 years, 11 months (the strongest reader in the group), achieved average standard scores expected of 6-year-old children on all subtests. Most of the other older children showed average performance for a child age 6 years, 11 months on the rhyme and alliteration tasks but showed difficulty on the phoneme level tasks. Group mean raw scores are reported in Table 9.2.

Most children demonstrated patterns expected of hearing children. That is, they found phoneme segmentation more difficult than the other tasks. This result also was consistent with findings for children with expressive phonological impairment but normal hearing who struggle with phoneme level tasks (see Chapter 5). One child, however, demonstrated an unusual pattern of development. A 7-year-old poor reader who demonstrated very weak performance on syllable, rhyme, alliteration, and phoneme isolation tasks was one of only two children in the group who performed well on the phoneme segmentation task (gaining a score of 7/12 items correct).

TABLE 9.2. Phonological Awareness Performance for Children with Cochlear Implants

	Syllable segmentation	Rhyme	Alliteration	Phoneme isolation	Phoneme segmentation
Mean	5.93	6.93	6.79	7.36	1.93
SD	2.59	3.77	3.19	4.13	3.12
Range	1–10	0–12	2–11	0–12	0–10

Note. Raw scores are reported with all subtests, which are comprised of 12 test items.

This result suggested that the child had an isolated strength in phoneme segmentation, possibly as a result of teaching methods.

In general, the PIPA proved to be a useful assessment measure for these children. Even though some of the children were much older than the population for whom the test was designed, the vocabulary and task type were suited to the children's level of language ability, and the picture cues helped with the presentation of the stimulus and practice items. None of the children reached ceiling on all of the subtests, and all children could complete at least some of the stimulus items correctly. Thus the test was useful for developing a profile of the children's phonological awareness strengths and weaknesses. A strong correlation (.83) was obtained between the children's combined phonological awareness raw score and performance on the word recognition task. The normative data provided a guide to estimate the level of phonological awareness exhibited by the children with hearing impairment against the level of phonological awareness abilities expected for 5- or 6-year-old children with normal hearing.

Intervention

Phonological awareness skills in children with prelingual hearing impairment cannot develop solely from exposure to a speaking environment (Miller, 1997). Exposure to speech does not fully compensate for the restricted auditory input that children with a hearing loss experience. It is likely that many children with hearing impairment, irrespective of degree of hearing loss or early language intervention, will require intervention that specifically targets phonological awareness development. Unfortunately, what has not yet been established in controlled research is whether phonological awareness interventions effective for children with normal hearing are optimum for children with a hearing impairment. However, given the significant and often dramatic effects of phonological awareness intervention on reading development in children with normal hearing who struggle to acquire efficient word recognition skills, this form of intervention should be considered for children with hearing loss who also exhibit word recognition deficits. Chapter 8 discusses a range of phonological awareness intervention strategies. In consultation with a child's advisor and speech–language pathologist, these activities could easily be adapted for children with hearing impairment.

Other types of phonological processing interventions also may prove promising for children with hearing loss. Schopmeyer, Mellon, Dobaj, Grant, and Niparko (2000) investigated the use of a computer software program, Fast ForWord, with 11 school-age children who had profound sensorineural hearing loss and were using cochlear implants. Fast ForWord, created by Scientific Learning Corporation, is an interactive computer-based training program that was developed in response to research indicating that children with specific language impairment exhibit deficits in the processing and integration of rapidly transient acoustic information (Merzenich et al., 1996; Nagarajan et al., 1999; Tallal, 1980; Tallal et al., 1996). These deficits are thought to prevent the development of stable phonological representations, which in turn lead to difficulties in phonological processing and literacy acquisition (Tallal, 1980). Fast ForWord consists of a series of exercises incorporating acoustically modified speech signals. As children advance through the program, processing demands are systematically adjusted so that they more closely resemble normal presentation. The program utilized by Schopmeyer et al. (2000) was intensive, with children participating in five 20-minute training sessions a day, 5 days a week, for approximately 8 weeks. The children in the study exhibited significant posttest improvement on five standardized measures of language and auditory processing abilities. The authors concluded that Fast ForWord may provide a beneficial adjunct to traditional therapy. Additional research is required, however, to evaluate the transfer of such gains to improved reading and spelling performance.

Another approach to facilitate phonological awareness development in children with hearing impairment may be "auditory verbal therapy" (Estabrooks, 1998), which focuses on the discrimination of sounds with minimal differences. Children are drilled and taught how to hear fine differences in sounds, such as hearing differences between words such as *goat* and *coat*. Such training may help children to focus on individual phonemes in words and build a stronger foundation from which to develop more specific phoneme awareness knowledge. If children with hearing impairment are unable to hear or access these fine differences between phonemes in words, supplementary cues (visual or tactile) need to be added to ensure that they receive the information.

Improving the Audibility of the Sound Signal in the Classroom

Research evidence supporting the benefit of phonological awareness instruction to early reading development has led to preschool and class teachers successfully integrating phonological awareness training into the language curriculum. Children with hearing impairment who are integrated into mainstream education may therefore be exposed to phonological awareness training within the classroom environment. An underlying assumption of classroom instruction is that children can clearly hear the teacher's speech (Flexer, 1997a). Unfortunately, there are two situations when this assumption is compromised. First, hearing loss, which has been described as an "invisible acoustic filter that distorts, smears or eliminates incoming sounds, especially sounds from a distance" (Flexer, 1997b, p. 7), means that a teacher does not know how well a child is hearing at any one time. Second, the modern classroom is frequently inadequate in terms of signal-to-noise ratio (SNR), reverberation, background noise levels, and distance from child to teacher (Arnhold & Canning, 1999; Blake & Busby, 1994; Flexer, 1997a, 1997b; Flynn, 2000) (Palmer, 1997). These conditions are disadvantageous to all children but especially those with a hearing impairment.

It is critical that a child with hearing loss receives the best auditory signal possible in the classroom, particularly when engaged in activities such as phonological awareness tasks that focus on listening to sounds within words. The first and most important aspect is to ensure that a child's hearing instruments are being worn, the settings are correct, and the batteries charged. Unfortunately, correctly fitted hearing aids may not always provide the total solution within the classroom, because the hearing aid amplifies the background classroom noise in addition to the teacher's voice (Flexer, 1997b). In these situations the student may use a personal listening device, which sends the signal directly from the teacher's mouth to the hearing aid via an FM radio wave or telecoil. This assistive listening device is crucial in ensuring that the child is able to hear the signal at the most appropriate level.

Not all children with hearing impairment wear hearing aids or can make use of assistive listening devices (e.g., the child with conductive hearing impairment). An option for these children is a sound-field amplification system, which is a small high-fidelity wireless public address system that is self-contained in a classroom (Flexer, 1997b). The aim is to amplify the teacher's voice so that it is delivered clearly and consistently to all pupils, no matter where they are seated. This device produces a consistent and favorable signal-to-noise ratio (SNR). Sound-field amplification is particularly appropriate for those with fluctuating conductive hearing loss. This technology greatly reduces the risk of children missing valuable learning experiences in the classroom because they cannot hear.

The results of sound-field amplification have been encouraging. Massie, Theodoros, Byrne, McPherson, and Smaldino (1999) observed children in classrooms with and without a sound-field system. In the classroom with a sound-field system, they found increases in children's spontaneous contributions, improvements in perception of speech, and an increase in the children's interaction with each other. Similarly, Arnhold and Canning (1999) examined the comprehension of 49 children (ages 8 years, 6 months–11 years, 4 months) under two conditions: with the sound-field system switched on and off. They found that when the sound-field was turned on, the children's comprehension was significantly higher than the unamplified condition. Bennetts and Flynn (2002) also found that for a group of children with Down syndrome and mild conductive hearing loss, providing sound-field amplification significantly improved their perception of speech in the classroom. Flexer, Biley, Hinkley, Harkema, and Holcomb (2002) showed improved phonological and phonemic awareness in preschool children related to the use of a sound-field system. Further studies are required to show the improvement that a positive SNR and an extra 10dB of volume from the teacher can foster in children's phonological awareness.

Summary

Children with hearing loss are a very diverse group. A range of variables undoubtedly affects their development of phonological awareness: the nature of their hearing loss, age of onset or identification of hearing loss, and the types of interventions and educational practices received. Children with hearing impairment, however, can demonstrate understanding of the sound structure of a spoken word. Even some children with a profound hearing loss can perform above chance levels on phonological awareness tasks at the syllable, rhyme, and phoneme level. Nevertheless, deficits in this development are to be expected. Poor phonological awareness, particularly at the phoneme level, is likely to restrict word recognition development in children with hearing impairment just as it does in children with normal hearing ability.

10

Concluding Remarks

We all want children to succeed in reading and writing. The pleasures of reading a favorite story, the enormous knowledge base accessible to efficient readers, and the communication systems that literate societies depend upon—all foster our desires for children to achieve high levels of literacy through the education process. Understanding variables that contribute to children's literacy success has received much research attention and has been the lifelong pursuit of many prominent investigators. Phonological awareness has emerged from this research as a critical factor in written language acquisition. The strength of research evidence supporting the relationship between phonological awareness and reading ability is unquestionable. A wide variety of research methodologies, research analyses, differing populations samples, and research in differing alphabetic languages all support the conclusion that phonological awareness (particularly at the phoneme level) contributes significantly to reading and spelling and that a severe deficit in phonological awareness is likely to result in persistent reading difficulty.

Many children acquire awareness of a word's sound structure and understand how sounds in words relate to letters on a page as a part of the language experiences to which they are exposed to at home and at school. For some children, though, this exposure is insufficient. Without specific instruction, these children exhibit weaknesses in phoneme awareness and in processing phonological information that will persist into adulthood. From a practical perspective, one of the most exciting research findings is that phonological awareness development is relatively simple to manipulate. Unlike some factors related to reading development, such as children's home language experiences, children's level of phonological awareness knowledge can be easily enhanced. Even a short period of well-planned intervention (e.g., 20 hours) can significantly improve a child's phonological awareness abilities and lead to improvements in both reading accuracy and comprehension.

Phonological awareness should be viewed within the broad context of a comprehensive language program. A range of other phonological, semantic, syntactic, morphological, and orthographic processing skills also must be developed and set within meaningful spoken and written language experiences.

The depth of research in phonological awareness interventions has led to many advantages for practitioners that are not necessarily afforded by other types of interventions. For example:

- Phonological awareness intervention is well grounded in theories of word recognition, reading comprehension, and spelling.
- Research has provided clear evidence for variables that increase the effectiveness of phonological awareness interventions.
- A range of tests to measure children's phonological awareness development reliably and accurately are available.
- Phonological awareness activities that can be easily developed or purchased have been subjected to controlled research intervention trials that have proven their effectiveness.
- The phonological awareness knowledge a child needs to acquire for successful reading and spelling can be presented in a wide variety of ways that captures children's interest and motivates their learning.

Understanding the importance of phonological awareness to written language is not only relevant for children with specific speech and language difficulties. Interest in its contribution to reading in other populations, such children with severe physical disabilities who use alternative communication systems, children who are blind and use Braille as their reading medium, children with cognitive impairment, and children with hearing loss is rapidly expanding. Continued research efforts will clarify directions for assessment and intervention in children with differing learning needs.

One of the goals of specialist services provided to children who struggle with reading and spelling is to "make a difference"—to make a difference in children's level of reading and spelling competency, the manner in which they perceive themselves as learners, and their enjoyment of learning and school experiences. If professionals working with children who have spoken and written language difficulties understand the contribution of phonological awareness to reading and spelling and have expertise in assessing, planning, implementing, and monitoring appropriate phonological awareness interventions, then they indeed will make a difference. They will make a difference to the lives of many young children who are at high risk for reading disorder or who struggle with reading and spelling. They will help these children enjoy success in understanding the written code.

APPENDIX

English Phonemes

Consonant phonemes		Vowel phonemes	
Phonetic symbol	Spelling example[a] (common graphemes)	Phonetic symbol	Spelling example[a] (common graphemes)
/p/	pie	/ei/	cake, rain, day, eight
/b/	bag	/i/	tree, eat, key, happy
/t/	tap	/ai/	my, tie, fine
/d/	dog	/ou/	go, toe, coat, snow
/m/	mat	/u/	boot, true blew
/n/	nail, know	/æ/	cat
/k/	cat, duck, key	/ɛ/	wet
/g/	go	/ɪ/	sit
/ŋ/	ring	/ɑ/	box
/f/	fir, phone, cuff	/ʌ/	cup
/v/	van	/ʊ/	book
/s/	sun, miss, science, city	/ɜ/	sir, her, fur
/z/	zoo, buzz	/ɔ/	for, saw, Paul
/θ/	teeth	/a/	car
/ð/	the, breathe	/ɔi/	coin, boy
/ʃ/	sheep, brush	/aʊ/	cow, out
/tʃ/	cheese, watch		

(continued)

Consonant phonemes	
Phonetic symbol	Spelling example[a] (common graphemes)
/ʒ/	measure
/dʒ/	jump, bridge
/l/	lake, bell
/r/	rain, write
/j/	yes
/w/	wet
/ʍ/	where
/h/	hat

[a]Examples children may encounter in the early school years are provided. Further examples and an in-depth discussion of English phonemes are provided by Moats (2000).

References

Adams, A., Foorman, B. R., Lundberg, I., & Beeler, C. (1997). *Phonemic awareness in young children: A classroom curriculum.* Baltimore: Brookes.

Adams, M. (1990). *Beginning to read: Thinking and learning about print.* Cambridge, MA: MIT Press.

Ahmed, S. T., Lombardino, L. J., & Leonard, C. M. (2001). Specific language impairment: Definitions, causal mechanisms, and neurobiological factors. *Journal of Medical Speech–Language Pathology, 9*(1), 1–15.

Alexander, A., Andersen, H., Heilman, P., Voeller, K., & Torgesen, J. (1991). Phonological awareness training and remediation of analytic decoding deficits in a group of severe dyslexics. *Annals of Dyslexia, 41,* 193–206.

Allen, M. C., Nikolopoulos, T. P., & O'Donoghue, G. M. (1998). Speech intelligibility in children after cochlear implantation. *American Journal of Otology, 19*(6), 742–746.

Allen, T. E. (1986). Patterns of academic achievement among hearing impaired students: 1974 and 1983. In M. A. Karchmer (Ed.), *Deaf children in America.* San Diego: College Hill Press.

American Speech–Language–Hearing Association. (2001). Roles and responsibilities of speech–language pathologists with respect to reading and writing in children and adolescents. *ASHA Supplement, 21,* 17–27.

Apel, K., & Masterson, J. J. (2001). Theory-guided spelling assessment and intervention: A case study. *Language, Speech, and Hearing Services in Schools, 32,* 182–195.

Arnhold, P., & Canning, D. (1999). Does classroom amplification aid comprehension? *British Journal of Audiology, 33*(3), 171–178.

Athey, L. (1977). Syntax, semantics and reading. In J. Guthrie (Ed.), *Cognition, curriculum and comprehension* (Vol. 1, pp. 71–98). Newark, DE: International Reading Association.

Ayres, L. (1995). The efficacy of three training conditions on phonological awareness of kindergarten children and the longitudinal effect of each on later reading. IRA Outstanding Dissertation award for 1994–95. *Reading Research Quarterly, 30*(4), 604–606.

Baker, E., Croot, K., McCleod, S., & Paul, R. (2001). Psycholinguistic models of speech development and their application to clinical practice. *Journal of Speech, Language and Hearing Research, 44,* 685–702.

Ball, E., & Blachman, B. (1988). Phoneme segmentation training: Effect on reading readiness. *Annals of Dyslexia, 38,* 208–225.

Ball, E., & Blachman, B. (1991). Does phoneme awareness training in kindergarten make a difference to early word recognition and developmental spelling? *Reading Research Quarterly, 26,* 49–66.

Barron, R. (1986). Word recognition in early reading: A review of the direct and indirect access hypothesis. *Cognition, 24,* 93–119.

Barry, C. (1994). *Spelling routes (or roots or rutes).* West Sussex, UK: Wiley.

Barsch, R. H., & Rudell, B. (1962). A study of reading development among 77 children with cerebral palsy. *Cerebral Palsy Review, 23*(2), 1–12.

Beech, J. R., & Harding, L. M. (1984). Phonemic processing and the poor reader from a developmental lag viewpoint. *Reading Research Quarterly, 19,* 357–366.

Bennetts, L. K., & Flynn, M. C. (2002). Improving the classroom listening skills of children with Down syndrome by using sound-field amplification. *Down Syndrome Research and Practice, 8*(1), 19–24.

Bentin, S., & Leshem, H. (1993). On the interaction between phonological awareness and reading acquisition: It's a two-way street. *Annals of dyslexia, 43,* 125–148.

Bernhardt, B., & Stoel-Gammon, C. (1994). Nonlinear phonology: Introduction and clinical application [tutorial]. *Journal of Speech and Hearing Research, 37*(1), 123–143.

Berninger, V. W., & Gans, B. M. (1986a). Language profiles in nonspeaking individuals of normal intelligence with severe cerebral palsy. *Augmentative and Alternative Communication, 2,* 45–50.

Berninger, V. W., & Gans, B. M. (1986b). Assessing word processing capability of the nonvocal, nonwriting. *Augmentative and Alternative Communication, 2,* 56–63.

Bernthal, J., & Bankson, N. (1998). *Articulation and phonological disorders.* Boston: Allyn & Bacon.

Bertelson, P. (1993). Reading acquisition and phonemic awareness testing: How conclusive are data from Down's syndrome? (Remarks on Cossu, Rossini, and Marshall, 1993). *Cognition, 48,* 281–283.

Bess, F. H., Dodd-Murphy, J., & Parker, R. A. (1998). Children with minimal sensorineural hearing loss: Prevalence, educational performance, and functional status. *Ear and Hearing, 19*(5), 339–354.

Beukelman, D. R., & Mirenda, P. (1998). Assessment of specific capabilities. In D. R. Beukelman & P. Mirenda (Eds.), *Augmentative and alternative communication: Management of severe communication disorders in children and adults* (2nd ed., pp. 171–220). Baltimore: Brookes.

Birch, H. (1962). Dyslexia and maturation of visual dysfunction. In J. Money (Ed.), *Reading disability: Progress and research needs in dyslexia* (pp. 161–169). Baltimore: Johns Hopkins Press.

Bird, J., Bishop, D., & Freeman, N. (1995). Phonological awareness and literacy development in children with expressive phonological impairments. *Journal of Speech and Hearing Research, 38,* 446–462.

Bishop, D. V. M. (1985). Spelling ability in congenital dysarthria: Evidence against articulatory coding in translating between phonemes and graphemes. *Cognitve Neuropsychology, 2*(3), 229–251.

Bishop, D. V. M., & Adams, C. (1990). A prospective study of the relationship between specific language impairment, phonological disorders and reading retardation. *Journal of Child Psychology and Psychiatry, 31,* 1027–1050.

Bishop, D. V. M., & Robson, J. (1989). Unimpaired short-term memory and rhyme judgment in congenitally speechless individuals: Implications for the notion of "articulatory coding". *Quarterly Journal of Experimental Psychology, 41A*(1), 123–140.

Bjaalid, I. K., Hoien, T., & Lundberg, I. (1997). Dual-route and connectionist models: A step towards a combined model. *Scandinavian Journal of Psychology, 38*(1), 73–82.

Blachman, B., Ball, E., Black, R., & Tangel, D. (1994). Kindergarten teachers develop phoneme awareness in low-income, inner-city classrooms. *Reading and Writing: An Interdisciplinary Journal, 6,* 1–18.

Blachman, B., Ball, E., Black, R., & Tangel, D. (2000). *Road to the code.* Baltimore: Brookes.

Blake, P., & Busby, S. (1994). Noise levels in New Zealand classrooms: Their impact on hearing and teaching. *New Zealand Medical Journal, 107,* 357–358.

Blamey, P. J., Sarant, J. Z., Paatsch, L. E., Barry, J. G., Bow, C. P., Wales, R. J., Wright, M., Psarros, C., Rattigan, K., & Tooher, R. (2001). Relationships among speech perception, production, language, hearing loss, and age in children with impaired hearing. *Journal of Speech, Language, and Hearing Research, 44*(2), 264–285.

Blischak, D. M. (1994). Phonologic awareness: Implications for individuals with little or no functional speech. *Augmentative and Alternative Communication, 10,* 245–254.

Boothroyd, A., & Eran, O. (1994). Auditory speech perception capacity of child implant users expressed as equivalent hearing loss. *Volta Review, 96*(5), 151–167.

Borstrom, I., & Elbro, C. (1997). Prevention of dyslexia in kindergarten: Effects of phoneme awareness training with children of dyslexic parents. In C. Hulme & M. Snowling (Eds.), *Dyslexia: Biology, cognition and intervention* (pp. 235–253). London: Whurr.

Boudreau, D. M. (2002). Literacy skills in children and adolescents with Down syndrome. *Reading and Writing: An Interdisciplinary Journal, 15,* 497–525.

Boudreau, D. M., & Hedberg, N. L. (1999). A comparison of the early literacy skills in children with specific language impairment and their typically developing peers. *American Journal of Speech–Language Pathology, 8*(3), 249–260.

Bourassa, D. C., & Treiman, R. (2001). Spelling development and disability: The importance of linguistic factors. *Language, Speech, and Hearing Services in Schools, 32*(3), 172–181.

Bowey, J. (1986). Syntactic awareness in relation to reading skill and ongoing reading comprehension monitoring. *Journal of Experimental Child Psychology, 41,* 282–299.

Bowey, J. (1994). Phonological sensitivity in novice readers and nonreaders. *Journal of Experimental Child Psychology, 58,* 134–159.

Bowey, J., Cain, M., & Ryan, S. (1992). A reading-level design study of phonological skills underlying fourth-grade children's word reading difficulties. *Child Development, 63,* 999–1011.

Bradley, L., & Bryant, P. (1978). Difficulties in auditory organization as a possible cause of reading backwardness. *Nature, 271,* 746–747.

Bradley, L., & Bryant, P. (1983). Categorizing sounds and learning to read: A causal connection. *Nature, 301,* 419–421.

Bradley, L., & Bryant, P. (1985). *Rhyme and reason in reading and spelling.* Ann Arbor, MI: University of Michigan Press.

Brady, S., Fowler, A., Stone, B., & Winbury, N. (1994). Training phonological awareness: A study with inner-city kindergarten children. *Annals of Dyslexia, 44,* 26–59.

Brennan, F., & Ireson, J. (1997). Training phonological awareness: A study to evaluate the effects of a program of metalinguistic games in kindergarten. *Reading and Writing: An Interdisciplinary Journal, 9,* 241–263.

Briscoe, J., Bishop, D. V. M., & Norbury, C. F. (2001). Phonological processing, language, and literacy: A comparison of children with mild-to-moderate sensorineural hearing loss and those with specific language impairment. *Journal of Child Psychology and Psychiatry, 42,* 329–340.

Brown, G., & Loosemore, R. (1994). Computational approaches to normal and impaired spelling. In G. Brown & N. Ellis (Eds.), *Handbook of spelling* (pp. 319–336). West Sussex, UK: Wiley.

Brown, L., Sherbenou, R., & Johnsen, S. (1990). *Test of Nonverbal Intelligence: A language-free measure of cognitive ability* (2nd ed.). Austin, TX: PRO-ED.

Bruce, B. (1964). The analysis of word sounds by young children. *British Journal of Educational Psychology, 34,* 158–170.

Bruck, M. (1992). Persistence of dyslexics' phonological awareness deficits. *Developmental Psychology, 28,* 874–886.

Bruck, M. (1993). Component spelling skills of college students with childhood diagnoses of dyslexia. *Learning Disability Quarterly, 16,* 171–184.

Bryant, P., Bradley, L., Maclean, M., & Crossland, J. (1989). Nursery rhymes, phonological skills and reading. *Journal of Child Language, 16,* 407–428.

Bryant, P. E., Maclean, M., Bradley, L. L., & Crossland, J. (1990). Rhyme and alliteration, phoneme detection, and learning to read. *Developmental Psychology, 26*(3), 429–438.

Burgess, S. R., & Lonigan, C. J. (1998). Bidirectional relations of phonological sensitivity and prereading abilities: Evidence from a preschool sample. *Journal of Experimental Child Psychology, 70*(2), 117–141.

Bus, A. (1986). Preparatory reading instruction in kindergarten: Some comparative research into methods of auditory and auditory–visual training of phonemic analysis and blending. *Perceptual and Motor skills, 62,* 11–24.

Byrne, B. (1993). Learning to read in the absence of phonemic awareness? A comment on Cossu, Rossini, and Marshall. *Cognition, 48*, 285–288.

Byrne, B., & Fielding-Barnsley, R. (1995). Evaluation of a program to teach phonemic awareness to young children: A 2- and 3-year follow-up and a new preschool trial. *Journal of Educational Psychology, 87*, 488–503.

Calder, H. (1992). *Reading Freedom Teacher's Manual*. Glebe, New South Wales, Australia: Pascal Press.

Calfee, R. C., Lindamood, P., & Lindamood, C. (1973). Acoustic–phonetic skills and reading: Kindergarten through twelfth grade. *Journal of Educational Psychology, 64*(3), 293–298.

Campbell, R., & Wright, H. (1988). Deafness, spelling and rhyme: How spelling supports written word and picture rhyming skills in deaf subjects. *Quarterly Journal of Experimental Psychology, 40*, 771–788.

Campbell, R., & Wright, H. (1990). Deafness and immediate memory for pictures: Dissociations between "inner speech" and the "inner ear"? *Journal of Experimental Child Psychology, 50*(2), 259–286.

Caravolas, M., & Bruck, M. (1993). The effect of oral and written language input on children's phonological awareness: A cross-linguistic study. *Journal of Experimental Child Psychology, 55*, 1–30.

Cardoso-Martins, C., Michalick, M. F., & Pollo, T. C. (2002). Is sensitivity to rhyme a developmental precursor to sensitivity to phoneme?: Evidence from individuals with Down syndrome. *Reading and Writing: An Interdisciplinary Journal, 15*, 439–454.

Carlisle, J. (1995). Morphological awareness and early reading achievement. In L. B. Feldman (Ed.), *Morphological aspects of language processing* (pp. 189–210). Hillsdale, NJ: Erlbaum.

Carney, A. E., & Moeller, M. P. (1998). Treatment efficacy: Hearing loss in children. *Journal of Speech, Language, and Hearing Research, 41*(1), S61–S84.

Carrillo, M. (1994). Development of phonological awareness and reading acquisition: A study in spanish language. *Reading and Writing: An Interdisciplinary Journal, 6*(3), 279–298.

Carrow-Woolfolk, E. (1985). *Test for Auditory Comprehension of Language—Revised*. Allen, TX: DLM Teaching Resources.

Carrow-Woolfolk, E. (1991). *Oral and Written Langauge Scales (OWLS)*. Circle Pines, MN: American Guidance Service.

Cary, L., & Verhaeghe, A. (1994). Promoting phonemic analysis ability among kindergarteners: Effects of different training programs. *Reading and Writing: An Interdisciplinary Journal, 6*, 251–278.

Castle, J. M., Riach, J., & Nicholson, T. (1994). Getting off to a better start in reading and spelling: The effects of phonemic awareness instruction within a whole language program. *Journal of Educational Psychology, 86*, 350–359.

Cataldo, S., & Ellis, N. (1988). Interactions in the development of spelling, reading and phonological skills. *Journal of Research in Reading, 11*, 86–109.

Catts, H. (1993). The relationship between speech–language impairments and reading disabilites. *Journal of Speech and Hearing Research, 36*, 948–958.

Catts, H., Fey, M., Zhang, X., & Tomblin, B. (2001). Estimating the risk of future reading difficulties in kindergarten children: A research-based model and its clinical implementation. *Language, Speech and Hearing Services in Schools, 32*, 38–51.

Catts, H., & Kamhi, A. (1999a). Causes of reading disabilities. In H. Catts & A. Kamhi (Eds.), *Language and reading disabilities* (pp. 95–127). Boston: Allyn & Bacon.

Catts, H., & Kamhi, A. (1999b). Defining reading disabilities. In H. Catts & A. Kamhi (Eds.), *Language and reading disabilities* (pp. 50–72). Boston: Allyn & Bacon.

Catts, H., & Kamhi, A. (1999c). Classification of reading disabilities. In H. Catts & A. Kamhi (Eds.), *Language and reading disabilities* (pp. 73–94). Boston: Allyn & Bacon.

Catts, H. W., & Vartianen, T. (1993). *Sounds abound: Listening, rhyming and reading*. East Moline, IL: LinguiSystems.

Catts, H. W. (1986). Speech production/phonological deficits in reading-disordered children. *Journal of Learning Disabilities, 19*, 504–508.

Catts, H. W., Gillispie, M., Leonard, L. B., Kail, R. V., & Miller, C. A. (2002). The role of speed of processing, rapid naming, and phonological awareness in reading achievement. *Journal of Learning Disabilities, 35*(6), 509–524.

Catts, H. W., Hogan, T. P., & Fey, M. E. (2003). Subgrouping poor readers on the basis of individual differences in reading-related abilities. *Journal of Learning Disabilities, 36*(2), 151–164.

Chaney, C. (1992). Language development, metalinguistic skills, and print awareness in 3-year-old children. *Applied Psycholinguistics, 13*(4), 485–514.

Chapman, J., & Tunmer, W. (1997). A longitudinal study of beginning reading achievement and reading self concept. *British Journal of Educational Psychology, 67*, 279–291.

Cheung, H., Chen, H. C., Lai, C. Y., Wong, O. C., & Hills, M. (2001). The development of phonological awareness: Effects of spoken language experience and orthography. *Cognition, 81*(3), 227–241.

Chiappe, P., & Siegel, L. S. (1999). Phonological awareness and reading acquisition in English- and Punjabi-speaking Canadian children. *Journal of Educational Psychology, 91*(1), 20–28.

Clark, H., & Clark, E. (1977). *Psychology and language: An introduction to psycholinguistics*. New York: Harcourt Brace Jovanovich.

Clarke-Klein, S. M. (1994). Expressive phonological deficiencies: Impact on spelling development. *Topics in Language Disorders, 14*(2), pp. 40–55.

Clay, M. (1991). *Becoming literate: The construction of inner control*. Auckland, NZ: Heinemann Education.

Coltheart, M. (1978). Lexical access in simple reading tasks. In G. Underwood (Ed.), *Strategies of information processing* (pp. 151–216). London: Academic Press.

Coltheart, M., Curtis, B., Atkins, P., & Haller, M. (1993). Models of reading aloud: Dual-route and parallel-distributed-processing approaches. *Psychological Review, 100*, 589–608.

Comeau, L., Cormier, P., Grandmaison, E., & Lacroix, D. (1999). A longitudinal study of phonological processing skills in children learning to read in a second language. *Journal of Educational Psychology, 91*(1), 29–43.

Conners, F., & Olsen, R. (1990). Reading comprehension in dyslexic and normal readers: A component skills analysis. In D. Balota, G. Flores d'Arcias, & K. Rayner (Eds.), *Comprehension processes in reading* (pp. 557–579). Hillsdale, NJ: Erlbaum.

Conti-Ramsden, G., & Botting, N. (1999). Characteristics of children attending language units in England: A national study of 7-year-olds. *International Journal of Language and Communication Disorders, 34*(4), 359–366.

Cossu, G., Rossini, R., & Marshall, J. (1993). When reading is acquired but phoneme awareness is not: A study of literacy in Down's syndrome. *Cognition, 48,* 297–303.

Cossu, G., Shankweiler, D., Liberman, I., Katz, L., & Tola, G. (1988). Awareness of phonological segments and reading ability in Italian children. *Applied Psycholinguistics, 9,* 1–16.

Cowan, W., & Moran, M. (1997). Phonological awareness skills of children with articulation disorders in kindergarten to third grade. *Journal of Children's Communication Development, 18*(2), 31–38.

Cunningham, A. (1990). Explicit versus implicit instruction in phonemic awareness. *Journal of Experimental Child Psychology, 50,* 429–444.

Cupples, L., & Iacono, T. (2000). Phonological awareness and oral reading skill in children with Down syndrome. *Journal of Speech, Language and Hearing Research, 43,* 595–608.

Cupples, L., & Iacono, T. (2002). The efficacy of "whole word" versus "analytic" reading instruction for children with Down syndrome. *Reading and Writing: An Interdisciplinary Journal, 54,* 549–574.

Dahlgren Sandberg, A. (2001). Reading and spelling, phonological awareness, and working memory in children with severe speech impairments: A longitudinal study. *Augmentative and Alternative Communication, 17,* 11–26.

Dahlgren Sandberg, A., & Hjelmquist, E. (1996a). Phonologic awareness and literacy abilities in nonspeaking preschool children with cerebral palsy. *Augmentative and Alternative Communication, 12,* 138–153.

Dahlgren Sandberg, A., & Hjelmquist, E. (1996b). A comparative, descriptive study of reading and writing skills among non-speaking children: A preliminary study. *European Journal of Disorders of Communication, 31,* 289–308.

Dahlgren Sandberg, A., & Hjelmquist, E. (1997). Language and literacy in nonvocal children with cerebral palsy. *Reading and Writing: An Interdisciplinary Journal, 9,* 107–133.

Danilova, L. A. (1983). *Methods of improving the cognitive and verbal development of children with cerebral palsy* (R. H. Silverman, Trans., Monograph No. 23). New York: World Rehabilitative Fund.

Danks, J. (1978). Models of language comprehension. *Polish Psychological Bulletin, 9,* 183–192.

Das, J., Mishra, R., & Kirby, J. (1994). Cognitive patterns of children with dyslexia: A comparison between groups with high and average nonverbal intelligence. *Journal of Learning Disabilities, 27,* 235–242.

Davis, J. M., Elfinbein, J., Schum, R., & Bentler, R. A. (1986). Effects of mild to moderate hearing impairments on language, educational, and psychosocial behavior of children. *Journal of Speech and Hearing Disorders, 51,* 53–62.

Dawson, P. W., Blamey, P. J., Rowland, L. C., Dettman, S. J., Clark, G. M., Busby, P., Brown, A. M., Dowell, R. C., & Rickards, F. W. (1992). Cochlear implants in children, adolescents, and prelinguistically deafened adults: Speech perception. *Journal of Speech and Hearing Research, 35,* 401–417.

Defior, S., & Tudela, P. (1994). Effect of phonological training on reading and writing acquisition. *Reading and Writing: An Interdisciplinary Journal, 6,* 299–320.

Denckla, M., & Rudel, R. (1976a). Rapid "automatized" naming (R.A.N): Dyslexia differentiated from other learning disabilities. *Neuropsychologia, 14,* 471–478.

Denckla, M., & Rudel, R. (1976b). Naming of object-drawings by dyslexic and other learning disabled children. *Brain and Language, 3,* 1–15.

Denckla, M. (1972). Color-naming deficits in dyslexic boys. *Cortex, 8,* 164–176.

Denton, C. A., Hasbrouck, J. E., Weaver, L. R., & Riccio, C. A. (2000). What do we know about phonological awareness in Spanish? *Reading Psychology, 21*(4), 335–352.

Derwing, B. L., Smith, M. L., & Wiebe, G. E. (1995). On the role of spelling in morpheme recognition: Experimental studies with children and adults. In L. B. Feldman (Ed.), *Morphological aspects of language processing* (pp. 3–28). Hillsdale, NJ: Erlbaum.

Dodd, B. (1980). The spelling abilities of profoundly pre-lingually deaf children. In U. Frith (Ed.), *Cognitive processes in spelling* (pp. 423–442). London: Academic Press.

Dodd, B. (1995). *Differential diagnosis and treatment of children with speech disorder.* London: Whurr.

Dodd, B., & Carr, A. (2003). Young children's letter-sound knowledge. *Language, Speech and Hearing Services in Schools, 34,* 128–137.

Dodd, B., & Conn, L. (2000). The effect of Braille's orthography on blind children's phonological awareness. *Journal of Research in Reading, 23*(1), 1–11.

Dodd, B., Crosbie, S., MacIntosh, B., Teitzel, T., & Ozanne, A. (2000). *Preschool and primary inventory of phonological awareness (PIPA).* London: Psychological Corporation.

Dodd, B., & Gillon, G. (1996). The nature of the phonological deficit underlying disorders of spoken and written language. In C. K. Leong & R. Malatesha Joshi (Eds.), *Cross-linguistic studies of learning to read and spell: Phonological and orthographic processing* (pp. 53–70). Dordrecht, Germany: Kluwer Academic.

Dodd, B., & Gillon, G. (2001). Exploring the relationship between phonological awareness, speech impairment and literacy. *Advances in Speech Language Pathology, 3*(2), 139–147.

Dodd, B., Gillon, G., Oerlemans, M., Russell, T., Syrmis, M., & Wilson, H. (1995). Phonological disorder and the acquisition of literacy. In B. Dodd (Ed.), *Differential diagnosis and treatment of children with speech disorder* (pp. 125–146). London: Whurr.

Dodd, B., & Hermelin, B. (1977). Phonological coding by the prelinguistically deaf. *Perception and Psychophysics, 21,* 413–417.

Dodd, B., Holm, A., Oerlemans, M., & McCormick, M. (1996). *Queensland Uni-*

versity Inventory of Literacy. University of Queensland, Australia: Department of Speech Pathology and Audiology.

Dodd, B., Sprainger, N., & Oerlemans, M. (1989). The phonological skills of spelling disordered children. *Reading and Writing: An Interdisciplinary Journal, 1,* 333–355.

Dorman, C. (1985). Classification of reading disability in a case of congenital brain damage. *Neuropsychologia, 23,* 393–402.

Dorman, C. (1987). Verbal, perceptual and intellectual factors associated with reading achievement in adolescents with CP. *Perceptual and Motor Skills, 64,* 671–678.

Downs, M. (1981). Contribution of mild hearing loss to auditory language problems. In M. Downs (Ed.), *Auditory disorders in school children.* New York: Thieme.

Duncan, L. G., & Johnston, R. S. (1999). How does phonological awareness relate to nonword reading amongst poor readers? *Reading and Writing: An Interdisciplinary Journal, 11,* 405–439.

Dunn, L., & Dunn, L. (1981). *Peabody Picture Vocabulary Test—Revised.* Circle Pines, MN: American Guidance Service.

Durgunoglu, A. Y., Nagy, W. E., & Hancin-Bhatt, B. J. (1993). Cross-language transfer of phonological awareness. *Journal of Educational Psychology, 85*(3), 453–465.

Ehri, L. (1987). Learning to read and spell words. *Journal of Reading Behavior, 19,* 1–31.

Ehri, L. (1989). The development of spelling knowledge and its role in reading acquisition and reading disability. *Journal of Learning Disabilities, 22,* 356–365.

Ehri, L. (1991). Development of the ability to read words. In R. Barr, M. Kamil, P. Mosenthal, & P. Pearson (Eds.), *Handbook of reading research* (Vol. 2, pp. 383–417). New York: Longman.

Ehri, L. (1992). Reconceptualizing the development of sight word reading and its relationship to recoding. In L. Gough & R. Treiman (Eds.), *Reading acquisition* (pp. 107–143). Hillsdale, NJ: Erlbaum.

Ehri, L. (1994). Development of the ability to read words: Update. In R. Ruddell, M. Ruddell, & H. Singer (Eds.), *Theoretical models and processes in reading* (4th ed., pp. 323–358). Newark, DE: International Reading Association.

Ehri, L. (2000). Learning to read and learning to spell: Two sides of a coin. *Topics in Language Disorders, 20*(3), 19–36.

Ehri, L. C., Nunes, S., Willows, D., Schuster, B., Yaghoub-Zadeh, & Shanahan, T. (2001). Phonemic awareness instruction helps children learn to read: Evidence from the National Reading Panel's meta-analysis. *Reading Research Quarterly, 36*(3), 250–287.

Elbro, C. (1996). Early linguistic abilities and reading development: A review and a hypothesis. *Reading and Writing, 8*(6), 453–485.

Elbro, C., & Arnbak, E. (1996). The role of morpheme recognition and morphological awareness in dyslexia. *Annals of Dyslexia, 46,* 209–240.

Elbro, C., Borstrom, I., & Petersen, D. K. (1998). Predicting dyslexia from kindergarten: The importance of distinctness of phonological representations of lexical items. *Reading Research Quarterly, 33*(1), 36–60.

Elkonin, D. (1973). U.S.S.R. In J. Downing (Ed.), *Comparative reading*. New York: MacMillan.

Elliott, J., Lee, S. W., & Tollefson, N. (2001). A reliability and validity study of the dynamic indicators of basic early literacy skills—modified. *School Psychology Review, 30*(1), 33–49.

Ellis, N. (1994). Longitudinal studies of spelling development. In G. Brown & N. Ellis (Eds.), *Handbook of spelling* (pp. 155–178). West Sussex, UK: Wiley.

Engen, L., & Hoien, T. (2002). Phonological skills and reading comprehension. *Reading and Writing: An Interdisciplinary Journal, 15*(7–8), 613–631.

Erikson, K. A., & Koppenhaver, D. A. (1995). Developing a literacy program for children with severe disabilities. *Reading Teacher, 48*(8), 676–684.

Erikson, K. A., & Koppenhaver, D. A. (2001). *Whole-to-part reading assessment.* Paper presented at the 9th Summer Seminar on Literacy in Augmentative and Alternative Communication, St. Peter, MN.

Erikson, K. A., Koppenhaver, D. A., Yoder, D. E., & Namce, J. (1997). Integrated communication and literacy instruction for a child with multiple disabilities. *Focus on Autism and Other Developmental Disorders, 12*(3), 142–150.

Estabrooks, W. (1998). Learning to listen with a cochlear implant: A model for children. In W. Estabrooks (Ed.), *Cochlear implants for kids*. Washington, DC: Bell.

Fawcett, A., & Nicholson, R. (1995). Persistence of phonological awareness deficits in older children with dyslexia. *Reading and Writing: An Interdisciplinary Journal, 7*, 361–376.

Fazio, B. (1997a). Learning a new poem: Memory for connected speech and phonological awareness in low-income children with and without specific language impairment. *Journal of Speech, Language, and Hearing Research, 40*, 1285–1297.

Fazio, B. (1997b). Memory for rote linguistic routines and sensitivity to rhyme: A comparison of low-income children with and without specific language impairment. *Applied Psycholinguistics, 18*(3), 345–372.

Felsenfeld, S., Broen, P., & McGrue, M. (1994). A 28 year follow-up of adults with a history of moderate phonological disorder. *Journal of Speech and Hearing Research, 37*, 1341–1353.

Fletcher, J. M., Shaywitz, S. E., Shankweiler, D., Katz, L., et al. (1994). Cognitive profiles of reading disability: Comparisons of discrepancy and low achievement profiles. *Journal of Educational Psychology, 86*, 6–23.

Fletcher-Flinn, C. M., & Johnston, R. (1999). *Do poor readers have a deficit in phonological awareness?* Paper presented at the Joint AARE–NZARE Conference, Melbourne, Australia.

Flexer, C. (1997a). Individual and sound-field FM systems: Rationale, description, and use. *Volta Review, 99*(3), 133–162.

Flexer, C. (1997b). Sound-field FM systems: Questions most often asked about classroom amplification. *Hearsay, 11*(2), 5–14.

Flexer, C., Biley, K. K., Hinkley, A., Harkema, C., & Holcomb, J. (2002). Using sound-field systems to teach phonemic awareness to pre-schoolers. *The Hearing Journal, 55*(3), 38–44.

Flynn, M. C. (2000). Square pegs in round holes: Do speech–language therapists have a role providing services for the hearing impaired? *New Zealand Journal of Speech–Language Therapy, 54,* 5–13.

Foley, B. E. (1993). The development of literacy in individuals with severe congenital speech and motor impairments. *Topics in Language Disorders, 13*(2), 16–32.

Foley, B. E., & Pollatsek, A. (1999). Phonological processing and reading abilities in adolescents and adults with severe congenital speech impairments. *Augmentative and Alternative Communication, 15,* 156–173.

Forster, K. (1976). Accessing the mental lexicon. In R. Wales & E. Walker (Eds.), *New approaches to language mechanisms.* Amsterdam: North Holland.

Fowler, A. (1991). *How early phonological development might set the stage for phonemic awareness.* Hillsdale, NJ: Erlbaum.

Fowler, A., & Liberman, I. (1995). The role of phonology and orthography in morphological awareness. In L. B. Feldman (Ed.), *Morphological aspects of language processing* (pp. 157–188). Hillsdale, NJ: Erlbaum.

Fox, B., & Routh, D. (1975). Analyzing spoken language into words, syllables and phonemes: A developmental study. *Journal of Psycholinguistic Research, 4,* 331–342.

Freil-Patti, S. (1990). Otitis media with effusion and the development of language: A review of the evidence. *Topics in Language Disorders, 11,* 11–22.

Fria, T. J., Cantekin, E. I., & Eicher, J. A. (1985). Hearing acuity of children with otitis media with effusion. *Archives of Otolaryngology, 111,* 10–16.

Frith, U. (1985). Beneath the surface of developmental dyslexia. In K. Patterson, J. Marshall, & M. Coltheart (Eds.), *Surface dyslexia* (pp. 301–331). Hillsdale, NJ: Erlbaum.

Frost, J. (2001). Phonemic awareness, spontaneous writing, and reading and spelling development from a preventive perspective. *Reading and Writing: An Interdisciplinary Journal, 14,* 487–513.

Fry, M., Johnson, C., & Muehl, S. (1970). Oral language production in relation to reading achievement among select second graders. In D. Bakker & P. Satz (Eds.), *Specific reading disability: Advances in theory and method* (pp. 123–159). Rotterdam: University Press.

Gierut, J. (1998). Treatment efficacy: Functional phonological disorders in children. *Journal of Speech, Language and Hearing Research, 41,* 85–100.

Gillon, G. (2000a). The efficacy of phonological awareness intervention for children with spoken language impairment. *Language, Speech, and Hearing Services in Schools, 31,* 126–141.

Gillon, G. (2000b, April). *Developing a " Speech to Print Profile" for children with spoken language impairment at risk for literacy failure.* Paper presented at the New Zealand Speech–Language Therapists' Association Biennial Conference, Napier, New Zealand.

Gillon, G. (2000c). *The Gillon Phonological Awareness Training Programme* (2nd ed.). Christchurch, New Zealand: Canterprise, University of Canterbury. Available at: *www.cmds.canterbury.ac.nz/people/gillon/gillon.html*

Gillon, G. (2002a). *Early phonological awareness development in children with speech impairment.* Paper presented at the American Speech–Langauge–Hearing Association Annual Convention, Atlanta, Georgia.

Gillon, G. (2002b). Follow-up study investigating benefits of phonological awareness intervention for children with spoken language impairment. *International Journal of Language and Communication Disorders, 37*(4), 381–400.

Gillon, G. (in press). Phonological awareness: A preventative framework for preschool children with spoken language impairment. In McCauley, R. and Fey, M. (Eds.) *Treatment of language disorders in children: Conventional and controversial approaches.* Baltimore, MD: Paul H. Brookes.

Gillon, G., & Dodd, B. (1994). A prospective study of the relationship between phonological, semantic and syntactic skills and specific reading disability. *Reading and Writing: An Interdisciplinary Journal, 6,* 321–345.

Gillon, G., & Dodd, B. (1995). The effects of training phonological, semantic and syntactic processing skills in spoken language on reading ability. *Language, Speech and Hearing Services in Schools, 26,* 58–68.

Gillon, G., & Dodd, B. (1997). Enhancing the phonological processing skills of children with specific reading disability. *European Journal of Disorders of Communication, 32,* 67–90.

Gillon, G., & Dodd, B. (1998). A developmental case study of a child with severe reading disability. *New Zealand Journal of Speech Language Therapy, 52,* 9–21.

Gillon, G. T., & Schwarz, I. E. (1999). *Resourcing speech and language needs in Special Education: Database and best practice validation.* Wellington, New Zealand: Ministry of Education.

Gillon, G. T., & Young, A. A. (2002). The phonological awareness skills of children who are blind. *Journal of Visual Impairment and Blindness, 96*(1), 38–49.

Gilmore, A., Croft, C., & Reid, N. (1981). *Burt Word Reading Test—New Zealand Revision.* Wellington, New Zealand: NZCER.

Glennan, S. (1992). Augmentative and alternative communication. In G. Church & S. Glennan (Eds.), *The handbook of assistive technology* (pp. 93–132). San Diego: Singular.

Glennan, S. (1997). Augmentative and alternative communication assessment strategies. In S. L. Glennan & D. C. DeCoste (Eds.), *Handbook of augmentative and alternative communication* (pp. 149–192). San Diego: Singular.

Glushko, R. (1979). The organization and activation of orthographic knowledge in reading aloud. *Journal of Educational Psychology: Human Perception and Performance, 5,* 674–691.

Goldman, R., & Fristoe, M. (1986). *Goldman–Fristoe Test of Articulation.* Circle Pines, MN: American Guidance Service.

Goldsworthy, C. (1998). *Sourcebook of phonological awareness activities: Children's classic literature.* San Diego: Singular.

Gombert, J. E. (2002). Children with Down syndrome use phonological knowledge. *Reading and Writing: An Interdisciplinary Journal, 15,* 455–469.

Gonzalez, J. E. J., & Garcia, C. R. H. (1995). Effects of word linguistic properties on phonological awareness in Spanish children. *Journal of Educational Psychology, 87*(2), 193–201.

Good, R. H., & Kaminski, R. A. E. (2002). *Dynamic indicators of basic early literacy skills* (6th ed.). Eugene, OR: Institute for the Development of Educational Achievement.

Goodman, K. (1970). Reading: A psycholinguistic guessing game. In H. Singer & R. Ruddell (Eds.), *Theoretical models and processes of reading* (pp. 259–271). Newark, DE: International Reading Association.

Goodman, K. (1985). A linguistic study of cues and miscues in reading. In H. Singer & R. Ruddell (Eds.), *Theoretical models and processes of reading* (3rd ed., pp. 129–134). Newark, DE: International Reading Association.

Goswami, U. (1991). Learning about spelling sequences: The role of onsets and rimes in analogies in reading. *Child Development, 62,* 1110–1123.

Goswami, U. (1994a). Reading by anaology: Theoretical and practical perspectives. In M. Snowling (Ed.), *Reading development and dyslexia* (pp. 18–30). London: Whurr.

Goswami, U. (1994b). Toward an interactive analogy of reading: Decoding vowel graphemes in beginning reading. *Journal of Experimental Child Psychology, 56,* 443–475.

Goswami, U., & Bryant, P. (1990). *Phonological skills and learning to read.* Hove, UK: Erlbaum.

Goswami, U., & Bryant, P. (1992). Rhyme, analogy, and children's reading. In L. Gough, L. Ehri, & R. Treiman (Eds.), *Reading acquisition* (pp. 49–63). Hillsdale, NJ: Erlbaum.

Goswami, U., & Mead, F. (1992). Onset and rime awareness and analogies in reading. *Reading Research Quarterly, 27*(2), 152–162.

Gough, P. (1972). One second of reading. In J. Kavanagh & I. Mattingly (Eds.), *Language by eye and ear: The relationship between speech and reading* (pp. 331–358). Cambridge, MA: MIT Press.

Gough, P., & Hillinger, M. (1980). Learning to read: An unnatural act. *Bulletin of the Orton Society, 30,* 179–196.

Gough, P., & Tunmer, W. (1986). Decoding, reading and reading disability. *Remedial and Special Education, 7*(1), 6–10.

Goulandris, N. K., Snowling, M. J., & Walker, I. (2000). Is dyslexia a form of specific language impairment? A comparison of dyslexic and language impaired children as adolescents. *Annals of Dyslexia, 50,* 103–120.

Gravel, J. S., & Wallace, I. F. (1992). Listening and language at 4 years of age: Effects of early otitis media. *Journal of Speech and Hearing Research, 35,* 588–595.

Gravel, J. S., & Wallace, I. F. (2000). Effects of otitis media with effusion on hearing in the first 3 years of life. *Journal of Speech, Language, and Hearing Research, 43,* 631–644.

Greaney, J., Hill, E., & Tobin, M. (1998). *Neale Analysis of Reading Ability: University of Birmingham Braille Version.* Birmingham, UK: Royal National Institute for the Blind.

Green, C. F. (1996). Some issues concerning access to information by blind and partially sighted pupils. In *Sustaining the vision. selected papers from the annual conference of the International Association of School Librarianship*, Worcester, England, July 17–21, 1995.

Groenen, P., Crul, P., Maassen, B., & van Bon, W. (1996). Perception of voicing cues by children with early otitis media with and without language impairment. *Journal of Speech, Language, and Hearing Research, 39,* 43–54.

References

Grundy, K. (1989). Developmental speech disorders. In K. Grundy (Ed.), *Linguistics in clinical practice* (pp. 255–280). London: Taylor & Francis.

Hanley, J. R., Reynolds, C. J., & Thornton, A. (1997). Orthographic analogies and developmental dyslexia. *British Journal of Psychology, 88*, 423–440.

Hanson, V., & Fowler, C. (1987). Phonological coding in word reading: Evidence from hearing and deaf readers. *Memory and Cognition, 15*, 199–207.

Hanson, V., & McGarr, N. (1989). Rhyme generation in deaf adults. *Journal of Speech and Hearing Research, 32*, 2–11.

Harm, M. W., & Seidenberg, M. S. (1999). Phonology, reading acquisition, and dyslexia: Insights from connectionist models. *Psychological Review, 106*(3), 491–528.

Hart, J. T., Guthrie, J. T., & Winfield, L. (1980). Black English phonology and learning to read. *Journal of Educational Psychology, 72*(5), 635–646.

Hatcher, P. J. (1994). *Sound linkage: An integrated programme for overcoming reading difficulties*. London: Whurr.

Hatcher, P. J., Hulme, C., & Ellis, A. (1994). Ameliorating early reading failure by integrating the teaching of reading and phonological skills: The phonological linkage hypothesis. *Child Development, 65*, 41–57.

Henderson, E., & Beers, J. E. (1980). *Developmental and cognitive aspects of learning to spell: A reflection of word knowledge*. Newark, DE: International Reading Association.

Hesketh, A., Adams, C., Nightingale, C., & Hall, R. (2000). Phonological awareness therapy and articulatory training approaches for children with phonological disorders: A comparative study. *International Journal of Language and Communication Disorders, 35*, 337–354.

Hinshelwood, J. (1900). Congenital word-blindness. *Lancet, 1*, 1506–1508.

Hodson, B., & Paden, E. (1991). *Targeting intelligible speech: A phonological approach to remediation* (2nd ed.). Austin, TX: PRO-ED.

Hoien, T., Lundberg, I., Stanovich, K. E., & Bjaalid, I. K. (1995). Components of phonological awareness. *Reading and Writing: An Interdisciplinary Journal, 7*(2), 171–188.

Holm, A., & Dodd, B. (1996). The effect of first written language on the acquisition of literacy. *Cognition, 59*, 119–147.

Hoover, W., & Gough, P. (1990). The simple view of reading. *Reading and Writing: An Interdisciplinary Journal*, 127–160.

Hulme, C., Hatcher, P. J., Nation, K., Brown, A., Adams, J., & Stuart, G. (2002). Phoneme awareness is a better predictor of early reading skill than onset-rime awareness. *Journal of Experimental Child Psychology, 82*(1), 2–28.

Humphreys, G., & Evett, L. (1985). Are there independent lexical and nonlexical routes in word processing? An evaluation of the dual-route theory of reading. *Behavioral and Brain Sciences, 8*, 689–740.

Hurford, D., Darrow, L., Edwards, T., Howerton, C., Mote, C., Schauf, J., & Coffey, P. (1993). An examination of phonemic processing abilities in children during their first-grade year. *Journal of Learning Disabilities, 26*, 167–177.

Iacono, T. (1998). Analysis of the phonological skills of children with Down syndrome from single word and connected speech samples. *International Journal of Disability, Development and Education, 45*, 57–73.

International Dyslexia Association. (1994). Online: *www.interdys.org.*

Idol, L. (1988). Johnny can't read: Does the fault lie with the book, the teacher, or Johnny? *Remedial and Special Education, 9*(1), 8–25, 35.

Invernizzi, M., & Meier, J. (2002). *PALS 1–3: Phonological Awareness Literacy Screening.* Charlottesville, VA: Virginia State Department of Education, University of Virginia.

Invernizzi, M., Meier, J., Swank, L., & Juel, C. (2002). *PALS-K Phonological Awareness Literacy Screening.* Charlottesville, VA: Virginia State Department of Education, University of Virginia.

Invernizzi, M., Sullivan, A., & Meier, J. (2002). *PALS-PreK Phonological Awareness Literacy screening.* Charlottesville, VA: The Virginia State Department of Education, The University of Virginia.

Joanisse, M. F., Manis, F. R., Keating, P., & Seidenberg, M. S. (2000). Language deficits in dyslexic children: Speech perception, phonology, and morphology. *Journal of Experimental Child Psychology, 77*(1), 30–60.

Johnson, C. J., Beitchman, J. H., Young, A., Escobar, M., Atkinson, L., Wilson, B., Brownlie, E. B., Douglas, L., Taback, N., Lam, I., & Wang, M. (1999). Fourteen year follow-up of children with and without speech/language impairments: Speech/language stability and outcomes. *Journal of Speech, Language, and Hearing Research, 42*, 744–760.

Johnson, L. (1996). The Braille literacy crisis for children. *Journal of Visual Impairment and Blindness, 90*, 276–278.

Johnston, R., Andersen, M., Perrett, D., & Holligan, C. (1990). Perceptual dysfunction in poor readers: Evidence for visual and auditory segmentation problems in subgroups of poor readers. *British Journal of Educational Psychology, 60*, 212–219.

Johnston, R. S., Anderson, M., & Holligan, C. (1996). Knowledge of the alphabet and explicit awareness of phonemes in pre-readers: The nature of the relationship. *Reading and Writing, 8*(3), 217–234.

Jones, M. H., Dayton, G. O., Jr., Bernstein, L., Strommen, E. A., Osborne, M., & Watanabe, K. (1996). Pilot study of reading problems in cerebral palsied adults. *Developmental Medicine and Child Neurology, 8*, 417–427.

Juel, C., Griffith, P., & Gough, P. (1986). Acquisition of literacy: A longitudinal study of children in first and second grade. *Journal of Educational Psychology, 78*, 243–255.

Jusczyk, P. (1992). Developing phonological categories from the speech signal. In C. Ferguson, L. Menn, & C. Stoel-Gammon (Eds.), *Phonological development: Models, research, implications* (pp. 17–64). Timonium, MD: York Press.

Justice, L. M., Invernizzi, M. A., & Meier, J. D. (2002). Designing and implementing an early literacy screening protocol: Suggestions for the speech–language pathologist. *Language, Speech, and Hearing Services in Schools, 33*(2), 84–101.

Kamhi, A., Catts, H., & Mauer, D. (1990). Explaining speech production deficits in poor readers. *Journal of Learning Disabilities, 23*, 632–636.

Kamhi, A., & Hinton, L. N. (2000). Explaining individual differences in spelling abilities. *Topics in Language Disorders, 20*(3), 37–49.

Kaminski, R. A., & Good, R. H. (1996). Toward a technology for assessing basic early literacy skills. *School Psychology Review, 25*, 215–227.

Katz, R. (1986). Phonological deficiencies in children with reading disability: Evidence from an object-naming task. *Cognition, 22,* 225–257.

Kay-Raining Bird, E., & Chapman, R. S. (1994). Sequential recall in individuals with Down syndrome. *Journal of Speech and Hearing Research, 37,* 1369–1380.

Kay-Raining Bird, E., Cleave, P. L., & McConnell, L. (2000). Reading and phonological awareness in children with Down syndrome: A longitudinal study. *American Journal of Speech–Language Pathology, 9,* 19–330.

Kess, J. F. (1992). *Psycholinguistics, linguistics and the study of natural language.* Philadelphia: Benjamins.

Kindig, J. S., & Richards, H. C. (2000). Otitis media: Precursor of delayed reading. *Journal of Pediatric Psychology, 25,* 15–18.

Koke, S., & Neilson, J. (1987). *The effect of auditory feedback on the spelling of nonspeaking physically disabled individuals.* Unpublished master's thesis, University of Toronto, Toronto, Canada.

Koppenhaver, D. A., Evans, D. A., & Yoder, D. E. (1991). Childhood reading and writing experiences of literate adults with severe speech and motor impairments. *Augmentative and Alternative Communication, 7,* 20–33.

Koppenhaver, D. A., & Yoder, D. E. (1992). Literacy issues in persons with severe speech and physical impairments. In R. Gaylord-Ross (Ed.), *Issues and research in special education* (Vol. 2, pp. 156–201). New York: Columbia University Teachers College Press.

Koppenhaver, D. A., & Yoder, D. E. (1993). Classroom literacy instruction for children with severe speech and physical impairments (SSPI): What is and what might be. *Topics in Language Disorders, 13*(2), 1–15.

Korkman, K., & Peltomma, A. (1993). Preventative treatment of dyslexia by a preschool training program for children with language impairments. *Journal of Clinical Child Psychology, 22,* 227–287.

Kroese, J. M., Hynd, G. W., Knight, D. F., Hiemenz, J. R., & Hall, J. (2000). Clinical appraisal of spelling ability and its relationship to phonemic awareness (blending, segmenting, elision, and reversal), phonological memory, and reading in reading disabled, ADHD, and normal children. *Reading and Writing: An Interdisciplinary Journal, 13*(1–2), 105–131.

LaBerge, D., & Samuels, S. (1974). Toward a theory of automatic information processing in reading. *Cognitive Psychology, 6,* 293–323.

Lamb, G. (1996). Beginning Braille: A whole language-based strategy. *Journal of Visual Impairment and Blindness, 90*(3), 184–189.

Larrivee, L., & Catts, H. (1999). Early reading achievement in children with expressive phonological disorders. *American Journal of Speech–Language Pathology, 8,* 137–148.

Leitao, S., Hogben, J., & Fletcher, J. (1997). Phonological processing skills in speech and language impaired children. *European Journal of Disorders of Communication, 32,* 73–93.

Lenchner, O., Gerber, M., & Routh, D. (1990). Phonological awareness tasks as predictors of decoding ability: Beyond segmentation. *Journal of Learning Difficulties, 23,* 240–246.

Leonard, C. M., Lombardino, L. J., Walsh, K., Eckert, M. A., Mockler, J. L., Rowe, L. A., Williams, S., & DeBose, C. B. (2002). Anatomical risk factors that distinguish dyslexia from SLI predict reading skill in normal children. *Journal of Communication Disorders, 35*(6), 501–531.

Leong, C. K., & Sheh, S. (1982). Knowing about language: Some evidence from readers.

Levitt, H., McGarr, N. S., & Geffner, D. (1987). *Development of language and communication skills in hearing impaired children.* Rockville, MD: American Speech–Language–Hearing Association.

Lewis, B. A., Freebairn, L. A., & Taylor, H. G. (2000). Follow-up of children with early expressive phonology disorders. *Journal of Learning Disabilities, 33*, 433–444.

Lewis, B. A., Freebairn, L. A., & Taylor, H. G. (2002). Correlates of spelling abilities in children with early speech sound disorders. *Reading and Writing: An Interdisciplinary Journal, 15*, 389–407.

Lewkowicz, N. K. (1980). Phonemic awareness training: What to teach and how to teach it. *Journal of Educational Psychology, 72*, 686–700.

Liberman, A., Cooper, F., Shankweiler, D., & Studdert-Kennedy, M. (1967). Perception of the speech code. *Psychological Review, 74*(6), 431–461.

Liberman, I. Y. (1991). Phonology and beginning reading revisited. In M. Studdert-Kennedy (Ed.), *Status report on speech research, January–June 1991.* New Haven, CT: Haskins Labs.

Liberman, I. Y. (1971). Basic research in speech and lateralization of language: Some implications for reading disability. *Bulletin of the Orton Society, 21*, 71–87.

Liberman, I. Y., Shankweiler, D., Fischer, F., & Carter, B. (1974). Explicit syllable and phoneme segmentation in the young child. *Journal of Experimental Child Psychology, 18*(2), 201–212.

Liberman, I. Y., Shankweiler, D., & Liberman, A. M. (1989). The alphabetic principle and learning to read. In M. Studdert-Kennedy (Ed.), *Status Report on Speech Research. January–June 1990.* New Haven, CT: Haskins Labs.

Light, J., & Kelford Smith, A. (1993). Home literacy experiences of preschoolers who use AAC systems and of their nondisabled peers. *Augmentative and Alternative Communication, 9*, 10–25.

Light, J., & McNaughton, D. (1993). Literacy and augmentative communication (AAC): The expectation and priorities of parents and teachers. *Topics in Language Disorders, 13*(2), 33–46.

Lindamood, C., & Lindamood, P. (1975). *Auditory discrimination in depth* (rev. ed.). Austin, TX: DLM Teaching Resources.

Lindamood, C., & Lindamood, P. (1979). *Lindamood Auditory Conceptualization Test.* Austin, TX: DLM Teaching Resources.

Lindamood, C., & Lindamood, P. (1998). *The Lindamood Phoneme Sequencing Program for Reading, Spelling, and Speech: The LiPS Program.* Austin, TX: PRO-ED.

Ling, D. (1989). *Foundations of spoken language for hearing impaired children.* Washington, DC: Bell.

Liow, S. J. R., & Poon, K. K. L. (1998). Phonological awareness in multilingual Chinese children. *Applied Psycholinguistics, 19*(3), 339–362.

Long, S., Fey, M., & Channell, R. (2002). Profile of phonology (PROPH). Computerized profiling. *www.computerizedprofiling.org.*

Lonigan, C., Burgess, S., Anthony, J., & Barker, T. (1998). Development of phonological sensitivity in 2– to 5– year-old children. *Journal of Educational Psychology, 90*(2), 294–311.

Love, E., & Reilly, S. (1995). *A sound way: Phonological awareness—activities for early literacy.* Melbourne, Australia: Longman.

Lovett, M. W., & Steinbach, K. (1997). The effectiveness of remedial programs for reading disabled children of different ages: Does the benefit decrease for older children? *Learning Disability Quarterly, 20,* 189–210.

Lovett, M. W., Borden, S., Deluca, T., Lacerenza, L., Benson, N., & Brackstone, D. (1994). Treating the core deficits of developmental dyslexia: evidence of transfer of learning after phonologically- and strategy-based reading training programs. *Developmental Psychology, 30,* 805–822.

Lovett, M. W., Lacerenza, L., & Borden, S. L. (2000). Putting struggling readers on the PHAST track: A program to integrate phonological and strategy-based remedial reading instruction and maximize outcomes. *Journal of Learning Disabilities, 33*(5), 458–476.

Lovett, M. W., Steinbach, K., & Frijters, J. (2000). Remediating the core deficits of developmental reading disability: A double deficit hypothesis. *Journal of Learning Disabilities, 33,* 334–358.

Lundberg, I., Frost, J., & Petersen, O. P. (1988). Effects of an intensive program for stimulating phonological awareness in preschool children. *Reading Research Quarterly, 23,* 263–284.

Lundberg, I., Olofsson, A., & Wall, S. (1980). Reading and spelling skills in the first years predicted from phonemic awareness skills in kindergarten. *Scandanavian Journal of Psychology, 21,* 159–173.

MacDonald, G. W., & Cornwall, A. (1995). The relationship between phonological awareness and reading and spelling acheivement eleven years later. *Journal of Learning Disabilities, 28,* 523–527.

Maclean, M., Bryant, P., & Bradley, L. (1987). Rhymes, nursery rhymes and reading in early childhood. *Merrill–Palmer Quarterly, 33,* 255–282.

Magnusson, E., & Naucler, K. (1990). Reading and spelling in language-disordered children—linguistic and metalinguistic prerequisites: Report on a longitudinal study. *Clinical Linguistics and Phonetics, 4,* 49–61.

Major, E. M., & Bernhardt, B. H. (1998). Metaphonological skills of children with phonological disorders before and after phonological and metaphonological intervention. *International Journal of Language and Communication Disorders, 33*(4), 413–444.

Mangold, S. (1977). *The Mangold Developmental Program of Tactile Perception and Braille Letter Recognition.* Castro Valley, CA: Exceptional Teaching Aids.

Manis, F., Custodio, R., & Szeszulski, P. (1993). Development of phonological and orthographic skill: A 2–year longitudinal study of dyslexic children. *Journal of Experimental Child Psychology, 56,* 64–86.

Mann, V. (1987). Phonological awareness: The role of reading experience. In P. Bertelson (Ed.), *The onset of literacy: Cognitive processes in reading acquisition* (pp. 65–91). Cambridge, MA: MIT Press.

Marcel, T. (1980). Surface dyslexia and beginning reading: A revised hypothesis of the pronunciation of print and its impairments. In M. Coltheart, K. Patterson, & J. Marshall (Eds.), *Deep dyslexia* (pp. 227–258). London: Routledge & Kegan Paul.

Marcell, M., & Armstrong, V. (1982). Auditory and sequential memory of Down syndrome and nonretarded children. *American Journal of Mental Retardation, 87,* 86–95.

Marsh, G., Desberg, P., & Cooper, J. (1977). Developmental strategies in reading. *Journal of Reading Behavior, 9,* 391–394.

Marsh, G., Friedman, M., Welch, V., & Desberg, P. (1980). A cognitive-developmental approach to reading acquisition. In G. MacKinnon & T. Waller (Eds.), *Reading research: Advances in theory and practice* (Vol. 3, pp. 199–221). San Diego: Academic Press.

Marshall, J., & Newcombe, F. (1973). Patterns of paralexia: A psycholinguistic approach. *Journal of Psycholinguistic Research, 2,* 175–199.

Martin, D., Colesby, C., & Jhamat, K. (1997). Phonological awareness in Panjabi/English children with phonological difficulties. *Child Language Teaching and Therapy, 4,* 59–72.

Massie, R., Theodoros, D., Byrne, D., McPherson, B., & Smaldino, J. (1999). The effects of sound-field classroom amplification on the communicative interactions of Aboriginal and Torres Strait Islander children. *Australian and New Zealand Journal of Audiology, 21*(2), 93–109.

Masterson, J. J., & Apel, K. (2000). Spelling assessment: Charting a path to optimal intervention. *Topics in Language Disorders, 20*(3), 50–65.

Mattingly, I. G. (1972). Reading, the linguistic process, and linguistic awareness. In J. F. Kavanagh & I. G. Mattingly (Eds.), *Language by ear and by eye: The relationships between speech and reading* (pp. 133–147). Cambridge, MA: MIT Press.

Maughan, B. (1994). Behavioural development and reading disabilities. In C. Hulme & M. Snowling (Eds.), *Reading development and dyslexia* (pp. 128–143). London: Whurr.

Mauk, G. W., & Behrens, T. R. (1993). Historical, political, and technological contexts associated with early identification of hearing loss. *Seminars in Hearing, 14,* 1–17.

Mayringer, H., & Wimmer, H. (2000). Pseudoname learning by German-speaking children with dyslexia: Evidence for a phonological learning deficit. *Journal of Experimental Child Psychology, 75*(2), 116–133.

McArthur, G. M., Hogben, J. H., Edwards, V. T., Heath, S. M., & Mengler, E. D. (2000). On the "specifics" of specific reading disability and specific language impairment. *Journal of Child Psychology and Psychiatry and Allied Disciplines, 41*(7), 869–874.

McCabe, P., Rosenthal, J. B., & McLeod, S. (1998). Features of developmental dyspraxia in the general speech-impaired population. *Clinical Linguistics and Phonetics, 12*(2), 105–126.

McCauley, R., & Swisher, L. (1984). Psychometric review of language and articulation tests for preschool children. *Journal of Speech and Hearing Disorders, 49,* 34–42.

McCormick, M. (1994). A nonreader becomes a reader: A case study of literacy acquisition by a severely disabled reader. *Reading Research Quarterly, 29*, 157–176.

McMahon, A. (2002). An introduction to English Phonology. New York: Oxford University Press.

McGuinness, D., McGuinness, C., & Donohue, J. (1995). Phonological training and the alphabet principle: Evidence for reciprocal causality. *Reading Research Quarterly, 30*(4), 830–852.

Merzenich, M. M., Jenkins, W. M., Johnston, P., Schreiner, C., Miller, S. L., & Tallal, P. (1996). Temporal processing deficits of language-learning impaired children ameliorated by training. *Science, 271*, 77–81.

Metsala, J. L. (1999a). The development of phonemic awareness in reading-disabled children. *Applied Psycholinguistics, 20*(1), 149–158.

Metsala, J. L. (1999b). Young children's phonological awareness and nonword repetition as a function of vocabulary development. *Journal of Educational Psychology, 91*(1), 3–19.

Metsala, J. L., & Walley, A. C. (1998). Spoken vocabulary growth and the segmental restructuring of lexical representations: Precursors to phoneme awareness and early raeding ability. In J. L. Metsala & L. C. Ehri (Eds.), *Word recognition in beginning literacy* (pp. 89–120). Mahwah, NJ: Erlbaum.

Meyer, T. A., Svirsky, M. A., Kirk, K. I., & Miyamoto, R. T. (1998). Improvements in speech perception by children with profound prelingual hearing loss: Effects of device, communication mode, and chronological age. *Journal of Speech, Language, and Hearing Research, 41*(4), 846–858.

Miller, P. (1997). The effect of communication mode on the development of phonemic awareness in prelingually deaf students. *Journal of Speech, Language and Hearing Research, 40*, 1151–1163.

Miyamoto, R. T., Kirk, K. I., Svirsky, M. A., & Sehgal, S. T. (1999). Communication skills in pediatric cochlear implant recipients. *Acta Oto-Laryngologica, 119*(2), 219–224.

Mizuko, M., Reichle, J., Ratcliffe, A., & Esser, J. (1994). Effects of selection techniques and array sizes on short-term visual memory. *Augmentative and Alternative Communication, 10*, 237–244.

Moats, L. C. (2000). *Speech to print: Language essentials for teachers.* Baltimore, MD: Brookes.

Moog, J. S., & Geers, A. E. (1999). Speech and language acquisition in young children after cochlear implantation. *Otolaryngologic Clinics of North America, 32*(6), 1127–1141.

Moores, D. F. (1997). Psycholinguistics and deafness. *American Annals of the Deaf, 142*(3), 80–89.

Morais, J., Bertelson, P., Cary, L., & Alegria, J. (1986). Literacy training and speech segmentation. *Cognition, 24*, 45–64.

Morais, J., Cary, L., Alegria, J., & Bertelson, P. (1979). Does awareness of speech as a sequence of phones arise spontaneously? *Cognition, 7*, 323–331.

Morais, J., Cluytens, M., & Alegria, J. (1984). Segmentation abilities of dyslexics and normal readers. *Perceptual and Motor Skills, 58*, 221–222.

Morgan, W. (1896). A case of congenital word-blindness. *British Medical Journal, 11*, 378.

Morice, R., & Slaghuis, W. (1985). Language performance and reading ability at 8 years of age. *Applied Psycholinguistics, 6*, 141–160.

Morris, R. D., Stuebing, K. K., Fletcher, J. M., Shaywitz, S. E., Lyon, G. R., Shankweiler, D. P., Katz, L., Francis, D. J., & Shaywitz, B. A. (1998). Subtypes of reading disability: Variability around a phonological core. *Journal of Educational Psychology, 90*(3), 347–373.

Morton, J., & Patterson, K. (1980). A new attempt at an interpretation, or, an attempt at a new interpretation. In M. Coltheart, K. Patterson, & J. Marshall (Eds.), *Deep dyslexia* (pp. 91–118). London: Routledge & Kegan Paul.

Muter, V. (1994). Influence of phonological awareness and letter knowledge on beginning reading and spelling. In C. Hulme & M. Snowling (Eds.), *Reading development and dyslexia* (pp. 45–62). London: Whurr.

Muter, V., Hulme, C., & Snowling, M. (1997). *Phonological Abilities Test (PAT)*. London: Psychological Corporation.

Muter, V., Hulme, C., Snowling, M., & Taylor, S. (1997). Segmentation, not rhyming, predicts early progress in learning to read. *Journal of Experimental Child Psychology, 65*, 370–396.

Muter, V., & Snowling, M. (1998). Concurrent and longitudinal predictors of reading: The role of metalinguistic and short-term memory skills. *Reading Research Quarterly, 33*(3), 320–337.

Myklebust, H., & Johnson, D. (1962). Dyslexia in children. *Exceptional Children, 29*, 14–25.

Nagarajan, D., Mahncke, H., Salz, T., Tallal, P., Roberts, T., & Merzenich, M. M. (1999). Cortical auditory signal processing in poor readers. *Proceedings of the National Academy of Science of the USA, 96*(11), 6483–6488.

Neale, M. (1988). *Neale Analysis of Reading Ability—Revised*. Victoria, Australia: ACER.

Nelson, N. W. (1992). Performance is the prize: Language competence and performance among AAC users. *Augmentative and Alternative Communication, 8*, 3–18.

Nippold, M. (1998). *Later language development: The school age and adolescent years*. Austin, TX: PRO-ED.

Nittrouer, S. (1996). The relationship between speech perception and phonological awareness: Evidence from low SES children and children with chronic OM. *Journal of Speech and Hearing Research, 39*, 1059–1070.

Norris, D., & Brown, G. (1985). Race models and analogy theories: A dead heat? Reply to Seidenberg. *Cognition, 20*, 155–168.

NotariSyverson, A., O'Connor, R., & Vadasy, P. (1998). *Ladders to literacy: A preschool activity book*. Baltimore: Brookes.

The Nuffield Centre Dyspraxia Program. (1994). London: The Nuffield Hearing and Speech Centre.

O'Connor, R., Jenkins, J., Leicester, N., & Slocum, T. (1993). Teaching phonological awareness to young children with learning disabilities. *Exceptional Children, 59*, 532–546.

Oerlemans, M., & Dodd, B. (1993). Development of spelling ability and letter-sound orientation in primary school children. *European Journal of Disorders of Communication, 28*, 349–367.

Olofsson, A., & Lundberg, I. (1983). Can phonemic awareness be trained in kindergarten? *Scandinavian Journal of Psychology, 24*, 35–44.

Olswang, L. B., & Bain, B. A. (1996). Assessment information for predicting upcoming change in language production. *Journal of Speech and Hearing Research, 39*(2), 414–423.

Ozanne, A. (1995). The search for developmental verbal dyspraxia. In B. Dodd (Ed.), *Differential diagnosis and treatment of children with speech disorder* (pp. 91–109). London: Whurr.

Palmer, C. V. (1997). Hearing and listening in a typical classroom. *Language, Speech, and Hearing Services in Schools, 28*(3), 213–218.

Patterson, K., & Morton, J. (1985). From orthography to phonology: An attempt at an old interpretation. In K. Patterson & M. Coltheart (Eds.), *Surface dyslexia* (pp. 335–359). Hillsdale, NJ: Erlbaum.

Patterson, K., Seidenberg, M., & McClelland, J. (1989). Connections and disconnections: Dyslexia in a computational model of reading. In P. Morris (Ed.), *Parallel distributed processing: Implications for psychology and neuroscience* (pp. 131–181). London: Oxford University Press.

Paul, R. (1997). Facilitating transitions in language development for children using AAC. *Augmentative and Alternative Communication, 13*, 141–148.

Paul, R. (2001). *Language disorders from infancy through adolescence*. St Louis, MO: Mosby.

Perfetti, C. A. (1985). *Reading ability*. New York: Oxford University Press.

Perfetti, C. A., Beck, I., Ball, L. C., & Hughes, C. (1987). Phonemic knowledge and learning to read are reciprocal: A longitudinal study of first grade children. *Merrill–Palmer Quarterly, 33*, 283–319.

Perfetti, C. A., & Hogaboam, T. (1975). The relationship between single word decoding and reading comprehension. *Journal of Educational Psychology, 56*, 461–469.

Perfetti, C. A., & Lesgold, A. (1979). Coding and comprehension in skilled reading and implications for reading instruction. In L. Resnick & P. Weaver (Eds.), *Theory and practice of early reading* (Vol. 1, pp. 57–84). Hillsdale, NJ: Erlbaum.

Peters, S. A. F., Grievink, E. H., van Bon, W., Vab den Bercken, J. H. L., & Schilder, A. G. M. (1997). The contribution of risk factors to the effect of early otitis media with effusion on later language, reading and spelling. *Developmental Medicine and Child Neurology, 39*, 31–39.

Poskiparta, E., Niemi, P., & Vauras, M. (1999). Who benefits from training in linguistic awareness in the first grade, and what components show training effects? *Journal of Learning Disabilities, 32*, 437–446.

Pratt, A. C., & Brady, S. (1988). Relation of phonological awareness to reading disability in children and adults. *Journal of Educational Psychology, 80*(3), 319–323.

Pring, L. (1982). Phonological and tactual coding of Braille by blind children. *British Journal of Psychology, 73*, 351–359.

Pring, L. (1994). Touch and go: Learning to read Braille. *Reading Research Quarterly, 29*, 67–74.

Prior, M. (1989). Reading disability: "Normative" or "pathological"? *Australian Journal of Psychology, 41*, 135–157.

Quigley, S. P., & Kretschmer, R. E. (1978). *The education of deaf children.* Baltimore: University Park Press.

Rabinovich, R. (1959). Reading and learning disabilities. In S. Arieti (Ed.), *American handbook of psychiatry* (Vol. 1, pp. 857–869). New York: Basic Books.

Rabinovich, R. (1968). Reading problems in children: Definitions and classification. In A. Keeney & V. Keeney (Eds.), *Dyslexia: Diagnosis and treatment of reading disorders* (pp. 1–10). St. Louis, MO: Mosby.

Rack, J., Snowling, M., & Olsen, R. (1992). The nonword reading deficit in developmental dyslexia: A review. *Reading Research Quarterly, 27*, 28–53.

Ramkalawan, T. W., & Davis, A. C. (1992). The effects of hearing loss and age at intervention on some language metrics in young hearing impaired children. *British Journal of Audiology, 26*, 97–107.

Read, C., Zhang, Y., Nie, H., & Ding, B. (1986). The ability to manipulate speech sounds depends on knowing alphabetic writing. *Cognition, 24*, 31–44.

Rice, M. L., & Wexler, K. (1996). Toward tense as a clinical marker of specific language impairment in English-speaking children. *Journal of Speech and Hearing Research, 39*(6), 1239–1257.

Rispens, J. (1990). Comprehension problems in dyslexia. In D. Balota, G. Flores d'Arcias, & K. Rayner (Eds.), *Comprehension processes in reading* (pp. 603–620). Hillsdale, NJ: Erlbaum.

Roberts, J. E., Wallace, I. F., & Henderson, F. W. (1997). *Otitis media in young children: Medical, developmental, and educational considerations.* Baltimore, MD: Brookes.

Robertson, C., & Salter, W. (1997). *The phonological awareness test.* East Moline, IL: LinguiSystems.

Robinshaw, H. M. (1995). Early intervention for hearing impairment: Differences in the timing of communicative and linguistic development. *British Journal of Audiology, 29*, 315–334.

Rosner, J. (1999). *Phonological Awareness Skills Program Test.* Austin, Texas: PRO-ED.

Rosner, J., & Simon, D. P. (1971). The auditory analysis test: An initial report. *Journal of Learning Disabilities, 4*(7), 384–392.

Roth, F., & Spekman, N. (1989). Higher order language processes and reading disabilities. In A. Kamhi & H. Catts (Eds.), *Reading disabilities. A developmental language perspective* (pp. 159–198). Boston: Little, Brown.

Roth, P., Speece, D. L., & Cooper, D. H. (2002). A longitudinal analysis of the connection between oral language and early reading. *Journal of Educational Research, 95*(5), 259–272.

Royal College of Speech and Language Therapists. (1996). *Communicating quality: Professional standards for speech and language therapists* (2nd ed.). London: Royal College of Speech and Language Therapists.

Rozin, P., & Gleitman, L. R. (1977). The structure and acquisition of reading, II: The reading process and the acquisition of the alphabetic principle of reading.

In D. L. Scarborough (Ed.), *Towards the psychology of reading.* Hillsdale, NJ: Erlbaum.

Rudel, R. (1983). Definition of dyslexia: Language and motor deficits. In F. Duffy & N. Geschwind (Eds.), *Dyslexia, current status and future directions.* Boston: Little, Brown.

Rumelhart, D. (1977). Toward an interactive model of reading. In S. Dornic (Ed.), *Attention and performance* (Vol. 6, pp. 573–603). Hillsdale, NJ: Erlbaum.

Rumelhart, D., & McClelland, J. (Eds.). (1986). *Parallel distributed processing: Explorations in the microstructure of cognition* (Vol. 1). Cambridge, MA: MIT Press.

Sawyer, D. (1985). Language problems observed in poor readers. In C. Simon (Ed.), *Communication skills and classroom success: Assessement of language learning disabled children* (pp. 317–335). San Diego: College Hill Press.

Sawyer, D. (1992). Language abilities, reading acquisition and developmental dyslexia: A discussion of hypothetical and observed relationships. *Journal of Learning Disabilities, 25,* 82–95.

Scarborough, H. (1990). Very early language deficits in dyslexic children. *Child Development, 61,* 1728–1743.

Scarborough, H. (1998). Early identification of children at risk for reading disabilities: Phonological awareness and some other promising predictors. In B. K. Shapiro, P. J. Accardo, & A. J. Capute (Eds.), *Specific reading disabilities: A view of the spectrum* (pp. 75–119). Timonium, MD: York Press.

Schatschneider, C., Francis, D. J., Foorman, B. R., Fletcher, J. M., & Mehta, P. (1999). The dimensionality of phonological awareness: An application of item response theory. *Journal of Educational Psychology, 91*(3), 439–449.

Schneider, W., Ennemoser, M., Roth, E., & Kuspert, P. (1999). Kindergarten prevention of dyslexia: Does training in phonological awareness work for everybody? *Journal of Learning Disabilities, 32,* 429–436.

Schneider, W., Kuspert, P., Roth, E., & Vise, M. (1997). Short and long term effects of training phonological awareness in kindergarten: Evidence from two German studies. *Journal of Experimental Child Psychology, 66,* 311–340.

Schonell, F. E. (1956). *Educating spastic children: The education and guidance of the cerebral palsied.* London: Oliver & Boyd.

Schopmeyer, B., Mellon, N., Dobaj, H., Grant, G., & Niparko, J. K. (2000). Use of Fast ForWord to enhance language development in children with cochlear implants. *Annals of Otology, Rhinology, and Laryngology, 109*(12), 95–98.

Seidenberg, M. (1985). Constraining models of word recognition. *Cognition, 20,* 169–190.

Seidenberg, M. (1989). Word recognition and naming: A computational model and its implications. In W. Marlsen-Wilson (Ed.), *Lexical representation and process* (pp. 25–73). Cambridge, MA: MIT Press.

Seidenberg, M., Bruck, M., Fornarolo, G., & Backman, J. (1985). Word recognition processes of poor and disabled readers: Do they necessarily differ? *Applied Psycholinguistics, 6,* 161–180.

Seidenberg, M., & McClelland, J. (1989). A distributed, developmental model of word recognition and naming. *Psychological Review, 96,* 523–568.

Semel, E., & Wiig, E. (1975). Comprehension of syntactic structures and critical verbal elements by children with learning disabilities. *Journal of Learning Disabilities, 8,* 53–58.

Semel, E., Wiig, E., & Secord, W. (1987). *Clinical evaluation of language fundamentals* (2nd ed.). San Antonio, TX: Psychological Corporation.

Share, D. (1995). Phonological recoding and self-teaching: Sine qua non of reading acquisition. *Cognition, 55,* 151–218.

Share, D., Jorm, A., Maclean, R., & Matthews, R. (1984). Sources of individual differences in reading acquisition. *Journal of Educational Psychology, 76,* 1309–1324.

Share, D., & Stanovich, K. (1995). Cognitive processes in early reading development: Accommodating individual differences into a model of acquisition. *Issues in Education, 1*(1), 1–57.

Shriberg, L. D., Aram, D. M., & Kwiatkowski, J. (1997). Developmental apraxia of speech: 1. Descriptive and theoretical perspectives. *Journal of Speech, Language, and Hearing Research, 40*(2), 273–285.

Shriberg, L. D., Friel-Patti, S., Flipsen, P., Jr., & Brown, R. L. (2000). Otitis media, fluctuant hearing loss, and speech–language outcomes: A preliminary structural equation model. *Journal of Speech, Language, and Hearing Research, 43*(1), 100–120.

Shriberg, L. D., Tomblin, J. B., & McSweeny, J. L. (1999). Prevalence of speech delay in 6–year-old children and comorbidity with language impairment. *Journal of Speech, Language, and Hearing Research, 42*(6), 1461–1481.

Siegel, L. S. (1992). An evaluation of the discrepancy definition of dyslexia. *Journal of Learning Disabilities, 25,* 618–629.

Siegel, L. S., & Ryan, E. (1984). Reading disability as a language disorder. *Reading and Special Education, 5*(3), 28–33.

Silva, P. A., Chalmers, D., & Stewart, I. (1986). Some audiological, psychological, educational and behavioral characteristics of children with bilateral otitis media with effusion: A longitudinal study. *Journal of Learning Disabilities, 3,* 165–169.

Slocum, T., O'Connor, R., & Jenkins, J. (1993). Transfer among phonological manipulation skills. *Journal of Educational Psychology, 85,* 618–630.

Smith, F. (1971). *Understanding reading: A psycholinguistic analysis of reading and learning to read.* New York: Holt, Reinhart & Winston.

Smith, M. M. (1989). Reading without speech: A study of children with cerebral palsy. *Irish Journal of Psychology, 10*(4), 601–614.

Snow, C. E., Cancino, H., Gonzalez, P., & Shriberg, E. (1989). Giving formal definitions: An oral language correlate of literacy. In D. Bloom (Ed.), *Classroom literacy* (pp. 233–249). Norwood, NJ: Ablex.

Snow, C. E., Tabors, P. O., Nicholson, P. E., & Kurland, B. F. (1995). SHELL: Oral language and early literacy in kindergarten and first-grade children. *Journal of Research in Childhood Education, 10,* 37–47.

Snowling, M. J., Adams, J. W., Bishop, D. V. M., & Stothard, S. E. (2001). Educational attainments of school leavers with a preschool history of speech–language impairments. *International Journal of Language and Communication Disorders, 36*(2), 173–183.

Snowling, M. J., Bishop, D. V. M., & Stothard, S. E. (2000). Is preschool language impairment a risk factor for dyslexia in adolescence? *Journal of Child Psychology and Psychiatry and Allied Disciplines, 41*(5), 587–600.

Snowling, M. J., & Hulme, C. (1989). A longitudinal case study of developmental phonological dyslexia. *Cognitive Neuropsychology, 6*, 379–401.

Snowling, M. J., Hulme, C., & Mercer, R. C. (2002). A deficit in rime awareness in children with Down syndrome. *Reading and Writing: An Interdisciplinary Journal, 15*, 471–495.

Snowling, M. J., van Wagtendonk, B., & Stafford, C. (1988). Object-naming deficits in developmental dyslexia. *Journal of Research in Reading, 11*, 67–85.

Sowell, V., & Sledge, A. (1986). Miscue analysis of Braille readers. *Journal of Visual Impairment and Blindness, 80*(10), 989–992.

Spring, C. (1976). Encoding speed and memory span in dyslexic readers. *Journal of Special Education, 10*, 35–40.

Spring, C., & Capps, C. (1974). Encoding speed rehearsal and probed recall of dyslexic boys. *Journal of Educational Psychology, 66*, 780–786.

Stackhouse, J. (1982). An investigation of reading and spelling performance in speech disordered children. *British Journal of Disorders of Communication, 17*, 53–60.

Stackhouse, J. (1992). Developmental verbal dyspraxia. *European Journal of Disorders of Communication, 27*, 19–34.

Stackhouse, J., & Wells, B. (1997). *Children's speech and literacy difficulties: A psycholinguistic framework.* London: Whurr.

Stahl, S. A., & Murray, B. A. (1994). Defining phonological awareness and its relationship to early reading. *Journal of Educational Psychology, 86*(2), 221–234.

Stanovich, K. (1980). Toward an interactive–compensatory model of individual differences in the development of reading fluency. *Reading Research Quarterly, 16*, 32–71.

Stanovich, K. (1984). The interactive–compensatory model of reading: A confluence of developmental, experimental, and educational psychology. *Remedial and Special Education, 5*(3), 11–19.

Stanovich, K. (1985). Explaining the variance in reading ability in terms of psychological processes: What have we learned? *Annals of Dyslexia, 35*, 67–69.

Stanovich, K. (1991a). Discrepancy definitions of reading disability: Has intelligence led us astray? *Reading Research Quarterly, 26*, 7–29.

Stanovich, K. (1991b). Word recognition: Changing perspectives. In R. Barr, M. Kamil, P. Mosenthal, & P. Pearson (Eds.), *Handbook of reading research* (Vol. 2, pp. 418–452). New York: Longman.

Stanovich, K. (2000). *Progress in understanding reading: Scientific foundations and new frontiers.* New York: Guilford Press.

Stanovich, K. (1988). Explaining the differences between the dyslexic and the garden-variety poor reader: The phonological-core variable-difference model. *Journal of Learning Disabilities, 21*(10), 590–604, 612.

Stanovich, K., Cunningham, A., & Cramer, B. (1984). Assessing phonological awareness in kindergarten children: Issues of task comparability. *Journal of Experimental Child Psychology, 38*, 175–190.

Stanovich, K., Nathan, R., & Vala-Rossi, M. (1986). Developmental changes in the cognitive correlates of reading ability and the developmental lag hypothesis. *Reading Research Quarterly, 21*(3), 267–283.

Stanovich, K., Nathan, R., & Zolman, J. (1988). The developmental lag hypothesis in reading: Longitudinal and matched-reading level comparisons. *Child Development, 59*, 71–86.

Stemberger, J. (1992). A connectionist view of child phonology: Phonological processing without phonological processes. In C. Ferguson, L. Menn, C. Stoel-Gammon (Eds.), *Phonological development: Models, research, implications.* Timonium, MD: York Press.

Sterne, A., & Goswami, U. (2000). Phonological awareness of syllables, rhymes, and phonemes in deaf children. *Journal of Child Psychology and Psychiatry, 41*, 609–625.

Stone, J. (2002). *Animated-literacy approach to integrated language arts instruction.* La Mesa, CA: Stone Creations.

Stothard, S. E., Snowling, M. J., Bishop, D. V. M., Chipchase, B. B., & Kaplan, C. A. (1998). Language-impaired preschoolers: A follow-up into adolescence. *Journal of Speech, Language, and Hearing Research, 41*(2), 407–418.

Stuart, M. (1995). Prediction and qualitative assessment of five- and six-year-old children's reading: A longitudinal study. *British Journal of Educational Psychology, 65*, 287–296.

Svirsky, M. A., & Meyer, T. A. (1999). Comparison of speech perception in pediatric CLARION cochlear implant and hearing aid users. *Annals of Otology, Rhinology, and Laryngology, 108*(4), 104–109.

Svirsky, M. A., Robbins, A. M., Kirk, K. I., Pisoni, D. B., & Miyamoto, R. T. (2000). Language development in profoundly deaf children with cochlear implants. *Psychological Science, 11*(2), 153–158.

Swan, D., & Goswami, U. (1997). Phonological awareness deficits in developmental dyslexia and the phonological representations hypothesis. *Journal of Experimental Child Psychology, 66*(1), 18–41.

Swanson, H. L., Mink, J., & Bocian, K. M. (1999). Cognitive processing deficits in poor readers with symptoms of reading disabilities and ADHD: More alike than different? *Journal of Educational Psychology, 91*(2), 321–333.

Swenson, A. M. (1991). A process approach to teaching Braille writing at the primary level. *Journal of Visual Impairment and Blindness, 85*(5), 217–221.

Tallal, P. (1980). Auditory temporal perception, phonics, and reading disabilities in children. *Brain and Language, 9*(2), 182–198.

Tallal, P., Miller, S. L., Bedi, G., Byma, G., Wang, X., Nagarajan, S. S., Schreiner, C., Jenkins, W. M., & Merzenich, M. M. (1996). Language comprehension in language-learning impaired children improved with acoustically modified speech. *Science, 271*, 81–84.

Thompson, L. J. (1971). Language disabilities in men of eminence. *Journal of Learning Disabilities, 4*(1), 39–45.

Tomblin, J. B., Smith, E., & Zhang, X. Y. (1997). Epidemiology of specific language impairment: Prenatal and perinatal risk factors. *Journal of Communication Disorders, 30*(4), 325–344.

Torgesen, J., & Bryant, B. (1994). *Test of Phonological Awareness.* Austin, Texas: PRO-ED.

Torgesen, J., Wagner, R., Rashotte, C., Alexander, A., & Conway, C. (1997). Preventive and remedial interventions for children with severe reading disabilities. *Learning Disabilities: A Multi-Disciplinary Journal, 8*(1) 51–61.

Torgesen, J., Morgan, S., & Davis, C. (1992). Effects of two types of phonological awareness training on word learning in kindergarten children. *Journal of Educational Psychology, 84,* 364–370.

Torgesen, J., Wagner, R., & Rashotte, C. (1994). Longitudinal studies of phonological processing and reading. *Journal of Learning Disabilities, 27,* 276–286.

Torgesen, J., Wagner, R., Rashotte, C., Lindamood, P., Rose, E., Conway, T., & Garvan, C. (1999). Preventing reading failure in young children with phonological processing disabilities: Group and individual responses to instruction. *Journal of Educational Psychology, 91,* 579–593.

Torneus, M. (1984). Phonological awareness and reading: A chicken and egg problem? *Journal of Educational Psychology, 76,* 1346–1358.

Treiman, R. (1992). The role of intrasyllabic units in learning to read and spell. In P. Gough, L. Ehri, & R. Treiman (Eds.), *Reading acquisition* (pp. 65–106). Hillsdale, NJ: Erlbaum.

Treiman, R. (1993). *Beginning to spell.* New York: Oxford University Press.

Treiman, R., & Barry, C. (2000). Dialect and authography: Some differences between American and British spellers. *Journal of Experimental Psychology–Learning, Memory, and Cognition, 26*(6), 1423–1430.

Treiman, R., & Bourassa, D. C. (2000). The development of spelling skill. *Topics in Language Disorders, 20*(3), 1–18.

Treiman, R., Goswami, U., Tincoff, R., & Leevers, H. (1997). Effects of dialect on American and British children's spelling. *Child Development, 68*(2), 229–245.

Treiman, R., & Zukowsky, A. (1991). Levels of phonological awareness. In S. A. Brady & D. P. Shankweiler (Eds.), *Phonological processes in literacy: A tribute to Isabelle Y. Liberman* (pp. 67–83). Hillsdale, NJ: Erlbaum.

Truch, S. (1994). Simulating basic reading processes using auditory discrimination in depth. *Annals of Dyslexia, 44,* 60–80.

Trybus, R., & Karchmer, M. A. (1977). School achievement scores of hearing impaired children: National data on achievement status and growth patterns. *American Annals of the Deaf, 122,* 62–69.

Tunmer, W., & Hoover, W. (1992). Cognitive and linguistic factors in learning to read. In R. Treiman, L. Ehri, & P. Gough (Eds.), *Reading acquisition* (pp. 175–214). Hillsade, NJ: Erlbaum.

Tunmer, W. E., Herriman, M. L., & Nesdale, A. R. (1988). Metalinguistic abilities and beginning reading. *Reading Research Quarterly, 23*(2), 134–158.

Tunmer, W. W., & Fletcher, C. M. (1981). The relationship between conceptual tempo, phonological awareness, and word recognition in beginning readers. *Journal of Reading Behavior, 13*(2), 173–185.

Uhry, J. K., & Ehri, L. (1999). Ease of segmenting two- and three- phoneme words in kindergarten: Rime cohesion or vowel salience? *Journal of Educational Psychology, 9,* 594–603.

Vandervelden, M., & Siegel, L. S. (1999). Phonological processing and literacy in AAC users and students with motor speech impairments. *Augmentative and Alternative Communication, 15,* 191–209.

Vandervelden, M., & Siegel, L. S. (2001). Phonological procesing in written learning: Assessment for children who use augmentative and alternative communication. *Augmentative and Alternative Communication, 17,* 37–51.

van IJzendoorn, M., & Bus, A. (1994). Meta-analytic confirmation of the nonword reading deficit in developmental dyslexia. *Reading Research Quarterly, 29*, 266–275.

van Kleeck, A., Gillam, R., & McFadden, T. (1998). A study of classroom-based phonological awareness training for preschoolers with speech and/or language disorders. *American Journal of Speech–Language Pathology, 7*(3), 65–76.

Vardi, I. (1991). *Phonological profile for the hearing impaired*. Perth, Australia: Edith Crowan University.

Velleman, S., & Strand, K. (1994). Developmental verbal dyspraxia. In J. Bernthal & N. Bankson (Eds.), *Child phonology: Characteristics, assessment, and intervention with special populations* (pp. 110–139). New York: Thieme.

Vellutino, F. (1979). *Dyslexia: Theory and research*. Cambridge, MA: MIT Press.

Vellutino, F., & Scanlon, D. (1987). Phonological coding, phonological awareness, and reading ability: Evidence from a longitudinal and experimenetal study. *Merrill–Palmer Quarterly, 33*, 321–363.

Vogel, S. (1974). Syntactic abilities in normal and dyslexic children. *Journal of Learning Disabilities, 7*, 103–109.

Wagner, R., & Torgesen, J. (1987). The nature of phonological processing and its causal role in the acquisition of reading skills. *Psychological Bulletin, 101*, 192–212.

Wagner, R., Torgesen, J., Laughon, P., Simmons, K., & Rashotte, C. (1993). Development of young readers' phonological processing abilities. *Journal of Educational Psychology, 85*, 83–103.

Wagner, R. K., Torgesen, J. K., & Rashotte, C. A. (1994). The development of reading-related phonological processing abilities: New evidence of bi-directional causality from a latent variable longitudinal study. *Developmental Psychology, 30*, 73–87.

Wagner, R., Torgesen, J., & Rashotte, C. (1999). *Comprehensive Test of Phonological Processing, CTOPP*. Austin, TX: PRO-ED.

Walker, N., & Wigglesworth, G. (2002). The effect of conductive hearing loss on phonological awareness, reading and spelling of urban Aboriginal students. *Australian and New Zealand Journal of Audiology, 23*(1), 37–51.

Wallach, M. A., & Wallach, L. (1976). Teaching all children to read.

Walley, A. C., Metsala, J. L., & Garlock, V. M. (2003). Spoken vocabulary growth: Its role in the development of phoneme awareness and early reading ability. *Reading and Writing: An Interdisciplinary Journal, 16*, 5–20.

Warrick, N., Rubin, H., & Rowe-Walsh, S. (1993). Phoneme awareness in language delayed children: Comparative studies and intervention. *Annals of Dyslexia, 43*, 153–173.

Watson, B., & Gillon, G. (1999). *Responses of children with developmental verbal dyspraxia to phonological awareness training*. Paper presented at the Speech Pathology Australia National Conference, Sydney, Australia.

Webster, P., & Plante, A. (1992). Effects of phonological impairment on word, syllable and phoneme segmentation and reading. *Language, Speech and Hearing Services in Schools, 23*, 176–182.

Webster, P., & Plante, A. (1995). Productive phonology and phonological awareness in preschool children. *Applied Psycholinguistics, 16*, 43–57.

Webster, P., Plante, A., & Couvillion, L. (1997). Phonologic impairment and pre-reading: Update on a longitudinal study. *Journal of Learning Disabilities, 30,* 365–375.

Wiig, E., & Roach, M. (1975). Immediate recall of semantically varied "sentences" by learning-disabled adolescents. *Perceptual and Motor Skills, 40,* 119–125.

Wiig, E., & Semel, E. (1984). *Language assessment and intervention for the learning disabled* (2nd ed.). Columbus, OH: Merrill.

Wiig, E., Semel, E., & Crouse, M. (1973). The use of English morphology by high-risk and learning disabled children. *Journal of Learning Disabilities, 6,* 457–465.

Windsor, J. (2000). The role of phonological opacity in reading achievement. *Journal of Speech, Language, and Hearing Research, 43*(1), 50–61.

Wishart, J. G. (1993). The development of learning difficulties in children with Down's syndrome. *Journal of Intellectual Disability Research, 37,* 389–403.

Wishart, J. G. (1998). Development in children with Down syndrome: Facts, findings, the future. *International Journal of Disability, Development, and Education, 43,* 343–363.

Wishart, J. G., & Duffy, L. (1990). Instability of performance on cognitive tests in infants and young children with Down's syndrome. *British Journal of Educational Psychology, 60,* 10–22.

Wittenstein, S. H., & Pardee, M. L. (1996). Teachers' voices: Comments on Braille and literacy from the field. *Journal of Visual Impairment and Blindness, 90,* 201–209.

Wolf, M., & Bowers, P. G. (1999). The double-deficit hypothesis for the developmental dyslexias. *Journal of Educational Psychology, 91*(3), 415–438.

Wolf, M., Bowers, P. G., & Biddle, K. (2000). Naming-speed processes, timing, and reading: A conceptual review. *Journal of Learning Disabilities, 33*(4), 387–407.

Wolf, M., Miller, L., & Donnelly, K. (2000). Retrieval, Automaticity, Vocabulary Elaboration, Orthography (RAVE-O): A comprehensive, fluency-based reading intervention program. *Journal of Learning Disabilities, 33*(4), 375–386.

Wood, C., & Terrell, C. (1998). Poor readers' ability to detect speech rhythm and perceive rapid speech. *British Journal of Developmental Psychology, 16,* 397–413.

Wood, F., & Felton, R. (1994). Separate linguistic and attentional factors in the development of reading. *Topics in Language Disorders, 14,* 42–57.

Yavas, M. S. (1998). *Phonology: Development and disorders.* San Diego: Singular Publishing.

Yopp, H. (1988). The validity and reliability of phonemic awareness tests. *Reading Research Quarterly, 23,* 159–177.

Yoshinaga-Itano, C. (1995). Efficacy of early identification and early intervention. *Seminars in Hearing, 16,* 115–123.

Yoshinaga-Itano, C., & Appuzzo, M. L. (1998). Identification of hearing loss after age 18 months is not early enough. *American Annals of the Deaf, 143,* 380–387.

Yoshinaga-Itano, C., Sedey, A. L., Coulter, D. K., & Mehl, A. L. (1998). Language of early- and later-identified children with hearing loss. *Pediatrics, 102,* 1161–1171.

Young, A., & Gillon, G. (2002). *A phonological awareness training programme for children who are blind.* Christchurch, New Zealand: Department of Communication Disorders, University of Canterbury.

Zecker, S., & Zinner, T. (1987). Semantic code deficit for reading disabled children on an auditory lexical decision task. *Journal of Reading Behavior, 19,* 177–190.

Zifcak, M. (1981). Phonological awareness and reading acquisition. *Contemporary Educational Psychology, 6*(2), 117–126.

Zinkus, P. W., Gottlieb, M. I., & Schapiro, M. (1978). Developmental and psychological sequelae of chronic otitis media. *American Journal of Diseases of Childhood, 132,* 1100–1104.

Index